FREE Test Taking Tips Video/DVD Offer

To better serve you, we created videos covering test taking tips that we want to give you for FREE. **These videos cover world-class tips that will help you succeed on your test.**

We just ask that you send us feedback about this product. Please let us know what you thought about it—whether good, bad, or indifferent.

To get your **FREE videos**, you can use the QR code below or email freevideos@studyguideteam.com with "Free Videos" in the subject line and the following information in the body of the email:

a. The title of your product

b. Your product rating on a scale of 1-5, with 5 being the highest

c. Your feedback about the product

If you have any questions or concerns, please don't hesitate to contact us at info@studyguideteam.com.

Thank you!

TOEFL Preparation Book 2022-2023

Exam Study Guide with 3 TOEFL iBT Practice Tests for Reading, Listening, Speaking, and Writing/Essay [Includes Audio Links]

Joshua Rueda

Written and edited by TPB Publishing.

TPB Publishing is not associated with or endorsed by any official testing organization. TPB Publishing is a publisher of unofficial educational products. All test and organization names are trademarks of their respective owners. Content in this book is included for utilitarian purposes only and does not constitute an endorsement by TPB Publishing of any particular point of view.

Interested in buying more than 10 copies of our product? Contact us about bulk discounts:
bulkorders@studyguideteam.com

ISBN 13: 9781637750476
ISBN 10: 1637750471

Table of Contents

//Test Prep Books|||

Quick Overview

As you draw closer to taking your exam, effective preparation becomes more and more important. Thankfully, you have this study guide to help you get ready. Use this guide to help keep your studying on track and refer to it often.

This study guide contains several key sections that will help you be successful on your exam. The guide contains tips for what you should do the night before and the day of the test. Also included are test-taking tips. Knowing the right information is not always enough. Many well-prepared test takers struggle with exams. These tips will help equip you to accurately read, assess, and answer test questions.

A large part of the guide is devoted to showing you what content to expect on the exam and to helping you better understand that content. In this guide are practice test questions so that you can see how well you have grasped the content. Then, answer explanations are provided so that you can understand why you missed certain questions.

Don't try to cram the night before you take your exam. This is not a wise strategy for a few reasons. First, your retention of the information will be low. Your time would be better used by reviewing information you already know rather than trying to learn a lot of new information. Second, you will likely become stressed as you try to gain a large amount of knowledge in a short amount of time. Third, you will be depriving yourself of sleep. So be sure to go to bed at a reasonable time the night before. Being well-rested helps you focus and remain calm.

Be sure to eat a substantial breakfast the morning of the exam. If you are taking the exam in the afternoon, be sure to have a good lunch as well. Being hungry is distracting and can make it difficult to focus. You have hopefully spent lots of time preparing for the exam. Don't let an empty stomach get in the way of success!

When travelling to the testing center, leave earlier than needed. That way, you have a buffer in case you experience any delays. This will help you remain calm and will keep you from missing your appointment time at the testing center.

Be sure to pace yourself during the exam. Don't try to rush through the exam. There is no need to risk performing poorly on the exam just so you can leave the testing center early. Allow yourself to use all of the allotted time if needed.

Remain positive while taking the exam even if you feel like you are performing poorly. Thinking about the content you should have mastered will not help you perform better on the exam.

Once the exam is complete, take some time to relax. Even if you feel that you need to take the exam again, you will be well served by some down time before you begin studying again. It's often easier to convince yourself to study if you know that it will come with a reward!

Test-Taking Strategies

1. Predicting the Answer

When you feel confident in your preparation for a multiple-choice test, try predicting the answer before reading the answer choices. This is especially useful on questions that test objective factual knowledge. By predicting the answer before reading the available choices, you eliminate the possibility that you will be distracted or led astray by an incorrect answer choice. You will feel more confident in your selection if you read the question, predict the answer, and then find your prediction among the answer choices. After using this strategy, be sure to still read all of the answer choices carefully and completely. If you feel unprepared, you should not attempt to predict the answers. This would be a waste of time and an opportunity for your mind to wander in the wrong direction.

2. Reading the Whole Question

Too often, test takers scan a multiple-choice question, recognize a few familiar words, and immediately jump to the answer choices. Test authors are aware of this common impatience, and they will sometimes prey upon it. For instance, a test author might subtly turn the question into a negative, or he or she might redirect the focus of the question right at the end. The only way to avoid falling into these traps is to read the entirety of the question carefully before reading the answer choices.

3. Looking for Wrong Answers

Long and complicated multiple-choice questions can be intimidating. One way to simplify a difficult multiple-choice question is to eliminate all of the answer choices that are clearly wrong. In most sets of answers, there will be at least one selection that can be dismissed right away. If the test is administered on paper, the test taker could draw a line through it to indicate that it may be ignored; otherwise, the test taker will have to perform this operation mentally or on scratch paper. In either case, once the obviously incorrect answers have been eliminated, the remaining choices may be considered. Sometimes identifying the clearly wrong answers will give the test taker some information about the correct answer. For instance, if one of the remaining answer choices is a direct opposite of one of the eliminated answer choices, it may well be the correct answer. The opposite of obviously wrong is obviously right! Of course, this is not always the case. Some answers are obviously incorrect simply because they are irrelevant to the question being asked. Still, identifying and eliminating some incorrect answer choices is a good way to simplify a multiple-choice question.

4. Don't Overanalyze

Anxious test takers often overanalyze questions. When you are nervous, your brain will often run wild, causing you to make associations and discover clues that don't actually exist. If you feel that this may be a problem for you, do whatever you can to slow down during the test. Try taking a deep breath or counting to ten. As you read and consider the question, restrict yourself to the particular words used by the author. Avoid thought tangents about what the author *really* meant, or what he or she was *trying* to say. The only things that matter on a multiple-choice test are the words that are actually in the question. You must avoid reading too much into a multiple-choice question, or supposing that the writer meant something other than what he or she wrote.

5. No Need for Panic

It is wise to learn as many strategies as possible before taking a multiple-choice test, but it is likely that you will come across a few questions for which you simply don't know the answer. In this situation, avoid panicking. Because most multiple-choice tests include dozens of questions, the relative value of a single wrong answer is small. As much as possible, you should compartmentalize each question on a multiple-choice test. In other words, you should not allow your feelings about one question to affect your success on the others. When you find a question that you either don't understand or don't know how to answer, just take a deep breath and do your best. Read the entire question slowly and carefully. Try rephrasing the question a couple of different ways. Then, read all of the answer choices carefully. After eliminating obviously wrong answers, make a selection and move on to the next question.

6. Confusing Answer Choices

When working on a difficult multiple-choice question, there may be a tendency to focus on the answer choices that are the easiest to understand. Many people, whether consciously or not, gravitate to the answer choices that require the least concentration, knowledge, and memory. This is a mistake. When you come across an answer choice that is confusing, you should give it extra attention. A question might be confusing because you do not know the subject matter to which it refers. If this is the case, don't eliminate the answer before you have affirmatively settled on another. When you come across an answer choice of this type, set it aside as you look at the remaining choices. If you can confidently assert that one of the other choices is correct, you can leave the confusing answer aside. Otherwise, you will need to take a moment to try to better understand the confusing answer choice. Rephrasing is one way to tease out the sense of a confusing answer choice.

7. Your First Instinct

Many people struggle with multiple-choice tests because they overthink the questions. If you have studied sufficiently for the test, you should be prepared to trust your first instinct once you have carefully and completely read the question and all of the answer choices. There is a great deal of research suggesting that the mind can come to the correct conclusion very quickly once it has obtained all of the relevant information. At times, it may seem to you as if your intuition is working faster even than your reasoning mind. This may in fact be true. The knowledge you obtain while studying may be retrieved from your subconscious before you have a chance to work out the associations that support it. Verify your instinct by working out the reasons that it should be trusted.

8. Key Words

Many test takers struggle with multiple-choice questions because they have poor reading comprehension skills. Quickly reading and understanding a multiple-choice question requires a mixture of skill and experience. To help with this, try jotting down a few key words and phrases on a piece of scrap paper. Doing this concentrates the process of reading and forces the mind to weigh the relative importance of the question's parts. In selecting words and phrases to write down, the test taker thinks about the question more deeply and carefully. This is especially true for multiple-choice questions that are preceded by a long prompt.

9. Subtle Negatives

One of the oldest tricks in the multiple-choice test writer's book is to subtly reverse the meaning of a question with a word like *not* or *except*. If you are not paying attention to each word in the question, you can easily be led astray by this trick. For instance, a common question format is, "Which of the following is...?" Obviously, if the question instead is, "Which of the following is not...?," then the answer will be quite different. Even worse, the test makers are aware of the potential for this mistake and will include one answer choice that would be correct if the question were not negated or reversed. A test taker who misses the reversal will find what he or she believes to be a correct answer and will be so confident that he or she will fail to reread the question and discover the original error. The only way to avoid this is to practice a wide variety of multiple-choice questions and to pay close attention to each and every word.

10. Reading Every Answer Choice

It may seem obvious, but you should always read every one of the answer choices! Too many test takers fall into the habit of scanning the question and assuming that they understand the question because they recognize a few key words. From there, they pick the first answer choice that answers the question they believe they have read. Test takers who read all of the answer choices might discover that one of the latter answer choices is actually *more* correct. Moreover, reading all of the answer choices can remind you of facts related to the question that can help you arrive at the correct answer. Sometimes, a misstatement or incorrect detail in one of the latter answer choices will trigger your memory of the subject and will enable you to find the right answer. Failing to read all of the answer choices is like not reading all of the items on a restaurant menu: you might miss out on the perfect choice.

11. Spot the Hedges

One of the keys to success on multiple-choice tests is paying close attention to every word. This is never truer than with words like almost, most, some, and sometimes. These words are called "hedges" because they indicate that a statement is not totally true or not true in every place and time. An absolute statement will contain no hedges, but in many subjects, the answers are not always straightforward or absolute. There are always exceptions to the rules in these subjects. For this reason, you should favor those multiple-choice questions that contain hedging language. The presence of qualifying words indicates that the author is taking special care with their words, which is certainly important when composing the right answer. After all, there are many ways to be wrong, but there is only one way to be right! For this reason, it is wise to avoid answers that are absolute when taking a multiple-choice test. An absolute answer is one that says things are either all one way or all another. They often include words like *every*, *always*, *best*, and *never*. If you are taking a multiple-choice test in a subject that doesn't lend itself to absolute answers, be on your guard if you see any of these words.

12. Long Answers

In many subject areas, the answers are not simple. As already mentioned, the right answer often requires hedges. Another common feature of the answers to a complex or subjective question are qualifying clauses, which are groups of words that subtly modify the meaning of the sentence. If the question or answer choice describes a rule to which there are exceptions or the subject matter is complicated, ambiguous, or confusing, the correct answer will require many words in order to be expressed clearly and accurately. In essence, you should not be deterred by answer choices that seem excessively long. Oftentimes, the author of the text will not be able to write the correct answer without

offering some qualifications and modifications. Your job is to read the answer choices thoroughly and completely and to select the one that most accurately and precisely answers the question.

13. Restating to Understand

Sometimes, a question on a multiple-choice test is difficult not because of what it asks but because of how it is written. If this is the case, restate the question or answer choice in different words. This process serves a couple of important purposes. First, it forces you to concentrate on the core of the question. In order to rephrase the question accurately, you have to understand it well. Rephrasing the question will concentrate your mind on the key words and ideas. Second, it will present the information to your mind in a fresh way. This process may trigger your memory and render some useful scrap of information picked up while studying.

14. True Statements

Sometimes an answer choice will be true in itself, but it does not answer the question. This is one of the main reasons why it is essential to read the question carefully and completely before proceeding to the answer choices. Too often, test takers skip ahead to the answer choices and look for true statements. Having found one of these, they are content to select it without reference to the question above. Obviously, this provides an easy way for test makers to play tricks. The savvy test taker will always read the entire question before turning to the answer choices. Then, having settled on a correct answer choice, he or she will refer to the original question and ensure that the selected answer is relevant. The mistake of choosing a correct-but-irrelevant answer choice is especially common on questions related to specific pieces of objective knowledge. A prepared test taker will have a wealth of factual knowledge at their disposal, and should not be careless in its application.

15. No Patterns

One of the more dangerous ideas that circulates about multiple-choice tests is that the correct answers tend to fall into patterns. These erroneous ideas range from a belief that B and C are the most common right answers, to the idea that an unprepared test-taker should answer "A-B-A-C-A-D-A-B-A." It cannot be emphasized enough that pattern-seeking of this type is exactly the WRONG way to approach a multiple-choice test. To begin with, it is highly unlikely that the test maker will plot the correct answers according to some predetermined pattern. The questions are scrambled and delivered in a random order. Furthermore, even if the test maker was following a pattern in the assignation of correct answers, there is no reason why the test taker would know which pattern he or she was using. Any attempt to discern a pattern in the answer choices is a waste of time and a distraction from the real work of taking the test. A test taker would be much better served by extra preparation before the test than by reliance on a pattern in the answers.

FREE Videos/DVD OFFER

Doing well on your exam requires both knowing the test content and understanding how to use that knowledge to do well on the test. We offer completely FREE test taking tip videos. **These videos cover world-class tips that you can use to succeed on your test.**

To get your **FREE videos**, you can use the QR code below or email freevideos@studyguideteam.com with "Free Videos" in the subject line and the following information in the body of the email:

> a. The title of your product
>
> b. Your product rating on a scale of 1-5, with 5 being the highest
>
> c. Your feedback about the product

If you have any questions or concerns, please don't hesitate to contact us at info@studyguideteam.com.

Thanks again!

Introduction to the TOEFL iBT

Function of the Test

The Test of English as a Foreign Language (TOEFL) internet Based Test (iBT) is an exam developed and administered by the Educational Testing Service (ETS) to measure test takers' ability to use and comprehend academic English at a university level. As such, the TOEFL iBT is a widely recognized English language credential for students planning to study in American colleges and universities, as well as in English language academic programs and institutions in over 130 countries. TOEFL scores may also be accepted by some immigration authorities for visas that require an English language proficiency component (policies vary by country and visa type).

According to ETS, over 30 million people have taken the TOEFL. Because of the diverse range of uses for a TOEFL iBT score, the exam is appropriate for a diverse range of test takers. In addition to providing credentials for school admissions and visa applications, TOEFL iBT scores may also be used for hiring criteria or simply for personal evaluation of language progress. (https://www.ets.org/toefl/ibt/about/)

Test Administration

The TOEFL iBT must be taken at an authorized ETS test center. Testing centers located around the world offer the TOEFL iBT more than 50 times a year. Test takers must preregister one week before the exam; walk-in registration is not permitted. Refer to the ETS TOEFL website for a list of local test centers and exam dates. (https://www.ets.org/toefl/ibt/register/centers_dates) Test takers are permitted to retake the exam as many times as they choose, but are limited to one test within a 12-day period.

On the day of the exam, test takers must present two valid forms of photo ID. Other personal belongings are not permitted in the testing room. Electronic devices like phones, cameras, and watches are prohibited, even during break time. Food and beverages may be accessed during break time, and longer breaks or extended access to snacks and drinks may be available for test takers in need of exam accommodations. The TOEFL iBT offers a variety of other accommodations for students with disabilities, such as screen magnification, sign language interpretation, and Braille or audio versions of the test. (https://www.ets.org/toefl/ibt/register/disabilities/accommodations)

Test Format

The TOEFL iBT consists of four sections: reading, listening, speaking, and writing. It is necessary to take the entire test at once (it is not possible to take specific sections of the test). One ten minute break is given after the reading and listening sections.

The type of questions, number of questions, and time limit varies between subjects:

Subject	Number of questions	Time
Reading	3-4 passages with 12-14 questions per passage	60-80 minutes
Listening	4-6 lectures with 6 questions per lecture 2-3 conversations with 5 questions per conversation	60-90 minutes
Speaking	6 questions 2 Independent Speaking tasks 2 Integrated Speaking tasks	~20 minutes Response time: Independent speaking: 45 seconds per question Integrated speaking: 60 seconds per question
Writing	2 questions 1 Integrated Writing task 1 Independent Writing task	Integrated writing: 20 minutes Independent writing: 30 minutes
Total test time: 4 hours		

Test content is based on academic English. Reading and listening passages come from college level textbooks or lectures. Conversations will be related to campus topics and school life. The listening, speaking, and writing sections all include listening components (lectures and/or conversations), and speakers may have accented English from North America, the UK, Australia, or New Zealand.

Because TOEFL iBT is internet based, it is administered via computer. Test takers will use a headset with a microphone to listen to test questions and record their responses. Writing responses must be typed. (https://www.ets.org/toefl/ibt/faq/)

Scoring

Test takers can check their scores via their TOEFL online account approximately 10 days after completing the exam. Each section of the test is scored between 0-30 points, with a cumulative score of 0–120 points. Scores are valid for two years, and test takers are able to choose which valid scores from the past two years they wish to report to score recipients (although test scores must be used in their entirety; it is not possible to combine section scores from different test dates).

There are no "passing" or "failing" scores; rather, each institution or program determines its own guidelines for evaluating scores. According to data from 2015 exams, the average TOEFL iBT score is approximately 80 points. (https://www.ets.org/s/toefl/pdf/94227_unlweb.pdf) Many institutions look for scores at or above 80-90 points, while competitive programs may require scores of 100 points or higher (http://www.msinus.com/content/toefl-cut-off-score-323/). Requirements vary greatly; refer to each institution for their evaluation criteria.

Recent/Future Developments

The TOEFL iBT is the newest version of the test. Previously, TOEFL was a paper based test (PBT). The TOEFL PBT may still be administered in areas without reliable internet connection. Unlike the TOEFL iBT, the TOEFL PBT has no speaking section and only requires one essay response on the writing section. (https://www.ets.org/toefl/pbt/about/content/)

Listening Section

We have recorded audio to go along with the listening practice questions. You can find all of our audio recordings by going to testprepbooks.com/toefl or by scanning the QR code below. The audio is only online. There is no CD.

Study Prep Plan for the TOEFL iBT

1 **Schedule -** Use one of our study schedules below or come up with one of your own.

2 **Relax -** Test anxiety can hurt even the best students. There are many ways to reduce stress. Find the one that works best for you.

3 **Execute -** Once you have a good plan in place, be sure to stick to it.

One Week Study Schedule		
Day 1	Reading	
Day 2	Listening & Speaking	
Day 3	Writing	
Day 4	Practice Test #1	
Day 5	Practice Test #2	
Day 6	Practice Test #3	
Day 7	Take Your Exam!	

Two Week Study Schedule			
Day 1	Reading	Day 8	Practice Test #1
Day 2	Main Idea	Day 9	Answer Explanations #1
Day 3	Literary Elements	Day 10	Practice Test #2
Day 4	Listening	Day 11	Answer Explanations #2
Day 5	Speaking	Day 12	Practice Test #3
Day 6	Writing	Day 13	Answer Explanations #3
Day 7	Punctuation	Day 14	Take Your Exam!

One Month Study Schedule					
Day 1	Reading	Day 11	Practice Questions	Day 21	Practice Test #1
Day 2	Analysis of Science Excerpts	Day 12	Writing	Day 22	Answer Explanations #1
Day 3	Main Idea	Day 13	Parts of Speech	Day 23	Take a Rest Day
Day 4	Transitional Words and Phrases	Day 14	Sentences	Day 24	Practice Test #2
Day 5	Literary Elements	Day 15	Phrases	Day 25	Answer Explanations #2
Day 6	Major Forms Within Each Genre	Day 16	Punctuation	Day 26	Take a Rest Day
Day 7	Practice Questions	Day 17	Word Confusion	Day 27	Practice Test #3
Day 8	Listening	Day 18	First Essay	Day 28	Answer Explanations #3
Day 9	Practice Questions	Day 19	Second Essay	Day 29	Take a Rest Day
Day 10	Speaking	Day 20	Take a Rest Day	Day 30	Take Your Exam!

Reading

The Reading section is the first section on the TOEFL iBT® and is designed to assess the test taker's ability to understand university-level academic texts. The section includes 3-4 passages, with approximately 10-14 questions pertaining to each passage, for a total of 34-56 questions. The total allotted time for the Reading section ranges from 60-80 minutes. These ranges exist because Educational Testing Service (ETS) sometimes includes additional questions in the Reading section that enable test developers to assess the viability of potential future scored questions or to compare outcomes of various administrations of the TOEFL across the country, as benchmark questions. While test takers are not alerted to which test questions fall under either of these conditions, the experimental questions are unscored and as such, they do not affect one's results either way.

Each passage and its associated question is timed separately and given 20 minutes, so test takers with three passages test for an hour and those with four passages will have a Reading section that lasts 80 minutes. It should be noted that the questions pertaining to the passage will not appear on the computer screen until the test taker has scrolled all the way to the end of the passage. At that point, the passage text moves to the right side of the screen and the associated questions are listed on left. The passage questions do not need to be answered in order and test takers can skim them and then refer back to the passage to determine the correct answer.

Each passage is approximately 700 words and comes from an introductory-level university course text from any number of subjects such as biology, sociology, business, and literature. Test takers do not need prior experience or knowledge of the subject to answer the questions successfully; all necessary information is contained within the passages themselves. The test taker only needs to demonstrate their ability to comprehend academic texts, rather than convey an advanced understanding of the specific subject matter.

Test takers should be prepared to critically analyze the point of view and structure of the passage, as there are often multiple perspectives presented, and typically at least one question per passage addresses the organizational structure of the reading exercise.

The questions in the Reading section are of three possible formats, but each passage will have at least one question of each type:

- Multiple-choice questions with four answer options, in which the test taker selects the single best choice.

- Multiple-choice questions that present a sentence in the question and then display four answer options, each which denotes a specific area within the text of the passage. Test takers must select the single best choice that correctly indicates the point in the passage where the new sentence should be inserted.

- "Reading to Learn" questions, which list more than four choices and have more than one correct response and ask test takers to sort the provided answers into gaps in a provided chart or summary statement. Such questions assess the test taker's ability to decode the text's structure or to link ideas from various parts of the passage together.

The first type of multiple-choice questions can address a variety of things. These questions may require that the test taker identify the passage's or main idea or specific factual details that were explicitly

stated in the text. Similarly, there are some questions in which the test taker must select the one detail that was *not* in the passage or is incorrectly presented in the answer choice in one way or another. Other questions may ask readers to identify the purpose of the passage in general or of specific statements, such that test takers need to decide *why* the author included a particular point. Some questions pull an entire sentence from the passage and then appear to simplify or paraphrase it in each of the four choices; incorrect choices will either omit important information from the original sentence or contain inaccurate details. Lastly, test takers may need to make logical inferences based on the passage or to determine the meaning of vocabulary words or pronouns referenced in the reading.

Analysis of History/Social Studies Excerpts

The TOEFL iBT® Reading section may include historically-based excerpts. The test may also include one or more passages from social sciences such as economics, psychology, or sociology.

For these types of questions, the test taker will need to utilize all the reading comprehension skills discussed below, but mastery of further skills will help. This section addresses those skills.

Comprehending Test Questions Prior to Reading

While preparing for a historical passage on a standardized test, first read the test questions, and then quickly scan the test answers prior to reading the passage itself. Notice there is a difference between the terms **read** and **scan.** Reading involves full concentration while addressing every word. Scanning involves quickly glancing at text in chunks, noting important dates, words, and ideas along the way. Reading test questions will help the test taker know what information to focus on in the historical passage. Scanning answers will help the test taker focus on possible answer options while reading the passage.

When reading standardized test questions that address historical passages, be sure to clearly understand what each question is asking. Is a question asking about vocabulary? Is another asking for the test taker to find a specific historical fact? Do any of the questions require the test taker to draw conclusions, identify an author's topic, tone, or position? Knowing what content to address will help the test taker focus on the information they will be asked about later. However, the test taker should approach this reading comprehension technique with some caution. It is tempting to only look for the right answers within any given passage. However, do not put on "reading blinders" and ignore all other information presented in a passage. It is important to fully read every passage and not just scan it. Strictly looking for what may be the right answers to test questions can cause the test taker to ignore important contextual clues that actually require critical thinking in order to identify correct answers. Scanning a passage for what appears to be wrong answers can have a similar result.

When reading test questions prior to tackling a historical passage, be sure to understand what skills the test is assessing, and then fully read the related passage with those skills in mind. Focus on every word in both the test questions and the passage itself. Read with a critical eye and a logical mind.

Reading for Factual Information

Standardized test questions that ask for factual information are usually straightforward. These types of questions will either ask the test taker to confirm a fact by choosing a correct answer, or to select a correct answer based on a negative fact question.

For example, the test taker may encounter a passage from Lincoln's Gettysburg address. A corresponding test question may ask the following:

> Which war is Abraham Lincoln referring to in the following passage?: "Now we are engaged in a great civil war, testing whether that nation, or any nation so conceived and so dedicated, can long endure."

This type of question is asking the test taker to confirm a simple fact. Given options such as World War I, the War of Spanish Succession, World War II, and the American Civil War, the test taker should be able to correctly identify the American Civil War based on the words "civil war" within the passage itself, and, hopefully, through general knowledge. In this case, reading the test question and scanning answer options ahead of reading the Gettysburg address would help quickly identify the correct answer. Similarly, a test taker may be asked to confirm a historical fact based on a negative fact question. For example, a passage's corresponding test question may ask the following:

> Which option is incorrect based on the above passage?

Given a variety of choices speaking about which war Abraham Lincoln was addressing, the test taker would need to eliminate all correct answers pertaining to the American Civil War and choose the answer choice referencing a different war. In other words, the correct answer is the one that contradicts the information in the passage.

It is important to remember that reading for factual information is straightforward. The test taker must distinguish fact from bias. Factual statements can be proven or disproven independent of the author and from a variety of other sources. Remember, successfully answering questions regarding factual information may require the test taker to re-read the passage, as these types of questions test for attention to detail.

Reading for Tone, Message, and Effect

The Reading section does not just address a test taker's ability to find facts within a reading passage; it also determines a reader's ability to determine an author's viewpoint through the use of tone, message, and overall effect. This type of reading comprehension requires inference skills, deductive reasoning skills, the ability to draw logical conclusions, and overall critical thinking skills. Reading for factual information is straightforward. Reading for an author's tone, message, and overall effect is not. It's key to read carefully when asked test questions that address a test taker's ability to these writing devices. These are not questions that can be easily answered by quickly scanning for the right information.

Tone

An author's **tone** is the use of particular words, phrases, and writing style to convey an overall meaning. Tone expresses the author's attitude towards a particular topic. For example, a historical reading passage may begin like the following:

> The presidential election of 1960 ushered in a new era, a new Camelot, a new phase of forward thinking in U.S. politics that embraced brash action and unrest and responded with admirable leadership.

From this opening statement, a reader can draw some conclusions about the author's attitude towards President John F. Kennedy. Furthermore, the reader can make additional, educated guesses about the state of the Union during the 1960 presidential election. By close reading, the test taker can determine that the repeated use of the word *new* and words such as *admirable leadership* indicate the author's

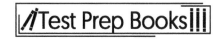

tone of admiration regarding President Kennedy's boldness. In addition, the author assesses that the era during President Kennedy's administration was problematic through the use of the words *brash action* and *unrest.* Therefore, if a test taker encountered a test question asking about the author's use of tone and their assessment of the Kennedy administration, the test taker should be able to identify an answer indicating admiration. Similarly, if asked about the state of the Union during the 1960s, a test taker should be able to correctly identify an answer indicating political unrest.

When identifying an author's tone, the following list of words may be helpful. This is not an inclusive list. Generally, parts of speech that indicate attitude will also indicate tone:

- Comical
- Angry
- Ambivalent
- Scary
- Lyrical
- Matter-of-fact
- Judgmental
- Sarcastic
- Malicious
- Objective
- Pessimistic
- Patronizing
- Gloomy
- Instructional
- Satirical
- Formal
- Casual

Message

An author's **message** is the same as the overall meaning of a passage. It is the main idea, or the main concept the author wishes to convey. An author's message may be stated outright, or it may be implied. Regardless, the test taker will need to use careful reading skills to identify an author's message or purpose.

Often, the message of a particular passage can be determined by thinking about why the author wrote the information. Many historical passages are written to inform and to teach readers established, factual information. However, many historical works are also written to convey biased ideas to readers. Gleaning bias from an author's message in a historical passage can be difficult, especially if the reader is presented with a variety of established facts as well. Readers tend to accept historical writing as factual. This is not always the case. Any discerning reader who has tackled historical information on topics such as United States political party agendas can attest that two or more works on the same topic may have completely different messages supporting or refuting the value of the identical policies. Therefore, it is important to critically assess an author's message separate from factual information.

One author, for example, may point to the rise of unorthodox political candidates in an election year based on the failures of the political party in office while another may point to the rise of the same candidates in the same election year based on the current party's successes. The historical facts of what has occurred leading up to an election year are not in refute. Labeling those facts as a failure or a success is a bias within an author's overall message, as is excluding factual information in order to further a particular point. In a standardized testing situation, a reader must be able to critically assess what the author is trying to say separate from the historical facts that surround their message.

Using the example of Lincoln's Gettysburg Address, a test question may ask the following:

What is the message the author is trying to convey through this address?

Then they will ask the test taker to select an answer that best expresses Lincoln's message to his audience. Based on the options given, a test taker should be able to select the answer expressing the idea that Lincoln's audience should recognize the efforts of those who died in the war as a sacrifice to preserving human equality and self-government.

Effect

The **effect** an author wants to convey is when an author wants to impart a particular mood in their message. An author may want to challenge a reader's intellect, inspire imagination, or spur emotion. An author may present information to appeal to a physical, aesthetic, or transformational sense. Take the following text as an example:

In 1963, Martin Luther King stated "I have a dream." The gathering at the Lincoln Memorial was the beginning of the Civil Rights movement and, with its reference to the Emancipation Proclamation, Dr. King's words electrified those who wanted freedom and equality while rising from hatred and slavery. It was the beginning of radical change.

The test taker may be asked about the effect this statement might have on King's audience. Through careful reading of the passage, the test taker should be able to choose an answer that best identifies an effect of grabbing the audience's attention. The historical facts are in place: King made the speech in 1963 at the Lincoln Memorial, kicked off the civil rights movement, and referenced the Emancipation Proclamation. The words *electrified* and *radical change* indicate the effect the author wants the reader to understand as a result of King's speech. In this historical passage, facts are facts. However, the author's message goes beyond the facts to indicate the effect the message had on the audience and, in addition, the effect the event should have on the reader.

When reading historical passages, the test taker should perform due diligence in their awareness of the test questions and answers up front. From there, the test taker should carefully, and critically, read all historical excerpts with an eye for detail, tone, message (biased or unbiased), and effect. Being able to synthesize these skills will result in success in a standardized testing situation.

Analysis of Science Excerpts

The Reading section may include passages that address the fundamental concepts of Earth science, biology, chemistry, or other sciences. Again, prior knowledge of these subjects is not necessary to determine correct test answers; instead, the test taker's ability to comprehend the passages is key to success. When reading scientific excerpts, the test taker must be able to examine quantitative information, identify hypotheses, interpret data, and consider implications of the material they are presented with. It is helpful, at this point, to reference the above section on comprehending test questions prior to reading. The same rules apply: read questions and scan questions, along with their answers, prior to fully reading a passage. Be informed prior to approaching a scientific text. A test taker should know what they will be asked and how to apply their reading skills. In this section of the test, it is also likely that a test taker will encounter graphs and charts to assess their ability to interpret scientific

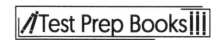

data with an appropriate conclusion. This section will determine the skills necessary to address scientific data presented through identifying hypotheses, through reading and examining data, and through interpreting data representation passages.

Examine Hypotheses

When presented with fundamental, scientific concepts, it is important to read for understanding. The most basic skill in achieving this literacy is to understand the concept of hypothesis and moreover, to be able to identify it in a particular passage. A **hypothesis** is a proposed idea that needs further investigation in order to be proven true or false. While it can be considered an educated guess, a hypothesis goes more in depth in its attempt to explain something that is not currently accepted within scientific theory. It requires further experimentation and data gathering to test its validity and is subject to change, based on scientifically conducted test results. Being able to read a science passage and understand its main purpose, including any hypotheses, helps the test taker understand data-driven evidence. It helps the test taker to be able to correctly answer questions about the science excerpt they are asked to read.

When reading to identify a hypothesis, a test taker should ask, "What is the passage trying to establish? What is the passage's main idea? What evidence does the passage contain that either supports or refutes this idea?" Asking oneself these questions will help identify a hypothesis. Additionally, hypotheses are logical statements that are testable and use very precise language.

Review the following hypothesis example:

> Consuming excess sugar in the form of beverages has a greater impact on childhood obesity and subsequent weight gain than excessive sugar from food.

While this is likely a true statement, it is still only a conceptual idea in a text passage regarding how sugar consumption affects childhood obesity, unless the passage also contains tested data that either proves or disproves the statement. A test taker could expect the rest of the passage to cite data proving that children who drink empty calories gain more weight, and are more likely to be obese, than children who eat sugary snacks.

A hypothesis goes further in that, given its ability to be proven or disproven, it may result in further hypotheses that require extended research. For example, the hypothesis regarding sugar consumption in drinks, after undergoing rigorous testing, may lead scientists to state another hypothesis such as the following:

> Consuming excess sugar in the form of beverages as opposed to food items is a habit found in mostly sedentary children.

This new, working hypothesis further focuses not just on the source of an excess of calories, but tries an "educated guess" that empty caloric intake has a direct, subsequent impact on physical behavior.

When reading a science passage to determine its hypothesis, a test taker should look for a concept that attempts to explain a phenomenon, is testable, logical, precisely worded, and yields data-driven results. The test taker should scan the presented passage for any word or data-driven clues that will help identify the hypothesis, and then be able to correctly answer test questions regarding the hypothesis based on their critical thinking skills.

Reading Strategies

A **reading strategy** is the way a reader interacts with text in order to understand its meaning. It is a skill set that a reader brings to the reading. It employs a reader's ability to use prior knowledge when addressing literature and utilizes a set of methods in order to analyze text. A reading strategy is not simply tackling a text passage as it appears. It involves a more complex system of planning and thought during the reading experience. Current research indicates readers who utilize strategies and a variety of critical reading skills are better thinkers who glean more interpretive information from their reading. Consequently, they are more successful in their overall comprehension.

Pre-Reading Strategies

Pre-reading strategies are important, yet often overlooked. Non-critical readers will often begin reading without taking the time to review factors that will help them understand the text. Skipping pre-reading strategies may result in a reader having to re-address a text passage more times than is necessary. Some pre-reading strategies include the following:

- Previewing the text for clues
- Skimming the text for content
- Scanning for unfamiliar words in context
- Formulating questions on sight
- Recognizing needed prior knowledge

Before reading a text passage, a reader can enhance their ability to comprehend material by **previewing the text for clues**. This may mean making careful note of any titles, headings, graphics, notes, introductions, important summaries, and conclusions. It can involve a reader making physical notes regarding these elements or highlighting anything he or she thinks is important before reading. Often, a reader will be able to gain information just from these elements alone. Of course, close reading is required in order to fill in the details. A reader needs to be able to ask what he or she is reading about and what a passage is trying to say. The answers to these general questions can often be answered in previewing the text itself.

It's helpful to use pre-reading clues to determine the main idea and organization. First, any titles, sub-headings, and chapter headings should be read, and the test taker should make note of the author's credentials if any are listed. It's important to deduce what these clues may indicate as it pertains to the focus of the text and how it's organized.

During pre-reading, readers should also take special note of how text features contribute to the central idea or thesis of the passage. Is there an index? Is there a glossary? What headings, footnotes, or other visuals are included and how do they relate to the details within the passage? Again, this is where any pre-reading notes come in handy, since a test taker should be able to relate supporting details to these textual features.

Next, a reader should **skim** the text for general ideas and content. This technique does not involve close reading; rather, it involves looking for important words within the passage itself. These words may have something to do with the author's theme. They may have to do with structure—for example, words such as *first, next, therefore,* and *last*. Skimming helps a reader understand the overall structure of a passage and, in turn, this helps him or her understand the author's theme or message.

From there, a reader should quickly **scan** the text for any unfamiliar words. When reading a print text, highlighting these words or making other marginal notation is helpful when going back to read text critically. A reader should look at the words surrounding any unfamiliar ones to see what contextual clues unfamiliar words carry. Being able to define unfamiliar terms through contextual meaning is a critical skill in reading comprehension.

A reader should also **formulate any questions** he or she might have before conducting close reading. Questions such as "What is the author trying to tell me?" or "Is the author trying to persuade my thinking?" are important to a reader's ability to engage critically with the text. Questions will focus a reader's attention on what is important in terms of ideas and supporting details.

Last, a reader should recognize that authors assume readers bring a prior knowledge set to the reading experience. Not all readers have the same experience, but authors seek to communicate with their readers. In turn, readers should strive to interact with the author of a particular passage by asking themselves what the passage demands they know during reading. If a passage is informational in nature, a reader should ask "What do I know about this topic from other experiences I've had or other works I've read?" If a reader can relate to the content, he or she will better understand it.

All of the above pre-reading strategies will help the reader prepare for a closer reading experience. They will engage a reader in active interaction with the text by helping to focus the reader's full attention on the details that he or she will encounter during the next round or two of critical, closer reading.

Strategies During Reading

After pre-reading, a test taker can employ a variety of other reading strategies while conducting one or more closer readings. These strategies include the following:

- Inferring the unspoken/unwritten text
- Clarifying during a close read
- Questioning during a close read
- Organizing the main ideas and supporting details
- Summarizing the text effectively

Inferring the unspoken or unwritten text demands the reader read between the lines in terms of an author's intent or message. The strategy asks that a reader not take everything he or she reads at face value, but instead, he or she will determine what the author is trying to say. A reader's ability to make inference relies on their ability to think clearly and logically about what he or she is reading. It does not ask that the reader make wild speculation or guess about the material but demands he or she be able to come to sound conclusion about the material, given the details provided and those not provided. A reader who can make logical inference from unstated text is achieving successful reading comprehension.

A reader needs to be able to **clarify** what he or she is reading. This strategy demands a reader think about how and what he or she is reading. This thinking should occur during and after the act of reading. For example, a reader may encounter one or more unfamiliar ideas during reading, then be asked to apply thoughts about those unfamiliar concepts after reading when answering test questions.

Questioning during a critical read is closely related to clarifying. A reader must be able to ask questions in general about what he or she is reading and questions regarding the author's supporting ideas. Questioning also involves a reader's ability to self-question. When closely reading a passage, it's not enough to simply try and understand the author. A reader must consider critical thinking questions to ensure he or she is comprehending intent. It's advisable, when conducting a close read, to write out margin notes and questions during the experience. These questions can be addressed later in the thinking process after reading and during the phase where a reader addresses the test questions. A reader who is successful in reading comprehension will iteratively question what he or she reads, search text for clarification, then answer any questions that arise.

A reader should **organize** main ideas and supporting details cognitively as he or she reads, as it will help the reader understand the larger structure at work. The use of quick annotations or marks to indicate what the main idea is and how the details function to support it can be helpful. Understanding the structure of a text passage is sometimes critical to answering questions about an author's approach, theme, messages, and supporting detail. This strategy is most effective when reading informational or nonfiction text. Texts that try to convince readers of a particular idea, that present a theory, or that try to explain difficult concepts are easier to understand when a reader can identify the overarching structure at work.

Post-Reading Strategies

After completing a text, a reader should be able to **summarize** the author's theme and supporting details in order to fully understand the passage. Being able to effectively restate the author's message, sub-themes, and pertinent, supporting ideas will help a reader gain an advantage when addressing standardized test questions. Employing all of these strategies will lead to fuller, more insightful reading comprehension.

Main Idea

It is very important to know the difference between the topic and the main idea of the text. Even though these two are similar because they both present the central point of a text, they have distinctive differences. A **topic** is the subject of the text; it can usually be described in a one- to two-word phrase and appears in the simplest form. On the other hand, the **main idea** is more detailed and provides the author's central point of the text. It can be expressed through a complete sentence and can be found in the beginning, middle, or end of a paragraph. In most nonfiction books, the first sentence of the passage usually (but not always) states the main idea. Take a look at the passage below to review the topic versus the main idea.

Cheetahs

Cheetahs are one of the fastest mammals on land, reaching up to 70 miles an hour over short distances. Even though cheetahs can run as fast as 70 miles an hour, they usually only have to run half that speed to catch up with their choice of prey. Cheetahs cannot maintain a fast pace over long periods of time because they will overheat their bodies. After a chase, cheetahs need to rest for approximately 30 minutes prior to eating or returning to any other activity.

In the example above, the topic of the passage is "Cheetahs" simply because that is the subject of the text. The main idea of the text is "Cheetahs are one of the fastest mammals on land but can only maintain this fast pace for short distances." While it covers the topic, it is more detailed and refers to the text in its entirety. The text continues to provide additional details called **supporting details**, which will be discussed in the next section.

Supporting Details

Supporting details help readers better develop and understand the main idea. Supporting details answer questions like *who, what, where, when, why,* and *how*. Different types of supporting details include examples, facts and statistics, anecdotes, and sensory details.

Persuasive and informative texts often use supporting details. In persuasive texts, authors attempt to make readers agree with their point of view, and supporting details are often used as "selling points." If authors make a statement, they should support the statement with evidence in order to adequately persuade readers. Informative texts use supporting details such as examples and facts to inform readers. Take another look at the previous "Cheetahs" passage to find examples of supporting details.

Cheetahs

Cheetahs are one of the fastest mammals on land, reaching up to 70 miles an hour over short distances. Even though cheetahs can run as fast as 70 miles an hour, they usually only have to run half that speed to catch up with their choice of prey. Cheetahs cannot maintain a fast pace over long periods of time because they will overheat their bodies. After a chase, cheetahs need to rest for approximately 30 minutes prior to eating or returning to any other activity.

In the example above, supporting details include:

- Cheetahs reach up to 70 miles per hour over short distances.
- They usually only have to run half that speed to catch up with their prey.
- Cheetahs will overheat their bodies if they exert a high speed over longer distances.
- Cheetahs need to rest for 30 minutes after a chase.

Look at the diagram below (applying the cheetah example) to help determine the hierarchy of topic, main idea, and supporting details.

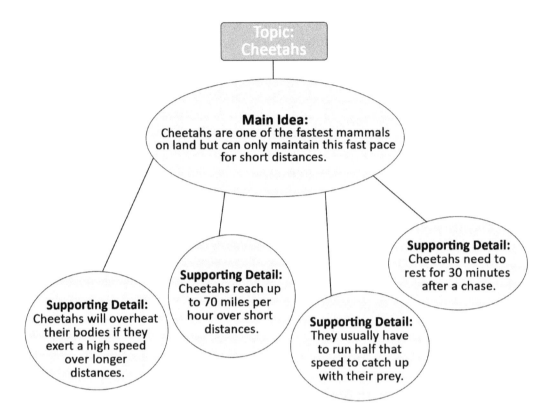

Analyzing Nuances of Word Meaning and Figures of Speech

Many words contain two levels of meaning: connotation and denotation. A word's **denotation** is its most literal meaning—the definition that can readily be found in the dictionary. A word's **connotation** includes all of its emotional and cultural associations.

In literary writing, authors rely heavily on connotative meaning to create mood and characterization. The following are two descriptions of a rainstorm:

- The rain slammed against the windowpane, and the wind howled through the fireplace. A pair of hulking oaks next to the house cast eerie shadows as their branches trembled in the wind.

- The rain pattered against the windowpane, and the wind whistled through the fireplace. A pair of stately oaks next to the house cast curious shadows as their branches swayed in the wind.

The first description paints a creepy picture for readers with strongly emotional words like *slammed*, connoting force and violence. *Howled* connotes pain or wildness, and *eerie* and *trembled* connote fear. Overall, the connotative language in this description serves to inspire fear and anxiety.

However, as can be seen in the second description, swapping out a few key words for those with different connotations completely changes the feeling of the passage. *Slammed* is replaced with the more cheerful *pattered*, and *hulking* has been swapped out for *stately*. Both words imply something large, but *hulking* is more intimidating whereas *stately* is more respectable. *Curious* and *swayed* seem

more playful than the language used in the earlier description. Although both descriptions represent roughly the same situation, the nuances of the emotional language used throughout the passages create a very different sense for readers.

Selective choice of connotative language can also be extremely impactful in other forms of writing, such as editorials or persuasive texts. Through connotative language, writers reveal their biases and opinions while trying to inspire feelings and actions in readers:

- Parents won't stop complaining about standardized tests.
- Parents continue to raise concerns about standardized tests.

Readers should be able to identify the nuance in meaning between these two sentences. The first one carries a more negative feeling, implying that parents are being bothersome or whiny. Readers of the second sentence, though, might come away with the feeling that parents are concerned and involved in their children's education. Again, the aggregate of even subtle cues can combine to give a specific emotional impression to readers, so from an early age, students should be aware of how language can be used to influence readers' opinions.

Another form of non-literal expression can be found in **figures of speech**. As with connotative language, figures of speech tend to be shared within a cultural group and may be difficult to pick up on for learners outside of that group. In some cases, a figure of speech may be based on the literal denotation of the words it contains, but in other cases, a figure of speech is far removed from its literal meaning. A case in point is **irony**, where what is said is the exact opposite of what is meant:

> The new tax plan is poorly planned, based on faulty economic data, and unable to address the financial struggles of middle class families. Yet legislators remain committed to passing this brilliant proposal.

When the writer refers to the proposal as brilliant, the opposite is implied—the plan is "faulty" and "poorly planned." By using irony, the writer means that the proposal is anything but brilliant by using the word in a non-literal sense.

Another figure of speech is **hyperbole**—extreme exaggeration or overstatement. Statements like, "I love you to the moon and back" or "Let's be friends for a million years" utilize hyperbole to convey a greater depth of emotion, without literally committing oneself to space travel or a life of immortality.

Figures of speech may sometimes use one word in place of another. **Synecdoche**, for example, uses a part of something to refer to its whole. The expression "Don't hurt a hair on her head!" implies protecting more than just an individual hair, but rather her entire body. "The art teacher is training a class of Picassos" uses Picasso, one individual notable artist, to stand in for the entire category of talented artists. Another figure of speech using word replacement is **metonymy**, where a word is replaced with something closely associated to it. For example, news reports may use the word "Washington" to refer to the American government or "the crown" to refer to the British monarch.

Meaning of Words in Context

There will be many occasions in one's reading career in which an unknown word or a word with multiple meanings will pop up. There are ways of determining what these words or phrases mean that do not require the use of the dictionary, which is especially helpful during a test where one may not be available. Even outside of the exam, knowing how to derive an understanding of a word via context clues will be a critical skill in the real world. The context is the circumstances in which a story or a passage is happening and can usually be found in the series of words directly before or directly after the word or phrase in question. The clues are the words that hint towards the meaning of the unknown word or phrase.

There may be questions that ask about the meaning of a particular word or phrase within a passage. There are a couple ways to approach these kinds of questions:

- Define the word or phrase in a way that is easy to comprehend (using context clues).
- Try out each answer choice in place of the word.

To demonstrate, here's an example from *Alice in Wonderland*:

> Alice was beginning to get very tired of sitting by her sister on the bank, and of having nothing to do: once or twice she <u>peeped</u> into the book her sister was reading, but it had no pictures or conversations in it, "and what is the use of a book," thought Alice, "without pictures or conversations?"

Q: As it is used in the selection, the word <u>peeped</u> means:

Using the first technique, before looking at the answers, define the word "peeped" using context clues and then find the matching answer. Then, analyze the entire passage in order to determine the meaning, not just the surrounding words.

To begin, imagine a blank where the word should be and put a synonym or definition there: "once or twice she _____ into the book her sister was reading." The context clue here is the book. It may be tempting to put "read" where the blank is, but notice the preposition word, "into." One does not read *into* a book, one simply reads a book, and since reading a book requires that it is seen with a pair of eyes, then "look" would make the most sense to put into the blank: "once or twice she <u>looked </u>into the book her sister was reading."

Once an easy-to-understand word or synonym has been supplanted, readers should check to make sure it makes sense with the rest of the passage. What happened after she looked into the book? She thought to herself how a book without pictures or conversations is useless. This situation in its entirety makes sense.

Now check the answer choices for a match:
    a. To make a high-pitched cry
    b. To smack
    c. To look curiously
    d. To pout

Since the word was already defined, Choice *C* is the best option.

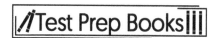

Using the second technique, replace the figurative blank with each of the answer choices and determine which one is the most appropriate. Remember to look further into the passage to clarify that they work, because they could still make sense out of context.

    a. Once or twice she <u>made a high pitched cry</u> into the book her sister was reading
    b. Once or twice she <u>smacked</u> into the book her sister was reading
    c. Once or twice she <u>looked curiously</u> into the book her sister was reading
    d. Once or twice she <u>pouted</u> into the book her sister was reading

For Choice *A*, it does not make much sense in any context for a person to yell into a book, unless maybe something terrible has happened in the story. Given that afterward Alice thinks to herself how useless a book without pictures is, this option does not make sense within context.

For Choice *B*, smacking a book someone is reading may make sense if the rest of the passage indicates a reason for doing so. If Alice was angry or her sister had shoved it in her face, then maybe smacking the book would make sense within context. However, since whatever she does with the book causes her to think, "what is the use of a book without pictures or conversations?" then answer Choice *B* is not an appropriate answer. Answer Choice *C* fits well within context, given her subsequent thoughts on the matter. Answer Choice *D* does not make sense in context or grammatically, as people do not "pout into" things.

This is a simple example to illustrate the techniques outlined above. There may, however, be a question in which all of the definitions are correct and also make sense out of context, in which the appropriate context clues will really need to be honed in on in order to determine the correct answer. For example, here is another passage from *Alice in Wonderland*:

> . . . but when the Rabbit actually took a watch out of its waistcoat pocket, and looked at it, and then hurried on, Alice <u>started</u> to her feet, for it flashed across her mind that she had never before seen a rabbit with either a waistcoat-pocket or a watch to take out of it, and burning with curiosity, she ran across the field after it, and was just in time to see it pop down a large rabbit-hole under the hedge.

Q: As it is used in the passage, the word started means
    a. To turn on
    b. To begin
    c. To move quickly
    d. To be surprised

All of these words qualify as a definition of "start," but using context clues, the correct answer can be identified using one of the two techniques above. It's easy to see that one does not turn on, begin, or be surprised to one's feet. The selection also states that she "ran across the field after it," indicating that she was in a hurry. Therefore, to move quickly would make the most sense in this context.

The same strategies can be applied to vocabulary that may be completely unfamiliar. In this case, focus on the words before or after the unknown word in order to determine its definition. Take this sentence, for example:

> Sam was such a <u>miser</u> that he forced Andrew to pay him twelve cents for the candy, even though he had a large inheritance and he knew his friend was poor.

Unlike with assertion questions, for vocabulary questions, it may be necessary to apply some critical thinking skills that may not be explicitly stated within the passage. Think about the implications of the passage, or what the text is trying to say. With this example, it is important to realize that it is considered unusually stingy for a person to demand so little money from someone instead of just letting their friend have the candy, especially if this person is already wealthy. Hence, a <u>miser</u> is a greedy or stingy individual.

Questions about complex vocabulary may not be explicitly asked, but this is a useful skill to know. If there is an unfamiliar word while reading a passage and its definition goes unknown, it is possible to miss out on a critical message that could inhibit the ability to appropriately answer the questions. Practicing this technique in daily life will sharpen this ability to derive meanings from context clues with ease.

Transitional Words and Phrases

There are approximately 200 transitional words and phrases that are commonly used in the English language. Below are lists of common transition words and phrases used throughout transitions.

Time
- after
- before
- during
- in the middle

Example about to be Given
- for example
- in fact
- for instance

Compare
- likewise
- also

Contrast
- however
- yet
- but

Addition
- and
- also
- furthermore
- moreover

Logical Relationships
- if
- then
- therefore
- as a result
- since

Steps in a Process
- first
- second
- last

Transitional words and phrases are important writing devices because they connect sentences and paragraphs. Transitional words and phrases present logical order to writing and provide more coherent meaning to readers.

Transition words can be categorized based on the relationships they create between ideas:

- General order: signaling elaboration of an idea to emphasize a point—e.g., *for example, for instance, to demonstrate, including, such as, in other words, that is, in fact, also, furthermore, likewise, and, truly, so, surely, certainly, obviously, doubtless*

- Chronological order: referencing the time frame in which main event or idea occurs—e.g., *before, after, first, while, soon, shortly thereafter, meanwhile*

- Numerical order/order of importance: indicating that related ideas, supporting details, or events will be described in a sequence, possibly in order of importance—e.g., *first, second, also, finally, another, in addition, equally important, less importantly, most significantly, the main reason, last but not least*

- Spatial order: referring to the space and location of something or where things are located in relation to each other—e.g., *inside, outside, above, below, within, close, under, over, far, next to, adjacent to*

- Cause and effect order: signaling a causal relationship between events or ideas—e.g., *thus, therefore, since, resulted in, for this reason, as a result, consequently, hence, for, so*

- Compare and contrast order: identifying the similarities and differences between two or more objects, ideas, or lines of thought—e.g., *like, as, similarly, equally, just as, unlike, however, but, although, conversely, on the other hand, on the contrary*

- Summary order: indicating that a particular idea is coming to a close—e.g., *in conclusion, to sum up, in other words, ultimately, above all*

Author's Use of Evidence to Support Claims

Authors utilize a wide range of techniques to tell a story or communicate information. Readers should be familiar with the most common of these techniques. Techniques of writing are also commonly known as rhetorical devices; these are different ways of using evidence to support claims.

In nonfiction writing, authors employ argumentative techniques to present their opinion to readers in the most convincing way. Persuasive writing usually includes at least one type of appeal: an appeal to logic (logos), emotion (pathos), or credibility and trustworthiness (ethos). When a writer appeals to logic, they are asking readers to agree with them based on research, evidence, and an established line of reasoning. An author's argument might also appeal to readers' emotions, perhaps by including personal stories and anecdotes (a short narrative of a specific event). A final type of appeal, appeal to authority, asks the reader to agree with the author's argument on the basis of their expertise or credentials. Consider three different approaches to arguing the same opinion:

Logic (Logos)
Below is an example of an appeal to logic. The author uses evidence to disprove the logic of the school's rule (the rule was supposed to reduce discipline problems, but the number of problems has not been reduced; therefore, the rule is not working) and call for its repeal.

> Our school should abolish its current ban on campus cell phone use. The ban was adopted last year as an attempt to reduce class disruptions and help students focus more on their lessons. However, since the rule was enacted, there has been no change in the number of disciplinary problems in class. Therefore, the rule is ineffective and should be done away with.

Emotion (Pathos)
An author's argument might also appeal to readers' emotions, perhaps by including personal stories and anecdotes.

The next example presents an appeal to emotion. By sharing the personal anecdote of one student and speaking about emotional topics like family relationships, the author invokes the reader's empathy in asking them to reconsider the school rule.

> Our school should abolish its current ban on campus cell phone use. If students aren't able to use their phones during the school day, many of them feel isolated from their loved ones. For example, last semester, one student's grandmother had a heart attack in the morning. However, because he couldn't use his cell phone, the student didn't know about his grandmother's condition until the end of the day—when she had already passed away, and it was too late to say goodbye. By preventing students from contacting their friends and family, our school is placing undue stress and anxiety on students.

Credibility (Ethos)
Finally, an appeal to authority includes a statement from a relevant expert. In this case, the author uses a doctor in the field of education to support the argument. All three examples begin from the same opinion—the school's phone ban needs to change—but rely on different argumentative styles to persuade the reader.

> Our school should abolish its current ban on campus cell phone use. According to Dr. Bartholomew Everett, a leading educational expert, "Research studies show that cell phone usage has no real impact on student attentiveness. Rather, phones provide a valuable technological resource for learning. Schools need to learn how to integrate this new technology into their curriculum." Rather than banning phones altogether, our school should follow the advice of experts and allow students to use phones as part of their learning.

Making Logical Inferences

Critical readers should be able to make inferences. Making an **inference** requires the reader to read between the lines and look for what is implied rather than what is explicitly stated. That is, using information that *is* known from the text, the reader is able to make a logical assumption about information that is not explicitly stated but is probably true. Read the following passage:

"Hey, do you wanna meet my new puppy?" Jonathan asked.

"Oh, I'm sorry but please don't—" Jacinta began to protest, but before she could finish Jonathan had already opened the passenger side door of his car and a perfect white ball of fur came bouncing towards Jacinta.

"Isn't he the cutest?" beamed Jonathan.

"Yes—achoo!—he's pretty—aaaachooo!!—adora—aaa—aaaachoo!" Jacinta managed to say in between sneezes. "But if you don't mind, I—I—achoo!—need to go inside."

Which of the following can be inferred from Jacinta's reaction to the puppy?
a. she hates animals
b. she is allergic to dogs
c. she prefers cats to dogs
d. she is angry at Jonathan

An inference requires the reader to consider the information presented and then form their own idea about what is probably true. Based on the details in the passage, what is the best answer to the question? Important details to pay attention to include the tone of Jacinta's dialogue, which is overall polite and apologetic, as well as her reaction itself, which is a long string of sneezes. Answer Choices *A* and *D* both express strong emotions ("hates" and "angry") that are not evident in Jacinta's speech or actions. Answer Choice *C* mentions cats, but there is nothing in the passage to indicate Jacinta's feelings about cats. Answer Choice *B*, "she is allergic to dogs," is the most logical choice—based on the fact that she began sneezing as soon as a fluffy dog approached her, it makes sense to guess that Jacinta might be allergic to dogs. So even though Jacinta never directly states, "Sorry, I'm allergic to dogs!" using the clues in the passage, it is still reasonable to guess that this is true.

Making inferences is crucial for readers of literature because literary texts often avoid presenting complete and direct information to readers about characters' thoughts or feelings, or they present this information in an unclear way, leaving it up to the reader to interpret clues given in the text. In order to make inferences while reading, readers should ask themselves:

- What details are being presented in the text?
- Is there any important information that seems to be missing?
- Based on the information that the author *does* include, what else is probably true?
- Is this inference reasonable based on what is already known?

Recognizing the Structure of Texts in Various Formats

Writing can be classified under four passage types: narrative, expository, descriptive (sometimes called technical), and persuasive. Though these types are not mutually exclusive, one form tends to dominate the rest. By recognizing the *type* of passage you're reading, you gain insight into *how* you should read. If you're reading a narrative, you can assume the author intends to entertain, which means you may skim the text without losing meaning. A technical document might require a close read because skimming the passage might cause the reader to miss salient details.

1. **Narrative writing**, at its core, is the art of storytelling. For a narrative to exist, certain elements must be present. First, it must have characters. While many characters are human, characters could be defined as anything that thinks, acts, and talks like a human. For example, many recent movies, such as *Lord of the Rings* and *The Chronicles of Narnia*, include animals, fantastical creatures, and even trees that behave like humans. Second, it must have a plot or sequence of events. Typically, those events follow a standard plot diagram, but recent trends start *in medias res* or in the middle (near the climax). In this instance, foreshadowing and flashbacks often fill in plot details. Finally, along with characters and a plot, there must also be conflict. Conflict is usually divided into two types: internal and external. Internal conflict indicates the character is in turmoil and is presented through the character's thoughts. External conflicts are visible. Types of external conflict include a person versus nature, another person, or society.

2. **Expository writing** is detached and to the point. Since expository writing is designed to instruct or inform, it usually involves directions and steps written in second person ("you" voice) and lacks any persuasive or narrative elements. Sequence words such as *first*, *second*, and *third*, or *in the first place*, *secondly*, and *lastly* are often given to add fluency and cohesion. Common examples of expository writing include instructor's lessons, cookbook recipes, and repair manuals.

3. Due to its empirical nature, **technical writing** is filled with steps, charts, graphs, data, and statistics. The goal of technical writing is to advance understanding in a field through the scientific method. Experts such as teachers, doctors, or mechanics use words unique to the profession in which they operate. These words, which often incorporate acronyms, are called **jargon**. Technical writing is a type of expository writing but is not meant to be understood by the general public. Instead, technical writers assume readers have received a formal education in a particular field of study and need no explanation as to what the jargon means. Imagine a doctor trying to understand a diagnostic reading for a car or a mechanic trying to interpret lab results. Only professionals with proper training will fully comprehend the text.

4. **Persuasive writing** is designed to change opinions and attitudes. The topic, stance, and arguments are found in the thesis, positioned near the end of the introduction. Later supporting paragraphs offer relevant quotations, paraphrases, and summaries from primary or secondary sources, which are then interpreted, analyzed, and evaluated. The goal of persuasive writers is not to stack quotes but to develop original ideas by using sources as a starting point. Good persuasive writing makes powerful arguments with valid sources and thoughtful analysis. Poor persuasive writing is riddled with bias and logical fallacies. Sometimes logical and illogical arguments are sandwiched together in the same piece. Therefore, readers should display skepticism when reading persuasive arguments.

Literary Elements

There is no one, final definition of what literary elements are. They can be considered features or characteristics of fiction, but they are really more of a way that readers can unpack a text for the purpose of analysis and understanding the meaning. The elements contribute to a reader's literary interpretation of a passage as to how they function to convey the central message of a work. The most common literary elements used for analysis are presented below.

Point of View

The **point of view** is the position the narrator takes when telling the story in prose. If a narrator is incorporated in a drama, the point of view may vary; in poetry, point of view refers to the position the speaker in a poem takes.

First Person

The **first person point of view** is when the writer uses the word "I" in the text. Poetry often uses first person, e.g., William Wordsworth's "I Wandered Lonely as a Cloud." Two examples of prose written in first person are Suzanne Collins' *The Hunger Games* and Anthony Burgess's *A Clockwork Orange*.

Second Person

The **second person point of view** is when the writer uses the pronoun "you." It is not widely used in prose fiction, but as a technique, it has been used by writers such as William Faulkner in *Absalom, Absalom!* and Albert Camus in *The Fall*. It is more common in poetry—e.g., Pablo Neruda's "If You Forget Me."

Third Person

Third person point of view is when the writer utilizes pronouns such as *him, her*, or *them*. It may be the most utilized point of view in prose as it provides flexibility to an author and is the one with which readers are most familiar. There are two main types of third person used in fiction. **Third person omniscient** uses a narrator that is all-knowing, relating the story by conveying and interpreting thoughts/feelings of all characters. In **third person limited**, the narrator relates the story through the perspective of one character's thoughts/feelings, usually the main character.

Plot

The **plot** is what happens in the story. Plots may be singular, containing one problem, or they may be very complex, with many sub-plots. All plots have an exposition, a conflict, a climax, and a resolution. The **conflict** drives the plot and is something that the reader expects to be resolved. The plot carries those events along until there is a resolution to the conflict.

Tone

The **tone** of a story reflects the author's attitude and opinion about the subject matter of the story or text. Tone can be expressed through word choice, imagery, figurative language, syntax, and other details. The emotion or mood the reader experiences relates back to the tone of the story. Some examples of possible tones are humorous, somber, sentimental, and ironic.

Setting

The **setting** is the time, place, or set of surroundings in which the story occurs. It includes time or time span, place(s), climates, geography—man-made or natural—or cultural environments. Emily Dickinson's poem "Because I could not stop for Death" has a simple setting—the narrator's symbolic ride with Death through town towards the local graveyard. Conversely, Leo Tolstoy's *War and Peace* encompasses numerous settings within settings in the areas affected by the Napoleonic Wars, spanning 1805 to 1812.

Characters

Characters are the story's figures that assume primary, secondary, or minor roles. Central or major characters are those integral to the story—the plot cannot be resolved without them. A central character can be a **protagonist** or hero. There may be more than one protagonist, and he/she doesn't always have to possess good characteristics. A character can also be an **antagonist**—the force against a protagonist.

Character development is when the author takes the time to create dynamic characters that add uniqueness and depth to the story. *Dynamic* characters are characters that change over the course of the plot time. **Stock** characters are those that appear across genres and embrace stereotypes—e.g., the cowboy of the Wild West or the blonde bombshell in a detective novel. A **flat** character is one that does not present a lot of complexity or depth, while a **rounded** character does. Sometimes, the **narrator** of a story or the **speaker** in a poem can be a character—e.g., Nick Carraway in F. Scott Fitzgerald's *The Great Gatsby* or the speaker in Robert Browning's "My Last Duchess." The narrator might also function as a character in prose, though not be part of the story—e.g., Charles Dickens' narrator of *A Christmas Carol*.

Development of Themes

Theme or Central Message

The **theme** is the central message of a fictional work, whether that work is structured as prose, drama, or poetry. It is the heart of what an author is trying to say to readers through the writing, and theme is largely conveyed through literary elements and techniques.

In literature, a theme can often be determined by considering the overarching narrative conflict with the work. Though there are several types of conflicts and several potential themes within them, the following are the most common:

- **Individual against the self**—relevant to themes of self-awareness, internal struggles, pride, coming of age, facing reality, fate, free will, vanity, loss of innocence, loneliness, isolation, fulfillment, failure, and disillusionment

- **Individual against nature**—relevant to themes of knowledge vs. ignorance, nature as beauty, quest for discovery, self-preservation, chaos and order, circle of life, death, and destruction of beauty

- **Individual against society**—relevant to themes of power, beauty, good, evil, war, class struggle, totalitarianism, role of men/women, wealth, corruption, change vs. tradition, capitalism, destruction, heroism, injustice, and racism

- **Individual against another individual**—relevant to themes of hope, loss of love or hope, sacrifice, power, revenge, betrayal, and honor

For example, in Hawthorne's *The Scarlet Letter*, one possible narrative conflict could be the individual against the self, with a relevant theme of internal struggles. This theme is alluded to through characterization—Dimmesdale's moral struggle with his love for Hester and Hester's internal struggles with the truth and her daughter, Pearl. It's also alluded to through plot—Dimmesdale's suicide and Hester helping the very townspeople who initially condemned her.

Sometimes, a text can convey a **message** or **universal lesson**—a truth or insight that the reader infers from the text, based on analysis of the literary and/or poetic elements. This message is often presented as a statement. For example, a potential message in Shakespeare's *Hamlet* could be "Revenge is what ultimately drives the human soul." This message can be immediately determined through plot and characterization in numerous ways, but it can also be determined through the setting of Norway, which is bordering on war.

How Authors Develop Theme

Authors employ a variety of techniques to present a theme. They may compare or contrast characters, events, places, ideas, or historical or invented settings to speak thematically. They may use analogies, metaphors, similes, allusions, or other literary devices to convey the theme. An author's use of diction, syntax, and tone can also help convey the theme. Authors will often develop themes through the development of characters, use of the setting, repetition of ideas, use of symbols, and through contrasting value systems. Authors of both fiction and nonfiction genres will use a variety of these techniques to develop one or more themes.

Regardless of the literary genre, there are commonalities in how authors, playwrights, and poets develop themes or central ideas.

Authors often do research, the results of which contributes to theme. In prose fiction and drama, this research may include real historical information about the setting the author has chosen or include elements that make fictional characters, settings, and plots seem realistic to the reader. In nonfiction, research is critical since the information contained within this literature must be accurate and, moreover, accurately represented.

In fiction, authors present a narrative conflict that will contribute to the overall theme. In fiction, this conflict may involve the storyline itself and some trouble within characters that needs resolution. In nonfiction, this conflict may be an explanation or commentary on factual people and events.

Authors will sometimes use character motivation to convey theme, such as in the example from *Hamlet* regarding revenge. In fiction, the characters an author creates will think, speak, and act in ways that effectively convey the theme to readers. In nonfiction, the characters are factual, as in a biography, but authors pay particular attention to presenting those motivations to make them clear to readers.

Authors also use literary devices as a means of conveying theme. For example, the use of moon symbolism in Mary Shelley's *Frankenstein* is significant as its phases can be compared to the phases that the Creature undergoes as he struggles with his identity.

The selected point of view can also contribute to a work's theme. The use of first-person point of view in a fiction or non-fiction work engages the reader's response differently than third person point of view. The central idea or theme from a first-person narrative may differ from a third-person limited text.

In literary nonfiction, authors usually identify the purpose of their writing, which differs from fiction, where the general purpose is to entertain. The purpose of nonfiction is usually to inform, persuade, or entertain the audience. The stated purpose of a non-fiction text will drive how the central message or theme, if applicable, is presented.

Authors identify an audience for their writing, which is critical in shaping the theme of the work. For example, the audience for J.K. Rowling's *Harry Potter* series would be different than the audience for a biography of George Washington. The audience an author chooses to address is closely tied to the purpose of the work. The choice of an audience also drives the choice of language and level of diction an author uses. Ultimately, the intended audience determines the level to which that subject matter is presented and the complexity of the theme.

Characteristics of Literary Genres

Classifying literature involves an understanding of the concept of genre. A **genre** is a category of literature that possesses similarities in style and in characteristics. Based on form and structure, there are four basic genres.

Fictional Prose

Fictional prose consists of fictional works written in standard form with a natural flow of speech and without poetic structure. Fictional prose primarily utilizes grammatically complete sentences and a paragraph structure to convey its message.

Drama

Drama is fiction that is written to be performed in a variety of media, intended to be performed for an audience, and structured for that purpose. It might be composed using poetry or prose, often straddling the elements of both in what actors are expected to present. Action and dialogue are the tools used in drama to tell the story.

Poetry

Poetry is fiction in verse that has a unique focus on the rhythm of language and focuses on intensity of feeling. It is not an entire story, though it may tell one; it is compact in form and in function. Poetry can be considered as a poet's brief word picture for a reader. Poetic structure is primarily composed of lines and stanzas. Together, poetic structure and devices are the methods that poets use to lead readers to feeling an effect and, ultimately, to the interpretive message.

Literary Nonfiction

Literary nonfiction is prose writing that is based on current or past real events or real people and includes straightforward accounts as well as those that offer opinions on facts or factual events.

Major Forms Within Each Genre

Fictional Prose

Fiction written in prose can be further broken down into **fiction genres**—types of fiction. Some of the more common genres of fiction are as follows:

- **Classical fiction**: a work of fiction considered timeless in its message or theme, remaining noteworthy and meaningful over decades or centuries—e.g., Charlotte Brontë's *Jane Eyre*, Mark Twain's *Adventures of Huckleberry Finn*

- **Fables**: short fiction that generally features animals, fantastic creatures, or other forces within nature that assume human-like characters and has a moral lesson for the reader—e.g., *Aesop's Fables*

- **Fairy tales**: children's stories with magical characters in imaginary, enchanted lands, usually depicting a struggle between good and evil, a sub-genre of folklore—e.g., Hans Christian Anderson's *The Little Mermaid*, *Cinderella* by the Brothers Grimm

- **Fantasy**: fiction with magic or supernatural elements that cannot occur in the real world, sometimes involving medieval elements in language, usually includes some form of sorcery or

witchcraft and sometimes set on a different world—e.g., J.R.R. Tolkien's *The Hobbit*, J.K. Rowling's *Harry Potter and the Sorcerer's Stone*, George R.R. Martin's *A Game of Thrones*

- **Folklore**: types of fiction passed down from oral tradition, stories indigenous to a particular region or culture, with a local flavor in tone, designed to help humans cope with their condition in life and validate cultural traditions, beliefs, and customs—e.g., William Laughead's *Paul Bunyan and The Blue Ox*, the Buddhist story of "The Banyan Deer"

- **Mythology**: closely related to folklore but more widespread, features mystical, otherworldly characters and addresses the basic question of why and how humans exist, relies heavily on allegory and features gods or heroes captured in some sort of struggle—e.g., Greek myths, Genesis I and II in the Bible, Arthurian legends

- **Science fiction**: fiction that uses the principle of extrapolation—loosely defined as a form of prediction—to imagine future realities and problems of the human experience—e.g., Robert Heinlein's *Stranger in a Strange Land*, Ayn Rand's *Anthem*, Isaac Asimov's *I, Robot*, Philip K. Dick's *Do Androids Dream of Electric Sheep?*

- **Short stories**: short works of prose fiction with fully-developed themes and characters, focused on mood, generally developed with a single plot, with a short period of time for settings—e.g., Edgar Allan Poe's "Fall of the House of Usher," Shirley Jackson's "The Lottery," Isaac Bashevis Singer's "Gimpel the Fool"

Drama

Drama refers to a form of literature written for the purpose of performance for an audience. Like prose fiction, drama has several genres. The following are the most common ones:

- **Comedy**: a humorous play designed to amuse and entertain, often with an emphasis on the common person's experience, generally resolved in a positive way—e.g., Richard Sheridan's *School for Scandal*, Shakespeare's *Taming of the Shrew*, Neil Simon's *The Odd Couple*

- **History**: a play based on recorded history where the fate of a nation or kingdom is at the core of the conflict—e.g., Christopher Marlowe's *Edward II*, Shakespeare's *King Richard III*, Arthur Miller's *The Crucible*

- **Tragedy**: a serious play that often involves the downfall of the protagonist. In modern tragedies, the protagonist is not necessarily in a position of power or authority—e.g., Jean Racine's *Phèdre*, Arthur Miller's *Death of a Salesman*, John Steinbeck's *Of Mice and Men*

- **Melodrama**: a play that emphasizes heightened emotion and sensationalism, generally with stereotypical characters in exaggerated or realistic situations and with moral polarization—e.g., Jean-Jacques Rousseau's *Pygmalion*

- **Tragi-comedy**: a play that has elements of both tragedy—a character experiencing a tragic loss—and comedy—the resolution is often positive with no clear distinctive mood for either—e.g., Shakespeare's *The Merchant of Venice*, Anton Chekhov's *The Cherry Orchard*

Poetry

The genre of **poetry** refers to literary works that focus on the expression of feelings and ideas through the use of structure and linguistic rhythm to create a desired effect.

Different poetic structures and devices are used to create the various major forms of poetry. Some of the most common forms are discussed in the following chart.

Type	Poetic Structure	Example
Ballad	A poem or song passed down orally which tells a story and in English tradition usually uses an ABAB or ABCB rhyme scheme	William Butler Yeats' "The Ballad of Father O'Hart"
Epic	A long poem from ancient oral tradition which narrates the story of a legendary or heroic protagonist	Homer's *The Odyssey* Virgil's *The Aeneid*
Haiku	A Japanese poem of three unrhymed lines with five, seven, and five syllables (in English) with nature as a common subject matter	Matsuo Bashō "An old silent pond . . . A frog jumps into the pond, splash! Silence again."
Limerick	A five-line poem written in an AABBA rhyme scheme, with a witty focus	From Edward Lear's *Book of Nonsense*: "There was a Young Person of Smyrna Whose grandmother threatened to burn her . . ."
Ode	A formal lyric poem that addresses and praises a person, place, thing, or idea	Edna St. Vincent Millay's "Ode to Silence"
Sonnet	A fourteen-line poem written in iambic pentameter	Shakespeare's Sonnets 18 and 130

Literary Nonfiction

Nonfiction works are best characterized by their subject matter, which must be factual and real, describing true life experiences. There are several common types of literary non-fiction.

Biography

A **biography** is a work written about a real person (historical or currently living). It involves factual accounts of the person's life, often in a re-telling of those events based on available, researched factual information. The re-telling and dialogue, especially if related within quotes, must be accurate and reflect reliable sources. A biography reflects the time and place in which the person lived, with the goal of creating an understanding of the person and their human experience. Examples of well-known biographies include *The Life of Samuel Johnson* by James Boswell and *Steve Jobs* by Walter Isaacson.

Autobiography

An **autobiography** is a factual account of a person's life written by that person. It may contain some or all of the same elements as a biography, but the author is the subject matter. An autobiography will be told in first person narrative. Examples of well-known autobiographies in literature include *Night* by Elie Wiesel and *Margaret Thatcher: The Autobiography* by Margaret Thatcher.

Memoir

A **memoir** is a historical account of a person's life and experiences written by one who has personal, intimate knowledge of the information. The line between memoir, autobiography, and biography is often muddled, but generally speaking, a memoir covers a specific timeline of events as opposed to the

other forms of nonfiction. A memoir is less all-encompassing. It is also less formal in tone and tends to focus on the emotional aspect of the presented timeline of events. Some examples of memoirs in literature include *Angela's Ashes* by Frank McCourt and *All Creatures Great and Small* by James Herriot.

Journalism

Some forms of **journalism** can fall into the category of literary non-fiction—e.g., travel writing, nature writing, sports writing, the interview, and sometimes, the essay. Some examples include Elizabeth Kolbert's "The Lost World, in the Annals of Extinction series for *The New Yorker* and Gary Smith's "Ali and His Entourage" for *Sports Illustrated*.

Figurative Language

Whereas literal language is the author's use of precise words, proper meanings, definitions, and phrases that mean exactly what they say, **figurative language** deviates from precise meaning and word definition—often in conjunction with other familiar words and phrases—to paint a picture for the reader. Figurative language is less explicit and more open to reader interpretation.

Some examples of figurative language are included in the following graphic.

	Definition	Example
Simile	Compares two things using "like" or "as"	Her hair was like gold.
Metaphor	Compares two things as if they are the same	He was a giant teddy bear.
Idiom	Using words with predictable meanings to create a phrase with a different meaning	The world is your oyster.
Alliteration	Repeating the same beginning sound or letter in a phrase for emphasis	The busy baby babbled.
Personification	Attributing human characteristics to an object or an animal	The house glowered menacingly with a dark smile.
Foreshadowing	Giving an indication that something is going to happen later in the story	I wasn't aware at the time, but I would come to regret those words.
Symbolism	Using symbols to represent ideas and provide a different meaning	The ring represented the bond between us.
Onomatopoeia	Using words that imitate sound	The tire went off with a bang and a crunch.
Imagery	Appealing to the senses by using descriptive language	The sky was painted with red and pink and streaked with orange.
Hyperbole	Using exaggeration not meant to be taken literally	The girl weighed less than a feather.

Figurative language can be used to give additional insight into the theme or message of a text by moving beyond the usual and literal meaning of words and phrases. It can also be used to appeal to the senses of readers and create a more in-depth story.

Practice Questions

Questions 1–5 are based upon the following passage:

I have thought that an example of the intelligence (instinct?) of a class of fish which has come under my observation during my excursions into the Adirondack region of New York State might possibly be of interest to your readers, especially as I am not aware that any one except myself has noticed it, or, at least, has given it publicity.

The female sun-fish (called, I believe, in England, the roach or bream) makes a "hatchery" for her eggs in this wise. Selecting a spot near the banks of the numerous lakes in which this region abounds, and where the water is about 4 inches deep, and still, she builds, with her tail and snout, a circular embankment 3 inches in height and 2 thick. The circle, which is as perfect a one as could be formed with mathematical instruments, is usually a foot and a half in diameter; and at one side of this circular wall an opening is left by the fish of just sufficient width to admit her body.

The mother sun-fish, having now built or provided her "hatchery," deposits her spawn within the circular inclosure, and mounts guard at the entrance until the fry are hatched out and are sufficiently large to take charge of themselves. As the embankment, moreover, is built up to the surface of the water, no enemy can very easily obtain an entrance within the inclosure from the top; while there being only one entrance, the fish is able, with comparative ease, to keep out all intruders.

I have, as I say, noticed this beautiful instinct of the sun-fish for the perpetuity of her species more particularly in the lakes of this region; but doubtless the same habit is common to these fish in other waters.

Excerpt from "The 'Hatchery' of the Sun-Fish"--- Scientific American, #711

1. What is the purpose of this passage?
    a. To show the effects of fish hatcheries on the Adirondack region
    b. To persuade the audience to study Ichthyology (fish science)
    c. To depict the sequence of mating among sun-fish
    d. To enlighten the audience on the habits of sun-fish and their hatcheries

2. What does the word *wise* in this passage most closely mean?
    a. Knowledge
    b. Manner
    c. Shrewd
    d. Ignorance

3. What is the definition of the word *fry* as it appears in the following passage?

> The mother sun-fish, having now built or provided her "hatchery," deposits her spawn within the circular inclosure, and mounts guard at the entrance until the fry are hatched out and are sufficiently large to take charge of themselves.

    a. Fish at the stage of development where they are capable of feeding themselves.
    b. Fish eggs that have been fertilized.
    c. A place where larvae is kept out of danger from other predators.
    d. A dish where fish is placed in oil and fried until golden brown.

4. How is the circle that keeps the larvae of the sun-fish made?
    a. It is formed with mathematical instruments.
    b. The sun-fish builds it with her tail and snout.
    c. It is provided to her as a "hatchery" by Mother Nature.
    d. The sun-fish builds it with her larvae.

5. The author included the third paragraph in the following passage to achieve which of the following effects?
    a. To complicate the subject matter
    b. To express a bias
    c. To insert a counterargument
    d. To conclude a sequence and add a final detail

Answer Explanations

1. D: To enlighten the audience on the habits of sun-fish and their hatcheries. Choice *A* is incorrect because although the Adirondack region is mentioned in the text, there is no cause or effect relationships between the region and fish hatcheries depicted here. Choice *B* is incorrect because the text does not have an agenda, but rather is meant to inform the audience. Finally, Choice *C* is incorrect because the text says nothing of how sun-fish mate.

2. B: The word *wise* in this passage most closely means *manner*. Choices *A* and *C* are synonyms of *wise*; however, they are not relevant in the context of the text. Choice *D*, *ignorance*, is opposite of the word *wise*, and is therefore incorrect.

3. A: Fish at the stage of development where they are capable of feeding themselves. Even if the word *fry* isn't immediately known to the reader, the context gives a hint when it says "until the fry are hatched out and are sufficiently large to take charge of themselves."

4. B: The sun-fish builds it with her tail and snout. The text explains this in the second paragraph: "she builds, with her tail and snout, a circular embankment 3 inches in height and 2 thick." Choice *A* is used in the text as a simile.

5. D: To conclude a sequence and add a final detail. The concluding sequence is expressed in the phrase "[t]he mother sun-fish, having now built or provided her 'hatchery.'" The final detail is the way in which the sun-fish guards the "inclosure." Choices *A, B,* and *C* are incorrect.

Listening

The Listening section test of the TOEFL iBT® lasts between 60 and 90 minutes and consists of 34–51 questions. These ranges exist because Educational Testing Service (ETS) sometimes includes additional questions in the Listening section that enable test developers to assess the viability of potential future scored questions or to compare outcomes of various administrations of the TOEFL across the country, as benchmark questions. While test takers are not alerted to which test questions fall under either of these conditions, the experimental questions are unscored and as such, they do not affect one's results either way.

As mentioned, there are 34–51 questions on the Listening section of the TOEFL iBT®, which follow each listening clip. There are six questions per lecture or academic discussion and five questions following each conversation. Depending on the inclusion of the unscored experimental section, the section includes 4–6 lectures and academic discussions, each of which is 3–5 minutes in duration, and 2–3 more casual conversations that each last approximately three minutes.

We have recorded audio to go along with the listening practice questions. You can find all of our audio recordings by going to testprepbooks.com/toefl or by scanning the QR code below. The audio is only online. There is no CD.

All of the questions are multiple choice; the majority offer four answer choices of which test takers must select the single best choice, although some multiple-choice questions may require selecting two or more correct answers. Some questions go beyond regurgitating the information that was presented in the recording and ask test takers to demonstrate deeper listening comprehension by making inferences or describing emotions or other implicit details. Some questions may involve categorizing items using charts or tables or require test takers to order steps or events in a sequence.

It should be noted that not all of the speakers in the audio recordings in the Listening section may speak with native North American English accents. Test takers may encounter English speakers with native accents from the United Kingdom, New Zealand, and Australia.

ETS test administrators model the TOEFL iBT® Listening section exercises after typical classroom lectures, discussions, or common administrative tasks that test takers will encounter in real-world settings long after passing the TOEFL iBT®. Lecture topics pull from a variety of academic disciplines in the arts and sciences, such as history, psychology, earth science, economics, and sociology. Some lecture exercises will be delivered by a single speaker, who is an instructor, or they may feature several speakers in a classroom discussion format, often between the instructor and a handful of students. For example, the instructor may give a short lecture about architecture and then pause to call on a couple of students to answer questions pertaining to the material just presented, or a student may ask the instructor a clarifying question. After the instructor answers the student's question, he or she may continue with the lecture or segue into an organic conversation that deviates from the original lecture topic but more fully answers the student's question.

The conversations revolve around typical interactions encountered around a university setting between a variety of individuals such as coaches, students, secretaries, administrators, and roommates. Topics may include conversations about registering for classes, purchasing textbooks, asking for directions or locating buildings around campus, meeting a roommate, receiving feedback on an assignment, and asking for academic support, among many others. The speech in the conversations is meant to sound natural and duplicate that which normally occurs between people, including imperfections and pauses. Characters may stumble over their words or even use the wrong word sometimes; test takers may be asked to point out these errors in the questions that follow the recording.

Test takers are allowed to listen to each exercise only one time, although they are encouraged to take notes while they listen, which they can refer to while answering the questions that follow the clip. If headsets are provided, they will have adjustable volume that test takers can experiment with prior to listening to the scored exercises. Each listening exercise begins with a picture of some sort to provide context for the conversation or lecture, and longer recordings will have additional pictures or diagrams scattered throughout the 3–5-minute clip.

ETS presents test takers with three categories of questions on the Listening section and both the lectures and conversations feature questions in each of these categories.

- **Basic Conversation Questions** are one of three types: **Gist-content questions** address the overall general content of the lecture, discussion, or conversation. Instead of addressing the broad content of the lectures or conversations, **gist-purpose questions** require test takers to identify the primary reasons for the given lectures or discussion. Lastly, **detail questions** ask test takers about specific facts provided in the lectures or regarding specific details from the conversations.

- **Pragmatic Understanding Questions** can be one of two types. In the first type, test takers must demonstrate their understanding of the speaker's purpose for delivering certain statements, or the function of what was said. In the second type, test takers must identify the speaker's emotions or preferences, often using nuances in tone of voice, inflection, and intonation to detect attitudes such as sarcasm, frustration, disappointment, or irony.

- **Connecting and Synthesizing Information Questions** can be one of three types. The **understanding organization** questions require test takers to select answer choices that correctly reflect the structure of the listening exercise or the function of specific statements delivered in the lecture or conversation. The **connecting content** questions are the only type of question that is solely found in the lecture-based exercises. It involves demonstrating relationships between explicit and implicit ideas presented in the lecture and often includes charts or tables that test takers must interpret to successfully answer the question. Finally, the **making inferences** questions involve using statements in the conversations or lectures to draw conclusions or surmise information that may not be explicitly discussed in the listening exercise.

Test takers often find the Listening section daunting, particularly because exercises can only be played once. However, the following are a couple of helpful strategies that successful test takers employ to achieve high scores in this section:

- **Use the pictures**: The initial picture helps set the stage and helps provide the context for conversation or lecture that test takers are about to hear. This picture is crucial in helping the listener imagine what is happening and visualize the speakers before the dialogue even begins. The additional pictures and visual aids that are presented during the course of the audio recordings appear in coordination with the statements or events in the lectures and conversations as they unfurl. Again, these are powerful aids to add context clues about the setting, speakers, and content, which, when taken with the audio information, helps provide test takers with a more complete and comprehensive understanding of the exercise.

- **Take notes**: Test takers can, and should, take notes while they listen to the recording that they can refer to while answering questions. While it is most important to devote attention towards critical listening, jotting down a few key points or details that seem important can help jog one's memory after the recording is over when the questions are presented. Some questions ask very specific information, and this is where careful listening with an ear towards details and a couple of key notes can be quite helpful. For example, from a conversation between two roommates buying course textbooks at the campus store, test takers may be asked to recall the specific subjects for which one speaker was buying books.

- **Practice**: The importance of practice cannot be overstated. Successful test takers listen to spoken English every chance they get and try to understand the main points, supporting details, and the emotions and attitudes of the speakers. There are a variety of mediums that present listening opportunities from television programs and movies to podcasts and audiobooks. In-person opportunities include class lectures, conversations with peers and friends, interactions with customer service agents, among others. While formal questions aren't presented after most listening opportunities, candidates can assess their understanding by listening to recordings several times or asking speakers of in-person conversations clarifying questions to verify understanding.

- **Listen for verbal cues**: Listeners can gather clues by appreciating the verbal cues from the recordings. Word emphasis, tone of voice, pauses interjected for effect, and changes in voice inflection can communicate implicit information such as the speaker's emotion (surprise, worry, frustration, etc.) or emphasize that something important is about to happen. Again, understanding these nuances in spoken language will help test takers more fully grasp the meaning of the conversation or lecture in the recordings.

Practice Questions

Directions: The Listening section measures your ability to understand conversations and lectures in English. In this test, you will listen to several pieces of content and answer questions after each one. The questions typically ask about the main idea and supporting details. Some questions ask about a speaker's purpose or attitude. Answer the questions based on what is stated or implied by the speakers.

Note that on the actual test, you can take notes while you listen and use your notes to help you answer the questions. Your notes will not be scored.

For your convenience, the transcript is provided after the answer explanations. However, on the actual test, no such transcript will be provided.

Practice Transcript: Lecture

Listen to all of these passages by going to <u>testprepbooks.com/toefl</u> or by scanning the QR code below:

1. What is the professor implying when they say, "Only persons, parents, and teachers, etc., have aims, not an abstract idea like education"?
    a. Abstract ideas are inconsistent with the purpose of education.
    b. People should have goals other than education.
    c. Education doesn't have its own agenda.
    d. Aims are more important than the people involved in education.

2. Identify TWO analogies the professor makes between farming and education.
    a. Educators must avoid causing harm just as farmers avoid rain failing and sun shining.
    b. Educators must consider conditions just as farmers consider the soil and climate.
    c. Educators must plan for obstacles just as farmers plan for insects and blight.
    d. Educators must use resources just as farmers use investments and technologies.

3. Aims should function like _____ to guide how educators observe and plan ahead.
    a. Agreements
    b. Mandates
    c. Rules
    d. Suggestions

4. Aims can do harm when they violate people's _____.
    a. Abstract ideas
    b. Common sense
    c. Observations
    d. Resources

For Questions 5–6, complete the plan provided below:

Guide to Planning a Curriculum

- Identify the 5. _____conditions that must be utilized.

- Identify all the resources that can be leveraged and combined.

- Identify potential 6. _____ that must be overcome.

a. Advantages

b. Chattels

c. Isolated

d. Obstacles

e. Reserves

f. Secondary

g. Various

Answer Explanations

1. C: The professor is saying that education is an abstract idea, and, therefore, it doesn't have its own aims. Instead, the people involved in education must set those aims. Thus, Choice *C* is the correct answer. Choice *A* is beside the point; the lecture is about how people have to take control of their education and set the aims. Similarly, Choice *B* is incorrect because the lecture is largely a discussion of how aims benefit education. The professor doesn't directly compare the value of aims and people. In addition, the professor seems to imply the opposite based on their claim that aims are derived from people. In any event, Choice *D* is incorrect.

2. B, C: During the first half of the lecture, the professor makes several analogies between teaching and farming. The professor mentions insects and blight, which pose obstacles to farming. In addition, the professor mentions soil and climate, which are conditions related to farming. Thus, Choice *B* and Choice *C* are the correct answers. Although the professor refers to rain falling and sun shining, it doesn't make sense for the farmers to avoid them. So, Choice *A* is incorrect. Choice *D* is incorrect because the professor never discusses investments and technologies.

3. D: Near the end of the lecture, the professor argues that aims should function as suggestions rather than as words to be strictly followed. Thus, Choice *D* is the correct answer. The professor likely believes that all of the stakeholders should agree on educational aims, but the professor never directly claims that aims function like agreements. Therefore, Choice *A* is incorrect. Mandates and rules are synonymous, and the professor argues that aims should function in the opposite way. So Choice *B* and Choice *C* are both incorrect.

4. B: In the latter half of the lecture, the professor asserts that aims can be harmful when they violate people's common sense, as when someone who lacks authority creates the aim. Thus, Choice *B* is the correct answer. Abstraction is not the reason that the professor believes aims can be harmful under some circumstances. Therefore, Choice *A* is incorrect. Aims could be harmful if they violate people's observations, but to observe is only to perceive, and perceptions might be wrong, as when I perceive the sun moving around the earth. The professor is concerned with violations of common sense, and common sense is what people know to be true. Thus, Choice *C* is incorrect. Violating resources doesn't make sense, and resources aren't included in the professor's warning about aims. Therefore, Choice *D* is incorrect.

5. G: These plans are described in detail at the beginning of the lesson. The professor instructs educators to identify all the various conditions at play, and conditions are always discussed in plural. Thus, Choice *G* is the correct answer. The professor doesn't mention any isolated conditions. Furthermore, the professor lists many conditions in the farming analogy, so it can be inferred that education also has numerous conditions. Therefore, Choice *C* is incorrect. Similarly, Choice *F* is incorrect because the professor doesn't list or distinguish between primary and secondary conditions. None of the other answer choices fit because they're nouns and not adjectives describing conditions.

6. D: Throughout the first half of the lecture and the farming analogy, the professor repeatedly implores educators to identify and overcome obstacles. Thus, Choice *D* is the correct answer. Choice *A* is incorrect because advantages would be utilized, not overcome. Chattels means property, which doesn't fit this context. Therefore, Choice *B* is incorrect. While the professor would agree with educators needing to identify reserves of resources, a reserve of obstacles doesn't make sense. Therefore, Choice *E* is incorrect. None of the other answer choices fit because they are all adjectives, not nouns.

Listening Transcript

Practice Transcript

(Narrator) Listen to the lecture and then answer the questions.

(Professor) Welcome back class! So far, we have learned about the varied purposes of education, ranging from its social function to its instructive content. Today we'll be discussing the importance of educational aims.

There is nothing peculiar about educational aims. They are just like aims in any directed occupation. The educator, like the farmer, has certain things to do, certain resources with which to do them, and certain obstacles with which to contend. The conditions with which the farmer deals, whether as obstacles or resources, have their own structure and operation independently of any purpose of his. Seeds sprout, rain falls, the sun shines, insects devour, blight comes, the seasons change. His aim is simply to utilize these various conditions; to make his activities and their energies work together, instead of against one another.

It would be absurd if the farmer set up a purpose of farming, without any reference to these conditions of soil, climate, characteristic of plant growth, etc. His purpose is simply a foresight of the consequences of his energies connected with those of the things about him, a foresight used to direct his movements from day to day. Foresight of possible consequences leads to more careful and extensive observation of the nature and performances of the things he had to do with, and to laying out a plan—that is, of a certain order in the acts to be performed.

It is the same with the educator, whether parent or teacher. It is as absurd for the latter to set up his "own" aims as the proper objects of the growth of the children as it would be for the farmer to set up an ideal of farming irrespective of conditions. Aims mean acceptance of responsibility for the observations, anticipations, and arrangements required in carrying on a function—whether farming or educating. Any aim is of value so far as it assists observation, choice, and planning in carrying on activity from moment to moment and hour to hour; if it gets in the way of the individual's own common sense (as it will surely do if imposed from without or accepted on authority) it does harm.

And it is well to remind ourselves that education as such has no aims. Only persons, parents, and teachers, etc., have aims, not an abstract idea like education. And consequently their purposes are indefinitely varied, differing with different children, changing as children grow and with the growth of experience on the part of the one who teaches. Even the most valid aims which can be put in words will, as words, do more harm than good unless one recognizes that they are not aims, but rather suggestions to educators as to how to observe, how to look ahead, and how to choose in liberating and directing the energies of the concrete situations in which they find themselves.

As I mentioned earlier, lesson plans will be our next topic. Please download the sample lesson plans, and we'll fill those out together next time.

This lecture has been adapted from <u>Democracy and Education</u> by John Dewey, 1916, found at
https://www.gutenberg.org/files/852/852-h/852-h.htm#link2HCH0008

Speaking

The TOEFL Speaking Section assesses the test taker's ability to communicate effectively in English. This section lasts 20 minutes and test takers will encounter six tasks; the first two involve listening to brief recordings on familiar topics, and the remaining four ask test takers to read short passages, lectures, or conversations. For each task, test takers have about 15–30 seconds to gather their thoughts and prepare, and then they must deliver their verbal response into a microphone. The response is typically expected to last approximately 45 seconds, which can be nearly 100 words for a fluent English speaker. Test takers are evaluated on their oral delivery, topic development, content, language use, and grammar of their responses.

While this can sound daunting, the good news is that the Speaking section of the TOEFL is the easiest one to prepare for because the opportunities to practice are endless. Candidates should take advantage of every opportunity to practice their English-speaking skills, not only to optimize their test performance, but also because they will be frequently conversing in English in diverse situations long after passing the exam. Nearly every situation presents a valid opportunity to practice—driving the car, walking the dog, commuting to work, visiting a friend, doing errands, etc.

In addition to capitalizing on every chance to practice speaking, there are some other helpful strategies that successful test takers employ for this section.

Practice, but Don't Memorize

As mentioned, it's impossible to over-practice and the more speaking time a test taker has under their belt, the better. However, memorizing responses, particularly for the first two tasks (which tend to pose only a handful of possible questions), is not recommended. For one thing, scorers are looking for a natural speaking style that feels conversational and relaxed. Rehearsing and memorizing a predetermined response will likely lower one's delivery score even if the content is good. It is better to sound authentic and organic in the delivery of the answer, even if it means slightly less content is delivered in the allotted time.

Listen and Read the Question Carefully

It's easy to jump to an answer when nervous, but successful test takers make sure to pay careful attention to the specific question posed in the task and ensure that their response addresses the exact points desired. For example, the first task usually asks general questions such as what do you enjoy doing in your spare time, what is your family like, or what are your favorite places to visit? Test takers who are overly rehearsed may begin to hear a familiar prompt and then assume they know what the question is asking and prepare to deliver their memorized response. However, this hastiness can lead to mistakes; oftentimes, there are slight changes in the wording of the questions such that the exact question test administrators are looking for is different than that assumed. Instead of what do you enjoy doing on your spare time, the question may be more specific and ask, what do you enjoy doing by yourself in your spare time? If a test taker did not listen carefully or jumped to a prepared answer about enjoying basketball with their team or shopping with friends, points would be deducted for inappropriate content for the intended answer.

Organize

Test takers should take advantage of the 15–30 seconds provided to reflect on the question and organize their thoughts before they have to deliver their response. Many people find it helpful to write down a couple of bullet points that they plan to highlight in their answer. These should be just a word or short phrase, rather than a whole sentence, so as to save time and sound organic and natural in the response. Reading fully composed sentences tends to sound overly rehearsed and may affect one's delivery score.

Speak Clearly and Simply

Many test takers feel anxious or self-conscious about delivering their responses with as little influence of an accent as possible. The good news is that the TOEFL does not expect candidates to speak with any sort of "American" accent and scores are not influenced by the responder's accent one way or another. What is important is that the response is clear, audible, and comprehensible. After all, if scorers cannot hear or understand the recorded answer, they cannot award it with high marks. Test takers should speak as fluidly as possible, without rushing or interjecting long pauses or words of varying volumes. As much as possible, words should be enunciated with all syllables present and emphasizing those necessary for proper pronunciation.

The more even and rhythmic the spoken answer, the better. One more point to note is that many test takers imagine that adding fancy vocabulary words will bolster their score. While demonstrating a rich vocabulary and strong command of English grammar and language skills is important, it is more important to ensure that words are used properly and that sentence structure and intended meaning is on point. If test takers are not confident in the meaning or proper usage of a word, it is better to use a seemingly simpler word whose meaning they are sure of.

Make Speech Flow

As mentioned, answers should flow as naturally fluidly as possible. With that said, short pauses should be interjected at the end of each sentence or where commas would be used in written text to help listeners understand the thoughts and the organization of the response. Rushing into each subsequent sentence without an adequate pause tends to make answers sound confusing. To connect thoughts together and create a logical flow to the response, test takers should demonstrate command of the use of conjunctions and employ effective connecting words and phrases such as: *because, due to, for example, after this, if…then,* and *however.*

Structure the Answer

Although spoken language is often not as formal as written communication, answers should still be organized, with well-developed thoughts presented in a logical order. Successful test takers generate their ideas and plan their delivery during the reflection time prior to recording their responses. It is wise to start the answer by stating the topic thought (like a topic sentence in a written essay) and then expand or describe that thought in the subsequent sentences. Adding a concluding sentence that ties back to the beginning thought gives the listener clarity and pulls all the details together into a comprehensive and intelligent answer.

Tell a Story

The most memorable conversations are those that include a captivating story. Speakers should try to make responses engaging and personal, when appropriate. This will not only make for a more enjoyable listen for scorers, but also can improve one's score by garnering more delivery points.

Be Confident

Everyone has important things to say. Test takers should not worry about saying something "stupid" or "boring." They should speak from the heart and be confident in their command of English as well as their comprehension of the posed question. There is no need to rush when delivering the response; there is plenty of time in 45 seconds to get out a complete answer. On that note, if there is extra time at the end of the allotted recording time, it is generally recommended to simply end the response when the question has been fully answered rather than fill every last second with speaking. It is unnecessary to speak aimlessly at the end, as this can reduce one's content score if the answer starts deviating from what was asked. Test takers should just pace themselves, stay relaxed, and speak with authority.

Practice Questions

1. Your friend Christina is a recent high school graduate with a big decision to make. She was offered a full-time job with good benefits and a $60,000-per year starting salary. Before she knew about this opportunity, she had applied and been admitted to her dream college. Tuition costs $50,000 per year plus living expenses, and the degree takes four years to complete. Christina is a terrific student, and the average starting salary for people holding her intended degree is $75,000.

Question: What advice would you give Christina? You should talk about the pros and cons of each side before reaching a conclusion.

- Preparation Time: 20 seconds
- Response Time: 45 seconds

2. Read the public service announcement and then answer the question that follows.

> Jose Ramirez is missing. He is in his late seventies, average height, medium build, dark complexion, and he has no memory. He was last seen two days ago, on July 4, 2018, at the fireworks festival near the docks. Jose wandered away from his family into the crowds and hasn't been seen since. It's likely that Jose is still in the local area due to his fear of new places.
>
> If you see anyone resembling Jose, please call 311 and someone will be right over. Please don't approach Jose. He's not dangerous, but he does suffer from Alzheimer's disease. Some days he doesn't remember his own name, so it's unclear how he'll respond to a stranger.

Question: Your friend is going down to the docks later today, but you know she didn't hear the public service announcement. Describe what happened to Jose and provide the relevant identifying information.

- Reading Time: 20 seconds
- Response Time: 45 seconds

3. Read the conversation between two students and then answer the question that follows.

> **(Martina)** Hi Charlie, how are you liking your classes so far?
>
> **(Charlie)** I like them a lot but I'm already falling behind because I don't have the textbooks yet.
>
> **(Martina)** Oh no! Have you not had a chance to go to the University bookstore to buy them?
>
> **(Charlie)** Well, it's not that. It's just that I don't know if I want to buy them there new or rent them online.
>
> **(Martina)** You can rent textbooks?
>
> **(Charlie)** Yeah. Basically, you pay less money and it's a digital subscription to the book for the duration of the semester, after which the book isn't available to you anymore. I've never done it before but it's much less expensive than buying them at the bookstore.
>
> **(Martina)** That's interesting but then you don't get to keep the book. What if you want to refer back to it in subsequent courses and semesters?

(Charlie) Yeah, then you don't have it anymore but buying books new is so expensive and honestly, I rarely use them again once the course is over. I mean, especially for classes outside of my major!

(Martina) That's true and they do take up a lot of room. Plus, they're heavy. My back hates me every time I tote them around. Since the rented ones are digital e-books, you don't have the weight.

(Charlie) Exactly! I hate lugging them around and I like reading on my tablet in bed, and this way I could just read them more comfortably. The one thing is that you can't highlight them. I like to highlight as I read instead of taking notes. I can't really do that if I don't have a physical textbook.

(Martina) Those are good points. Well, Charlie, I'd decide soon because either way, you'll want to get books soon so that you don't fall behind in class!

(Charlie) Yeah, you're right Martina. I'll think about it.

Question: Briefly summarize Charlie's problem and the two options. Then, state which solution you would recommend. Be sure to explain the reasons for your recommendation.

- Preparation Time: 20 seconds
- Response Time: 60 seconds

4. Read part of a lecture in an earth science course and then answer the question that follows. Note that test takers will listen to the lecture on the actual exam.

(Professor) Minor members of the solar system are those objects that are too small to be classified as planets, yet in aggregate, they make up a large percentage of the "stuff" in our solar system. Asteroids, meteors, and comets are examples of minor members. In addition to being smaller than planets, asteroids and comets have more irregular orbits and can even enter the Earth's atmosphere and collide with Earth, the moon, the Sun, or other planets.

Asteroids and comets are thought to be remnants from the same giant cloud of gas and dust that condensed to create the Sun, planets, and moons about 4.5 billion years ago during the Big Bang. Some people even theorize that the main asteroids, which lie in a tight belt between Mars and Jupiter, may all be fragments from another planet that was forming there that suffered some sort of major collision and broke into thousands of little pieces. Comets tend to be more scattered and found in the far-reaching edges of the Solar System. However, both of these minor bodies are subject to changes in gravitational pulls or perturbations, which can alter their trajectories and cause various collisions and changes in course.

Generally speaking, comets are smaller than asteroids and are not as confined to a particular region. They also tend to be more elliptical in shape and have chemical components that vaporize when heated, perhaps because they contain more ice than asteroids, which are mostly composed of chunks of rock. Some people describe them as "fuzzy looking," when observed through a telescope because they grow tails as a function of their elliptical orbit that the sun illuminates. Comets are not always visible in the night sky, although they sometimes streak across in bright glows, such as Halley's comet. Because of the irregularity of their orbits, they are subject to impacts with Earth. Astronomers also believe that there is a concentration of comets

near Neptune in what is called the Kuiper belt. Asteroids also can enter our atmosphere but many are quite small and burn up in the atmosphere on their way down. It is theorized that such a collision from a massive asteroid caused the extinction of the dinosaurs.

Question: Using points and information from the lecture, describe the two different examples of minor members of the Solar System detailed by the professor.

- Preparation Time: 20 seconds
- Response Time: 60 seconds

Answer Explanations

1. Christina, this is a really tough decision. I'm sure that's nothing you don't know. The full-time job starts at $60,000 with full benefits. That's quite an offer in this economy. Most of our parents don't make that much, and we all know how hard it is to get quality, affordable healthcare. The downside is you wouldn't be able to attend your dream college right now. You're such a great student, and I'm sure you'd be one of the top students, the ones who get a job right out of college for $75,000. Or even more, possibly; your potential is limitless with that degree. Still, the tuition costs $50,000 per year plus living expenses, and the degree takes four years to complete. So not only does it cost more than $200,000, you'd also lose out on at least $240,000 in salary. As such, I think you should accept the job offer. You're still a teenager and can always pursue a college degree in the future. Even if the job doesn't turn into a career, you'll be in a better position to afford college. Plus, you'll have more life experience and have a better idea of what you want to study.

2. Hey, I heard you were going down to the docks today. Before you leave you have to hear something. I was walking Fido, and while he was doing his business, I noticed a public service announcement taped to a pole. A man named Jose Ramirez is missing. He's in his late seventies, average height, medium build, and dark complexion. Jose has Alzheimer's disease, and he wandered away from his family into the crowd during that big fireworks festival on the Fourth down by the docks. He apparently hasn't been seen since, but the poster said he's likely still in the area. So make sure to look out for a guy in his late seventies of average height, medium build, and dark complexion. If you see someone matching Jose's description, call 311. That's a number to contact the police in nonemergency situations. The poster said not to approach him since he gets confused easily. Anyway, have fun at the docks. Tell everybody I say what's up.

3. Charlie needs to purchase textbooks for his courses but he's not sure whether to buy physical books from the University bookstore or rent digital textbooks online. The digital books are much less expensive than the bookstore books and they obviously don't have the weight and bulk of real books. However, students don't get to keep them after the term, which may be an issue if they want to refer back to them and they can't highlight them as they study. I would recommend that he buy physical textbooks for those classes that he's taking in his major and rent the digital books for classes he has to take for general education classes outside of his major. That way, he'll save some money by buying fewer physical books with the cheaper e-textbooks, but he'll have the hard copy books for classes in his major in case he wants to look back on them in future classes and he can highlight them while he's reading to make sure he's really understanding the material as he studies, which is very important for classes in his major.

4. This lecture described asteroids and comets, which are both minor members of the Solar System. This means that they are smaller than planets. Both asteroids and comets have more irregular orbits than the planets and they can enter the atmosphere and collide with the moon, Sun, Earth or other planets. In fact, it was likely an asteroid collision that caused the extinction of the dinosaurs! Scientists think asteroids and comets are ice and rock remains from when the planets formed during the Big Bang. Asteroids are mostly concentrated in one area between Mars and Jupiter, while comets tend to be more scattered throughout the Solar System and some are much further away. Comets are usually smaller than asteroids, more elliptical instead of round, and have tails, which make them look fuzzy when viewed through a microscope. They can streak across the sky. Asteroids are made of less ice and more rock than comets. Many small ones enter our atmosphere but they burn up before reaching the surface of the Earth.

Writing

The TOEFL writing section consists of two different writing questions. The first writing section gives you a passage to read about a topic. Then, you will listen to a short lecture around two minutes long over the same topic. Though the two different mediums are over the same topic, they may have differing opinions. You will then have twenty minutes to write an essay synthesizing the two pieces.

The second writing section consists of a single prompt. You will have thirty minutes to complete this prompt, and you should plan on writing at least 300 words. The question of this essay is usually in one of the following structures:

- Your opinion on an issue
- Do you agree or disagree?
- Which would you prefer?
- Do you support or oppose this idea?
- Use specific reasons and examples

Writing the Essay

Brainstorming

One of the most important steps in writing an essay is prewriting. Before drafting an essay, it's helpful to think about the topic for a moment or two, in order to gain a more solid understanding of the task. Then, spending about five minutes jotting down the immediate ideas that could work for the essay is recommended. It is a way to get some words on the page and offer a reference for ideas when drafting. Scratch paper is provided for writers to use any prewriting techniques such as webbing, free writing, or listing. The goal is to get ideas out of the mind and onto the page.

Considering Opposing Viewpoints

In the planning stage, it's important to consider all aspects of the topic, including different viewpoints on the subject. There are more than two ways to look at a topic, and a strong argument considers those opposing viewpoints. Considering opposing viewpoints can help writers present a fair, balanced, and informed essay that shows consideration for all readers. This approach can also strengthen an argument by recognizing and potentially refuting opposing viewpoint(s).

Drawing from personal experience may help to support ideas. For example, if the goal for writing is a personal narrative, then the story should come from the writer's own life. Many writers find it helpful to draw from personal experience, even in an essay that is not strictly narrative. Personal anecdotes or short stories can help to illustrate a point in other types of essays as well.

Moving from Brainstorming to Planning

Once the ideas are on the page, it's time to turn them into a solid plan for the essay. The best ideas from the brainstorming results can then be developed into a more formal outline. An outline typically has one main point (the thesis) and at least three sub-points that support the main point. Here's an example:

Main Idea

- Point #1
- Point #2
- Point #3

Of course, there will be details under each point, but this approach is the best for dealing with timed writing.

Staying on Track

Basing the essay on the outline aids in both organization and coherence. The goal is to ensure that there is enough time to develop each sub-point in the essay, roughly spending an equal amount of time on each idea. Keeping an eye on the time will help. If there are fifteen minutes left to draft the essay, then it makes sense to spend about 5 minutes on each of the ideas. Staying on task is critical to success and timing out the parts of the essay can help writers avoid feeling overwhelmed.

Parts of the Essay

The **introduction** has to do a few important things:

- Establish the **topic** of the essay in original wording (i.e., not just repeating the prompt)
- Clarify the significance/importance of the topic or purpose for writing (not too many details, a brief overview)
- Offer a **thesis statement** that identifies the writer's own viewpoint on the topic (typically one to two brief sentences as a clear, concise explanation of the main point on the topic)

Body paragraphs reflect the ideas developed in the outline. Three to four points is probably sufficient for a short essay, and they should include the following:

- A **topic sentence** that identifies the sub-point (e.g., a reason why, a way how, a cause or effect)
- A detailed **explanation** of the point, explaining why the writer thinks this point is valid
- Illustrative **examples**, such as personal examples or real-world examples, that support and validate the point (i.e., "prove" the point)
- A **concluding sentence** that connects the examples, reasoning, and analysis to the point being made

The **conclusion**, or final paragraph, should be brief and should reiterate the focus, clarifying why the discussion is significant or important. It is important to avoid adding specific details or new ideas to this paragraph. The purpose of the conclusion is to sum up what has been said to bring the discussion to a close.

Don't Panic!

Writing an essay can be overwhelming, and performance panic is a natural response. The outline serves as a basis for the writing and helps writers keep focused. Getting stuck can also happen, and it's helpful

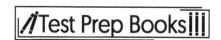

to remember that brainstorming can be done at any time during the writing process. Following the steps of the writing process is the best defense against writer's block.

Timed essays can be particularly stressful, but assessors are trained to recognize the necessary planning and thinking for these timed efforts. Using the plan above and sticking to it helps with time management. Timing each part of the process helps writers stay on track. Sometimes writers try to cover too much in their essays. If time seems to be running out, this is an opportunity to determine whether all of the ideas in the outline are necessary. Three body paragraphs are sufficient, and more than that is probably too much to cover in a short essay.

More isn't always *better* in writing. A strong essay will be clear and concise. It will avoid unnecessary or repetitive details. It is better to have a concise, five-paragraph essay that makes a clear point, than a ten-paragraph essay that doesn't. The goal is to write one to two pages of quality writing. Paragraphs should also reflect balance; if the introduction goes to the bottom of the first page, the writing may be going off-track or be repetitive. It's best to fall into the one to two-page range, but a complete, well-developed essay is the ultimate goal.

The Final Steps

Leaving a few minutes at the end to revise and proofread offers an opportunity for writers to polish things up. Putting one's self in the reader's shoes and focusing on what the essay actually says helps writers identify problems—it's a movement from the mindset of writer to the mindset of editor. The goal is to have a clean, clear copy of the essay. The following areas should be considered when proofreading:

- Sentence fragments
- Awkward sentence structure
- Run-on sentences
- Incorrect word choice
- Grammatical agreement errors
- Spelling errors
- Punctuation errors
- Capitalization errors

The Short Overview

The essay may seem challenging, but following these steps can help writers focus:

- Take one to two minutes to think about the topic.
- Generate some ideas through brainstorming (three to four minutes).
- Organize ideas into a brief outline, selecting just three to four main points to cover in the essay (eventually the body paragraphs).
- Develop essay in parts:
- Introduction paragraph, with intro to topic and main points
- Viewpoint on the subject at the end of the introduction
- Body paragraphs, based on outline
- Each paragraph: makes a main point, explains the viewpoint, uses examples to support the point
- Brief conclusion highlighting the main points and closing
- Read over the essay (last five minutes).
- Look for any obvious errors, making sure that the writing makes sense.

Parts of Speech

Nouns

A **common noun** is a word that identifies any of a class of people, places, or things. Examples include numbers, objects, animals, feelings, concepts, qualities, and actions. *A, an,* or *the* usually precedes the common noun. These parts of speech are called *articles*. Here are some examples of sentences using nouns preceded by articles.

A building is under construction.

The girl would like to move to *the* city.

A **proper noun** (also called a **proper name**) is used for the specific name of an individual person, place, or organization. The first letter in a proper noun is capitalized. "My name is *Mary*." "I work for *Walmart*."

Nouns sometimes serve as adjectives (which themselves describe nouns), such as "hockey player" and "state government."

Pronouns

A word used in place of a noun is known as a **pronoun**. Pronouns are words like *I, mine, hers,* and *us*.

Pronouns can be split into different classifications (as shown below) which make them easier to learn; however, it's not important to memorize the classifications.

- **Personal pronouns:** refer to people

- **First person pronouns:** we, I, our, mine

- **Second person pronouns:** you, yours

- **Third person pronouns:** he, she, they, them, it

- **Possessive pronouns:** demonstrate ownership (mine, his, hers, its, ours, theirs, yours)

- **Interrogative pronouns:** ask questions (what, which, who, whom, whose)

- **Relative pronouns:** include the five interrogative pronouns and others that are relative (whoever, whomever, that, when, where)

- **Demonstrative pronouns:** replace something specific (this, that, those, these)

- **Reciprocal pronouns:** indicate something was done or given in return (each other, one another)

- **Indefinite pronouns:** have a nonspecific status (anybody, whoever, someone, everybody, somebody)

Indefinite pronouns such as *anybody, whoever, someone, everybody*, and *somebody* command a singular verb form, but others such as *all, none,* and *some* could require a singular or plural verb form.

Antecedents

An **antecedent** is the noun to which a pronoun refers; it needs to be written or spoken before the pronoun is used. For many pronouns, antecedents are imperative for clarity. In particular, a lot of the personal, possessive, and demonstrative pronouns need antecedents. Otherwise, it would be unclear who or what someone is referring to when they use a pronoun like *he* or *this*.

Pronoun reference means that the pronoun should refer clearly to one, clear, unmistakable noun (the antecedent).

Pronoun-antecedent agreement refers to the need for the antecedent and the corresponding pronoun to agree in gender, person, and number. Here are some examples:

> The *kidneys* (plural antecedent) are part of the urinary system. *They* (plural pronoun) serve several roles.

> The kidneys are part of the *urinary system* (singular antecedent). *It* (singular pronoun) is also known as the renal system.

Pronoun Cases

The **subjective pronouns** —*I, you, he/she/it, we, they,* and *who*—are the subjects of the sentence.

> Example: *They* have a new house.

The **objective pronouns**—*me, you* (*singular*), *him/her, us, them,* and *whom*—are used when something is being done for or given to someone; they are objects of the action.

> Example: The teacher has an apple for *us*.

The **possessive pronouns**—*mine, my, your, yours, his, hers, its, their, theirs, our,* and *ours*—are used to denote that something (or someone) belongs to someone (or something).

> Example: It's *their* chocolate cake.

> Even Better Example: It's *my* chocolate cake!

One of the greatest challenges and worst abuses of pronouns concerns *who* and *whom*. Just knowing the following rule can eliminate confusion. *Who* is a subjective-case pronoun used only as a subject or subject complement. *Whom* is only objective-case and, therefore, the object of the verb or preposition.

> *Who* is going to the concert?

> You are going to the concert with *whom*?

Hint: When using *who* or *whom*, think of whether someone would say *he* or *him*. If the answer is *he*, use *who*. If the answer is *him*, use *whom*. This trick is easy to remember because *he* and *who* both end in vowels, and *him* and *whom* both end in the letter *M*.

Many possessive pronouns sound like contractions. For example, many people get *it's* and *its* confused. The word *it's* is the contraction for *it is*. The word *its* without an apostrophe is the possessive form of *it*.

> I love that wooden desk. It's beautiful. (contraction)

> I love that wooden desk. Its glossy finish is beautiful. (possessive)

If you are not sure which version to use, replace *it's/its* with *it is* and see if that sounds correct. If so, use the contraction (*it's*). That trick also works for *who's/whose*, *you're/your*, and *they're/their*.

Adjectives

"The *extraordinary* brain is the *main* organ of the central nervous system." The adjective *extraordinary* describes the brain in a way that causes one to realize it is more exceptional than some of the other organs while the adjective *main* defines the brain's importance in its system.

An **adjective** is a word or phrase that names an attribute that describes or clarifies a noun or pronoun. This helps the reader visualize and understand the characteristics—size, shape, age, color, origin, etc.— of a person, place, or thing that otherwise might not be known. Adjectives breathe life, color, and depth into the subjects they define. Life would be *drab* and *colorless* without adjectives!

Adjectives often precede the nouns they describe.

> S*he drove her <u>new</u> car.*

However, adjectives can also come later in the sentence.

> *Her car is <u>new</u>.*

Adjectives using the prefix *a–* can only be used after a verb.

> Correct: The dog was alive until the car ran up on the curb and hit him.

> Incorrect: The alive dog was hit by a car that ran up on the curb.

Other examples of this rule include *awake, ablaze, ajar, alike,* and *asleep.*

Other adjectives used after verbs concern states of health.

> The girl was finally *well* after a long bout of pneumonia.

> The boy was *fine* after the accident.

An adjective phrase is not a bunch of adjectives strung together, but a group of words that describes a noun or pronoun and, thus, functions as an adjective. Very happy is an adjective phrase; so are way too hungry and passionate about traveling.

Possessives

In grammar, *possessive nouns* show ownership, which was seen in previous examples like *mine, yours,* and *theirs*.

Singular nouns are generally made possessive with an apostrophe and an *s* (*'s*).

My *uncle's* new car is silver.

The *dog's* bowl is empty.

James's ties are becoming outdated.

Plural nouns ending in *s* are generally made possessive by just adding an apostrophe ('):

The pistachio nuts' saltiness is added during roasting. (The saltiness of pistachio nuts is added during roasting.)

The students' achievement tests are difficult. (The achievement tests of the students are difficult.)

If the plural noun does not end in an *s* such as *women,* then it is made possessive by adding an *apostrophe s* (*'s*)—*women's*.

Indefinite possessive pronouns such as *nobody* or *someone* become possessive by adding an *apostrophe s— nobody's* or *someone's*.

Verbs

A verb is the part of speech that describes an action, state of being, or occurrence.

A verb forms the main part of a predicate of a sentence. This means that the verb explains what the noun (which will be discussed shortly) is doing. A simple example is *time <u>flies</u>*. The verb *flies* explains what the action of the noun, *time,* is doing. This example is a *main* verb.

Helping (auxiliary) verbs are words like *have, do, be, can, may, should, must,* and *will*. "I *should* go to the store." Helping verbs assist main verbs in expressing tense, ability, possibility, permission, or obligation.

Particles are minor function words like *not, in, out, up,* or *down* that become part of the verb itself. "I might *not*."

Participles are words formed from verbs that are often used to modify a noun, noun phrase, verb, or verb phrase.

The *running* teenager collided with the cyclist.

Participles can also create compound verb forms.

He is *speaking*.

Verbs have five basic forms: the **base** form, the **-s** form, the **-ing** form, the **past** form, and the **past participle** form.

The past forms are either **regular** (*love/loved; hate/hated*) or **irregular** because they don't end by adding the common past tense suffix "-ed" (*go/went; fall/fell; set/set*).

Adverbs

Adverbs have more functions than adjectives because they modify or qualify verbs, adjectives, or other adverbs as well as word groups that express a relation of place, time, circumstance, or cause. Therefore, adverbs answer any of the following questions: *How, when, where, why, in what way, how often, how much, in what condition,* and/or *to what degree. How good looking is he? He is <u>very</u> handsome.*

Here are some examples of adverbs for different situations:

- how: quickly
- when: daily
- where: there
- in what way: easily
- how often: often
- how much: much
- in what condition: badly
- what degree: hardly

As one can see, for some reason, many adverbs end in *-ly.*

Adverbs do things like emphasize (*really, simply,* and *so*), amplify (*heartily, completely,* and *positively*), and tone down (*almost, somewhat,* and *mildly*).

Adverbs also come in phrases.

The dog ran as <u>though his life depended on it.</u>

Prepositions

Prepositions are connecting words and, while there are only about 150 of them, they are used more often than any other individual groups of words. They describe relationships between other words. They are placed before a noun or pronoun, forming a phrase that modifies another word in the sentence. **Prepositional phrases** begin with a preposition and end with a noun or pronoun, the **object of the preposition.** *A pristine lake is <u>near the store</u> and <u>behind the bank.</u>*

Some commonly used prepositions are *about, after, anti, around, as, at, behind, beside, by, for, from, in, into, of, off, on, to,* and *with.*

Complex prepositions, which also come before a noun or pronoun, consist of two or three words such as *according to, in regards to,* and *because of.*

Interjections

Interjections are words used to express emotion. Examples include *wow, ouch,* and *hooray.* Interjections are often separate from sentences; in those cases, the interjection is directly followed by an exclamation point. In other cases, the interjection is included in a sentence and followed by a comma. The punctuation plays a big role in the intensity of the emotion that the interjection is expressing. Using a comma or semicolon indicates less excitement than using an exclamation mark.

Conjunctions

Conjunctions are vital words that connect words, phrases, thoughts, and ideas. Conjunctions show relationships between components. There are two types:

Coordinating conjunctions are the primary class of conjunctions placed between words, phrases, clauses, and sentences that are of equal grammatical rank; the coordinating conjunctions are *for, and, nor, but, or, yet,* and *so*. A useful memorization trick is to remember that the first letter of these conjunctions collectively spell the word *fanboys*.

> I need to go shopping, *but* I must be careful to leave enough money in the bank.

> She wore a black, red, *and* white shirt.

Subordinating conjunctions are the secondary class of conjunctions. They connect two unequal parts, one **main** (or **independent**) and the other **subordinate** (or **dependent**). I must go to the store *even though* I do not have enough money in the bank.

> *Because* I read the review, I do not want to go to the movie.

Notice that the presence of subordinating conjunctions makes clauses dependent. *I read the review* is an independent clause, but *because* makes the clause dependent. Thus, it needs an independent clause to complete the sentence.

Sentences

First, let's review the basic elements of sentences.

A **sentence** is a set of words that make up a grammatical unit. The words must have certain elements and be spoken or written in a specific order to constitute a complete sentence that makes sense.

> 1. A sentence must have a **subject** (a noun or noun phrase). The subject tells whom or what the sentence is addressing (i.e. what it is about).

> 2. A sentence must have an **action** or **state of being** (*a* verb). To reiterate: A verb forms the main part of the predicate of a sentence. This means that it explains what the noun is doing.

> 3. A sentence must convey a complete thought.

When examining writing, be mindful of grammar, structure, spelling, and patterns. Sentences can come in varying sizes and shapes; so, the point of grammatical correctness is not to stamp out creativity or diversity in writing. Rather, grammatical correctness ensures that writing will be enjoyable and clear. One of the most common methods for catching errors is to mouth the words as you read them. Many typos are fixed automatically by our brain, but mouthing the words often circumvents this instinct and helps one read what's actually on the page. Often, grammar errors are caught not by memorization of grammar rules but by the training of one's mind to know whether something *sounds* right or not.

Types of Sentences

There isn't an overabundance of absolutes in grammar, but here is one: every sentence in the English language falls into one of four categories.

- Declarative: a simple statement that ends with a period

    The price of milk per gallon is the same as the price of gasoline.

- Imperative: a command, instruction, or request that ends with a period

    Buy milk when you stop to fill up your car with gas.

- Interrogative: a question that ends with a question mark

    Will you buy the milk?

- Exclamatory: a statement or command that expresses emotions like anger, urgency, or surprise and ends with an exclamation mark

    Buy the milk now!

Declarative sentences are the most common type, probably because they are comprised of the most general content, without any of the bells and whistles that the other three types contain. They are, simply, declarations or statements of any degree of seriousness, importance, or information.

Imperative sentences often seem to be missing a subject. The subject is there, though; it is just not visible or audible because it is *implied*. Look at the imperative example sentence.

    Buy the milk when you fill up your car with gas.

You is the implied subject, the one to whom the command is issued. This is sometimes called *the understood you* because it is understood that *you* is the subject of the sentence.

Interrogative sentences—those that ask questions—are defined as such from the idea of the word *interrogation*, the action of questions being asked of suspects by investigators. Although that is serious business, interrogative sentences apply to all kinds of questions.

To exclaim is at the root of **exclamatory sentences**. These are made with strong emotions behind them. The only technical difference between a declarative or imperative sentence and an exclamatory one is the exclamation mark at the end. The example declarative and imperative sentences can both become an exclamatory one simply by putting an exclamation mark at the end of the sentences.

    The price of milk per gallon is the same as the price of gasoline!
    Buy milk when you stop to fill up your car with gas!

After all, someone might be really excited by the price of gas or milk, or they could be mad at the person that will be buying the milk! However, as stated before, exclamation marks in abundance defeat their own purpose! After a while, they begin to cause fatigue! When used only for their intended purpose, they can have their expected and desired effect.

Independent and Dependent Clauses

Independent and dependent clauses are strings of words that contain both a subject and a verb. An **independent clause** *can* stand alone as complete thought, but a **dependent clause** *cannot*. A dependent clause relies on other words to be a complete sentence.

> Independent clause: The keys are on the counter.
> Dependent clause: If the keys are on the counter

Notice that both clauses have a subject (*keys*) and a verb (*are*). The independent clause expresses a complete thought, but the word *if* at the beginning of the dependent clause makes it *dependent* on other words to be a complete thought.

> Independent clause: If the keys are on the counter, please give them to me.

This example constitutes a complete sentence since it includes at least one verb and one subject and is a complete thought. In this case, the independent clause has two subjects (*keys* & an implied *you*) and two verbs (*are* & *give*).

> Independent clause: I went to the store.
> Dependent clause: Because we are out of milk,

> Complete Sentence: Because we are out of milk, I went to the store.
> Complete Sentence: I went to the store because we are out of milk.

Sentence Structures

A **simple sentence** has one independent clause.

> I am going to win.

A **compound sentence** has two independent clauses. A conjunction—*for, and, nor, but, or, yet, so*—links them together. Note that each of the independent clauses has a subject and a verb.

> I am going to win, but the odds are against me.

A **complex sentence** has one independent clause and one or more dependent clauses.

> I am going to win, even though I don't deserve it.

Even though I don't deserve it is a dependent clause. It does not stand on its own. Some conjunctions that link an independent and a dependent clause are *although, because, before, after, that, when, which*, and *while*.

A **compound-complex sentence** has at least three clauses, two of which are independent and at least one that is a dependent clause.

> While trying to dance, I tripped over my partner's feet, but I regained my balance quickly.

The dependent clause is *While trying to dance*.

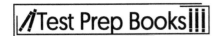

Run-Ons and Fragments

Run-Ons

A common mistake in writing is the run-on sentence. A **run-on** is created when two or more independent clauses are joined without the use of a conjunction, a semicolon, a colon, or a dash. We don't want to use commas where periods belong. Here is an example of a run-on sentence:

> Making wedding cakes can take many hours I am very impatient, I want to see them completed right away.

There are a variety of ways to correct a run-on sentence. The method you choose will depend on the context of the sentence and how it fits with neighboring sentences:

> Making wedding cakes can take many hours. I am very impatient. I want to see them completed right away. (Use periods to create more than one sentence.)

> Making wedding cakes can take many hours; I am very impatient—I want to see them completed right away. (Correct the sentence using a semicolon, colon, or dash.)

> Making wedding cakes can take many hours, and I am very impatient and want to see them completed right away. (Correct the sentence using coordinating conjunctions.)

> I am very impatient because I would rather see completed wedding cakes right away than wait for it to take many hours. (Correct the sentence by revising.)

Fragments

Remember that a complete sentence must have both a subject and a verb. Complete sentences consist of at least one independent clause. Incomplete sentences are called **sentence fragments**. A sentence fragment is a common error in writing. Sentence fragments can be independent clauses that start with subordinating words, such as *but, as, so that,* or *because,* or they could simply be missing a subject or verb.

You can correct a fragment error by adding the fragment to a nearby sentence or by adding or removing words to make it an independent clause. For example:

> Dogs are my favorite animals. Because cats are too lazy. (Incorrect; the word because creates a sentence fragment)

> Dogs are my favorite animals because cats are too lazy. (Correct; this is a dependent clause.)

> Dogs are my favorite animals. Cats are too lazy. (Correct; this is a simple sentence.)

Subject and Predicate

Every complete sentence can be divided into two parts: the subject and the predicate.

Subjects: We need to have subjects in our sentences to tell us who or what the sentence describes. Subjects can be simple or complete, and they can be direct or indirect. There can also be compound subjects.

Simple subjects are the noun or nouns the sentence describes, without modifiers. The simple subject can come before or after the verb in the sentence:

The big brown <u>dog</u> is the calmest one.

Complete subjects are the subject together with all of its describing words or modifiers.

The <u>big brown dog</u> is the calmest one. (The complete subject is big brown dog.)

Direct subjects are subjects that appear in the text of the sentence, as in the example above. **Indirect subjects** are implied. The subject is "you," but the word *you* does not appear.

Indirect subjects are usually in imperative sentences that issue a command or order:

Feed the short skinny dog first. (The understood you is the subject.)

Watch out—he's really hungry! (The sentence warns you to watch out.)

Compound subjects occur when two or more nouns join together to form a plural subject.

<u>Carson</u> and <u>Emily</u> make a great couple.

Predicates: Once we have identified the subject of the sentence, the rest of the sentence becomes the predicate. Predicates are formed by the verb, the direct object, and all words related to it.

We <u>went to see the Cirque du' Soleil performance</u>.

The gigantic green character <u>was funnier than all the rest</u>.

Direct objects are the nouns in the sentence that are receiving the action. Sentences don't necessarily need objects. Sentences only need a subject and a verb.

The clown brought the acrobat the <u>hula-hoop</u>. (What is getting brought? the hula-hoop)

Then he gave the trick pony a <u>soapy bath</u>. (What is being given? (a soapy bath)

Indirect objects are words that tell us to or for whom or what the action is being done. For there to be an indirect object, there first must always be a direct object.

The clown brought <u>the acrobat</u> the hula-hoop. (Who is getting the direct object? the hula-hoop)

Then he gave <u>the trick pony</u> a soapy bath. (What is getting the bath? a trick pony)

Phrases

A **phrase** is a group of words that go together but do not include both a subject and a verb. We use them to add information, explain something, or make the sentence easier for the reader to understand. Unlike clauses, phrases can never stand alone as their own sentence. They do not form complete thoughts. There are noun phrases, prepositional phrases, verbal phrases, appositive phrases, and absolute phrases. Here are some examples of phrases:

I know <u>all the shortest routes</u>.

<u>Before the sequel</u>, we wanted to watch the first movie. (introductory phrase)

The jumpers have hot cocoa <u>to drink right away</u>.

Subject-Verb Agreement

The subject of a sentence and its verb must agree. The cornerstone rule of subject-verb agreement is that subject and verb must agree in number. Whether the subject is singular or plural, the verb must follow suit.

Incorrect: The houses is new.

Correct: The houses are new.

Also Correct: The house is new.

In other words, a singular subject requires a singular verb; a plural subject requires a plural verb.

The words or phrases that come between the subject and verb do not alter this rule.

Incorrect: The houses built of brick is new.

Correct: The houses built of brick are new.

Incorrect: The houses with the sturdy porches is new.

Correct: The houses with the sturdy porches are new.

The subject will always follow the verb when a sentence begins with *here* or *there.* Identify these with care.

Incorrect: Here *is* the *houses* with sturdy porches.

Correct: Here *are* the *houses* with sturdy porches.

The subject in the sentences above is not *here*, it is *houses*. Remember, *here* and *there* are never subjects. Be careful that contractions such as *here's* or *there're* do not cause confusion!

Two subjects joined by *and* require a plural verb form, except when the two combine to make one thing:

Incorrect: Garrett and Jonathan is over there.

Correct: Garrett and Jonathan are over there.

Incorrect: Spaghetti and meatballs are a delicious meal!

Correct: Spaghetti and meatballs is a delicious meal!

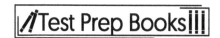

In the example above, *spaghetti and meatballs* is a compound noun. However, *Garrett and Jonathan* is not a compound noun.

Two singular subjects joined by *or, either/or,* or *neither/nor* call for a singular verb form.

Incorrect: Butter or syrup are acceptable.

Correct: Butter or syrup is acceptable.

Plural subjects joined by *or*, *either/or*, or *neither/nor* are, indeed, plural.

The chairs or the boxes are being moved next.

If one subject is singular and the other is plural, the verb should agree with the closest noun.

Correct: The chair or the boxes are being moved next.

Correct: The chairs or the box is being moved next.

Some plurals of money, distance, and time call for a singular verb.

Incorrect: Three dollars *are* enough to buy that.

Correct: Three dollars *is* enough to buy that.

For words declaring degrees of quantity such as *many of, some of,* or *most of,* let the noun that follows *of* be the guide:

Incorrect: Many of the books is in the shelf.

Correct: Many of the books are in the shelf.

Incorrect: Most of the pie *are* on the table.

Correct: Most of the pie *is* on the table.

For indefinite pronouns like anybody or everybody, use singular verbs.

Everybody *is* going to the store.

However, the pronouns *few, many, several, all, some,* and *both* have their own rules and use plural forms.

Some *are* ready.

Some nouns like *crowd* and *congress* are called *collective nouns* and they require a singular verb form.

Congress *is* in session.

The news *is* over.

Books and movie titles, though, including plural nouns such as *Great Expectations*, also require a singular verb. Remember that only the subject affects the verb. While writing tricky subject-verb arrangements, say them aloud. Listen to them. Once the rules have been learned, one's ear will become sensitive to them, making it easier to pick out what's right and what's wrong.

Dangling and Misplaced Modifiers

A **modifier** is a word or phrase meant to describe or clarify another word in the sentence. When a sentence has a modifier but is missing the word it describes or clarifies, it's an error called a **dangling modifier**. We can fix the sentence by revising to include the word that is being modified. Consider the following examples with the modifier underlined:

Incorrect: <u>Having walked five miles</u>, this bench will be the place to rest. (This implies that the bench walked the miles, not the person.)

Correct: <u>Having walked five miles</u>, Matt will rest on this bench. (*Having walked five miles* correctly modifies *Matt*, who did the walking.)

Incorrect: <u>Since midnight</u>, my dreams have been pleasant and comforting. (The adverb clause *since midnight* cannot modify the noun *dreams*.)

Correct: <u>Since midnight</u>, I have had pleasant and comforting dreams. (*Since midnight* modifies the verb *have had*, telling us when the dreams occurred.)

Sometimes the modifier is not located close enough to the word it modifies for the sentence to be clearly understood. In this case, we call the error a **misplaced modifier**. Here is an example with the modifier underlined.

Incorrect: We gave the hot cocoa to the children <u>that was filled with marshmallows</u>. (This sentence implies that the children are what are filled with marshmallows.)

Correct: We gave the hot cocoa <u>that was filled with marshmallows</u> to the children. (The cocoa is filled with marshmallows. The modifier is near the word it modifies.)

Parallel Structure in a Sentence

Parallel structure, also known as **parallelism**, refers to using the same grammatical form within a sentence. This is important in lists and for other components of sentences.

Incorrect: At the recital, the boys and girls were dancing, singing, and played musical instruments.
Correct: At the recital, the boys and girls were dancing, singing, and playing musical instruments.

Notice that in the second example, *played* is not in the same verb tense as the other verbs, nor is it compatible with the helping verb *were*. To test for parallel structure in lists, try reading each item as if it were the only item in the list.

The boys and girls were dancing.
The boys and girls were singing.
The boys and girls were played musical instruments.

Suddenly, the error in the sentence becomes very clear. Here's another example:

Incorrect: After the accident, I informed the police *that Mrs. Holmes backed* into my car, *that Mrs. Holmes got out* of her car to look at the damage, and *she was driving* off without leaving a note.

Correct: After the accident, I informed the police *that Mrs. Holmes backed* into my car, *that Mrs. Holmes got out* of her car to look at the damage, and *that Mrs. Holmes drove off* without leaving a note.

Correct: After the accident, I informed the police that Mrs. Holmes *backed* into my car, *got out* of her car to look at the damage, and *drove off* without leaving a note.

Note that there are two ways to fix the nonparallel structure of the first sentence. The key to parallelism is consistent structure.

Punctuation

Commas

A **comma** (,) is the punctuation mark that signifies a pause—breath—between parts of a sentence. It denotes a break of flow. As with so many aspects of writing structure, authors will benefit by reading their writing aloud or mouthing the words. This can be particularly helpful if one is uncertain about whether the comma is needed.

In a complex sentence—one that contains a subordinate (dependent) clause or clauses—the use of a comma is dictated by where the subordinate clause is located. If the subordinate clause is located before the main clause, a comma is needed between the two clauses.

I will not pay for the steak, *because I don't have that much money*.

Generally, if the subordinate clause is placed after the main clause, no punctuation is needed.

I did well on my exam because I studied two hours the night before.

Notice how the last clause is dependent because it requires the earlier independent clauses to make sense.

Use a comma on both sides of an interrupting phrase.

I will pay for the ice cream, *chocolate and vanilla*, and then will eat it all myself.

The words forming the phrase in italics are nonessential (extra) information. To determine if a phrase is nonessential, try reading the sentence without the phrase and see if it's still coherent.

A comma is not necessary in this next sentence because no interruption—nonessential or extra information—has occurred. Read sentences aloud when uncertain.

I will pay for his chocolate and vanilla ice cream and then will eat it all myself.

If the nonessential phrase comes at the beginning of a sentence, a comma should only go at the end of the phrase. If the phrase comes at the end of a sentence, a comma should only go at the beginning of the phrase.

Other types of interruptions include the following:

- interjections: Oh no, I am not going.
- abbreviations: Barry Potter, M.D., specializes in heart disorders.
- direct addresses: Yes, Claudia, I am tired and going to bed.
- parenthetical phrases: His wife, lovely as she was, was not helpful.
- transitional phrases: Also, it is not possible.

The second comma in the following sentence is called an Oxford comma.

I will pay for ice cream, syrup, and pop.

It is a comma used after the second-to-last item in a series of three or more items. It comes before the word *or* or *and*. Not everyone uses the Oxford comma; it is optional, but many believe it is needed. The comma functions as a tool to reduce confusion in writing. So, if omitting the Oxford comma would cause confusion, then it's best to include it.

Commas are used in math to mark the place of thousands in numerals, breaking them up so they are easier to read. Other uses for commas are in dates (*March 19, 2016*), letter greetings (*Dear Sally,*), and in between cities and states (*Louisville, KY*).

Apostrophes

This punctuation mark, the apostrophe ('), is a versatile little mark. It has a few different functions:

- Quotes: Apostrophes are used when a second quote is needed within a quote.

- In my letter to my friend, I wrote, "The girl had to get a new purse, and guess what Mary did? She said, 'I'd like to go with you to the store.' I knew Mary would buy it for her."

- Contractions: Another use for an apostrophe in the quote above is a contraction. *I'd* is used for *I would.*

  The basic rule for making *contractions* is one area of spelling that is pretty straightforward: combine the two words by inserting an apostrophe (') in the space where a letter is omitted. For example, to combine *you* and *are*, drop the *a* and put the apostrophe in its place: *you're*.

  he + is = he's

  you + all = y'all (informal but often misspelled)

- Possession: An apostrophe followed by the letter *s* shows possession (*Mary's* purse). If the possessive word is plural, the apostrophe generally just follows the word.

- The trees' leaves are all over the ground.

Ellipses

An **ellipsis** (...) consists of three handy little dots that can speak volumes on behalf of irrelevant material. Writers use them in place of words, lines, phrases, list content, or paragraphs that might just as easily

have been omitted from a passage of writing. This can be done to save space or to focus only on the specifically relevant material.

> Exercise is good for some unexpected reasons. Watkins writes, "Exercise has many benefits such as...reducing cancer risk."

In the example above, the ellipsis takes the place of the other benefits of exercise that are more expected.

The ellipsis may also be used to show a pause in sentence flow.

> "I'm wondering...how this could happen," Dylan said in a soft voice.

Semicolons

The **semicolon** (;) might be described as a heavy-handed comma. Take a look at these two examples:

> I will pay for the ice cream, but I will not pay for the steak.
> I will pay for the ice cream; I will not pay for the steak.

What's the difference? The first example has a comma and a conjunction separating the two independent clauses. The second example does not have a conjunction, but there are two independent clauses in the sentence, so something more than a comma is required. In this case, a semicolon is used.

Two independent clauses can only be joined in a sentence by either a comma and conjunction or a semicolon. If one of those tools is not used, the sentence will be a run-on. Remember that while the clauses are independent, they need to be closely related in order to be contained in one sentence.

Another use for the semicolon is to separate items in a list when the items themselves require commas.

> The family lived in Phoenix, Arizona; Oklahoma City, Oklahoma; and Raleigh, North Carolina.

Colons

Colons (:) have many miscellaneous functions. Colons can be used to precede further information or a list. In these cases, a colon should only follow an independent clause.

> Humans take in sensory information through five basic senses: sight, hearing, smell, touch, and taste.

The meal includes the following components:

- Caesar salad
- spaghetti
- garlic bread
- cake

The family got what they needed: a reliable vehicle.

While a comma is more common, a colon can also precede a formal quotation.

> He said to the crowd: "Let's begin!"

The colon is used after the greeting in a formal letter.

> Dear Sir:
> To Whom It May Concern:

In the writing of time, the colon separates the minutes from the hour (*4:45 p.m.*). The colon can also be used to indicate a ratio between two numbers (*50:1*).

Hyphens
The **hyphen** (-) is a little hash mark that can be used to join words to show that they are linked.

Hyphenate two words that work together as a single adjective (a compound adjective).

> honey-covered biscuits

Some words always require hyphens, even if not serving as an adjective.

> merry-go-round

Hyphens always go after certain prefixes like *anti-* & *all-*.

Hyphens should also be used when the absence of the hyphen would cause a strange vowel combination (*semi-engineer*) or confusion. For example, *re-collect* should be used to describe something being gathered twice rather than being written as *recollect*, which means to remember.

Parentheses and Dashes
Parentheses are half-round brackets that look like this: ( ). They set off a word, phrase, or sentence that is an afterthought, explanation, or side note relevant to the surrounding text but not essential. A pair of commas is often used to set off this sort of information, but parentheses are generally used for information that would not fit well within a sentence or that the writer deems not important enough to be structurally part of the sentence.

> The picture of the heart (see above) shows the major parts you should memorize.
> Mount Everest is one of three mountains in the world that are over 28,000 feet high (K2 and Kanchenjunga are the other two).

See how the sentences above are complete without the parenthetical statements? In the first example, *see above* would not have fit well within the flow of the sentence. The second parenthetical statement could have been a separate sentence, but the writer deemed the information not pertinent to the topic.

The **em-dash** (—) is a mark longer than a hyphen used as a punctuation mark in sentences and to set apart a relevant thought. Even after plucking out the line separated by the dash marks, the sentence will be intact and make sense.

> Looking out the airplane window at the landmarks—Lake Clarke, Thompson Community College, and the bridge—she couldn't help but feel excited to be home.

The dashes use is similar to that of parentheses or a pair of commas. So, what's the difference? Many believe that using dashes makes the clause within them stand out while using parentheses is subtler. It's advised to not use dashes when commas could be used instead.

Quotation Marks

Here are some instances where *quotation marks* should be used:

- Dialogue for characters in narratives. When characters speak, the first word should always be capitalized, and the punctuation goes inside the quotes. For example:

    Janie said, "The tree fell on my car during the hurricane."

- Around titles of songs, short stories, essays, and chapters in books
- To emphasize a certain word
- To refer to a word as the word itself

Capitalization

Here's a non-exhaustive list of things that should be capitalized.

- The first word of every sentence
- The first word of every line of poetry
- The first letter of proper nouns (World War II)
- Holidays (Valentine's Day)
- The days of the week and months of the year (Tuesday, March)
- The first word, last word, and all major words in the titles of books, movies, songs, and other creative works (In the novel, *To Kill a Mockingbird*, note that *a* is lowercase since it's not a major word, but *to* is capitalized since it's the first word of the title.)
- Titles when preceding a proper noun (President Roberto Gonzales, Aunt Judy)

When simply using a word such as president or secretary, though, the word is not capitalized.

    Officers of the new business must include a *president* and *treasurer*.

Seasons—spring, fall, etc.—are not capitalized.

North, *south*, *east*, and *west* are capitalized when referring to regions but are not when being used for directions. In general, if it's preceded by *the* it should be capitalized.

    I'm from the South.
    I drove south.

Word Confusion

That/Which

The pronouns *that* and *which* are both used to refer to animals, objects, ideas, and events—but they are not interchangeable. The rule is to use the word *that* in essential clauses and phrases that help convey the meaning of the sentence. Use the word *which* in nonessential (less important) clauses. Typically, *which* clauses are enclosed in commas.

    The morning <u>that I fell asleep in class</u> caused me a lot of trouble.

    This morning's coffee, <u>which had too much creamer</u>, woke me up.

Who/Whom

We use the pronouns *who* and *whom* to refer to people. We always use *who* when it is the subject of the sentence or clause. We never use *whom* as the subject; it is always the object of a verb or preposition.

<u>Who</u> hit the baseball for the home run? (subject)

The baseball fell into the glove of <u>whom</u>? (object of the preposition *of*)

The umpire called <u>whom</u> "out"? (object of the verb *called*)

To/Too/Two

to: a preposition or infinitive (*to walk, to run, walk to the store, run to the tree*)
too: means also, as well, or very (*She likes cookies, too.; I ate too much.*)
two: a number (*I have two cookies. She walked to the store two times.*)

There/Their/They're

there: an adjective, adverb, or pronoun used to start a sentence or indicate place (*There are four vintage cars over there.*)
their: a possessive pronoun used to indicate belonging (*Their car is the blue and white one.*)
they're: a contraction of the words "they are" (*They're going to enter the vintage car show.*)

Your/You're

your: a possessive pronoun (*Your artwork is terrific.*)
you're: a contraction of the words "you are" (*You're a terrific artist.*)

Its/It's

its: a possessive pronoun (*The elephant had its trunk in the water.*)
it's: a contraction of the words "it is" (*It's an impressive animal.*)

Affect/Effect

affect: as a verb means "to influence" (*How will the earthquake affect your home?*); as a noun means "emotion or mood" (*Her affect was somber.*)
effect: as a verb means "to bring about" (*She will effect a change through philanthropy.*); as a noun means "a result of" (*The effect of the earthquake was devastating.*)

Other mix-ups: Other pairs of words cause mix-ups but are not necessarily homonyms. Here are a few of those:

Bring/Take

bring: when the action is coming toward (*Bring me the money.*)
take: when the action is going away from (*Take her the money.*)

Can/May

can: means "able to" (*The child can ride a bike.*)
may: asks permission (*The child asked if he may ride his bike.*)

Than/Then

than: a conjunction used for comparison (*I like tacos better than pizza.*)

then: an adverb telling when something happened (*I ate and then slept.*)

Disinterested/Uninterested

disinterested: used to mean "neutral" (*The jury remains disinterested during the trial.*)

uninterested: used to mean "bored" (*I was uninterested during the lecture.*)

Percent/Percentage

percent: used when there is a number involved (*Five percent of us like tacos.*)

percentage: used when there is no number (*That is a low percentage.*)

Fewer/Less

fewer: used for things you can count (*He has fewer playing cards.*)

less: used for things you cannot count, as well as time (*He has less talent. You have less than a minute.*)

Farther/Further

farther: used when discussing distance (*His paper airplane flew farther than mine.*)

further: used to mean "more" (*He needed further information.*)

Lend/Loan

lend: a verb used for borrowing (*Lend me your lawn mower. He will lend it to me.*)

loan: a noun used for something borrowed (*She applied for a student loan.*)

Note

Some people have problems with these:

- regardless/irregardless
- a lot/alot

Irregardless and *alot* are always incorrect. Don't use them

First Essay

1. First read the article below. Then click the link below the article and watch the TED Talk video. Then review the prompt and write an essay synthesizing the two sources.

"Coping with Stress"

By the U.S. Centers for Disease Control and Prevention, (https://www.cdc.gov/violenceprevention/about/copingwith-stresstips.html)

(1) Stress is a reaction to a situation where a person feels threatened or anxious. Learning healthy ways to cope and getting the right care and support can help reduce stressful feelings and symptoms.

(2) After a traumatic event, people may have strong and lingering reactions. These events may include personal or environmental disasters, or threats with an assault. The symptoms may be physical or emotional. Common reactions to a stressful event can include:

- disbelief, shock, and numbness
- feeling sad, frustrated, and helpless
- difficulty concentrating and making decisions
- headaches, back pains, and stomach problems
- smoking or use of alcohol or drugs

Healthy Ways to Cope with Stress

(3) Feeling emotional and nervous or having trouble sleeping and eating can all be normal reactions to stress. Here are some healthy ways you can deal with stress:

- **Take care of yourself.** Eat healthy, exercise, get plenty of sleep, and give yourself a break if you feel stressed out.
- **Talk to others.** Share your problems and how you are feeling and coping with a parent, friend, counselor, doctor, or pastor.
- **Avoid drugs and alcohol.** These may seem to help, but they can create additional problems and increase the stress you are already feeling.
- **Take a break.** If news events are causing your stress, take a break from listening or watching the news.
- **Recognize when you need more help.** If problems continue or you are thinking about suicide, talk to a psychologist, social worker, or professional counselor.

Helping Children and Youth Cope with Stress

(4) Children and youth often struggle with how to cope with stress. Youth can be particularly overwhelmed when their stress is connected to a traumatic event—like a natural disaster, family loss, school shootings, or community violence. Parents, caregivers, and educators can take steps to provide stability and support that help young people feel better.

2. Listen to the following lecture:
https://www.ted.com/talks/kelly_mcgonigal_how_to_make_stress_your_friend#t-3091

3. Prompt: Give an overview of the article and the Ted Talk and then synthesize the two. What are some similarities they offer? Are there any major differences in the two sources?

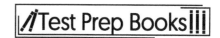

Cite evidence found in the passage by placing the relevant paragraph number in parentheses at the end of the sentence.

Second Essay

Prepare an essay of about 300–600 words on the topic below.

Technology has been invading cars for the last several years, but there are some new high tech trends that are pretty amazing. It is now standard in many car models to have a rear-view camera, hands-free phone and text, and a touch screen digital display. Music can be streamed from a paired cell phone, and some displays can even be programmed with a personal photo. Sensors beep to indicate there is something in the driver's path when reversing and changing lanes. Rain-sensing windshield wipers and lights are automatic, leaving the driver with little to do but watch the road and enjoy the ride. The next wave of technology will include cars that automatically parallel park, and self-driving cars are on the horizon. These technological advances make it a good time to be a driver.

Write an essay to someone who is considering buying a smart car. Take a side on the issue and argue whether or not he/she should invest in one. Use specific examples to support your argument.

Reading

Questions 1–6 are based upon the following passage:

My gentleness and good behaviour had gained so far on the emperor and his court, and indeed upon the army and people in general, that I began to conceive hopes of getting my liberty in a short time. I took all possible methods to cultivate this favourable disposition. The natives came, by degrees, to be less apprehensive of any danger from me. I would sometimes lie down, and let five or six of them dance on my hand; and at last the boys and girls would venture to come and play at hide-and-seek in my hair. I had now made a good progress in understanding and speaking the language. The emperor had a mind one day to entertain me with several of the country shows, wherein they exceed all nations I have known, both for dexterity and magnificence. I was diverted with none so much as that of the rope-dancers, performed upon a slender white thread, extended about two feet, and twelve inches from the ground. Upon which I shall desire liberty, with the reader's patience, to enlarge a little.

This diversion is only practised by those persons who are candidates for great employments, and high favour at court. They are trained in this art from their youth, and are not always of noble birth, or liberal education. When a great office is vacant, either by death or disgrace (which often happens,) five or six of those candidates petition the emperor to entertain his majesty and the court with a dance on the rope; and whoever jumps the highest, without falling, succeeds in the office. Very often the chief ministers themselves are commanded to show their skill, and to convince the emperor that they have not lost their faculty. Flimnap, the treasurer, is allowed to cut a caper on the straight rope, at least an inch higher than any other lord in the whole empire. I have seen him do the summerset several times together, upon a trencher fixed on a rope which is no thicker than a common packthread in England. My friend Reldresal, principal secretary for private affairs, is, in my opinion, if I am not partial, the second after the treasurer; the rest of the great officers are much upon a par.

This excerpt is an adaptation of Jonathan Swift's Gulliver's Travels into Several Remote Nations of the World

1. Which of the following statements best summarize the central purpose of this text?
    a. Gulliver details his fondness for the archaic yet interesting practices of his captors.
    b. Gulliver conjectures about the intentions of the aristocratic sector of society.
    c. Gulliver becomes acquainted with the people and practices of his new surroundings.
    d. Gulliver's differences cause him to become penitent around new acquaintances.

2. What is the word *principal* referring to in the following text?

> My friend Reldresal, principal secretary for private affairs, is, in my opinion, if I am not partial, the second after the treasurer; the rest of the great officers are much upon a par.

a. Primary or chief
b. An acolyte
c. An individual who provides nurturing
d. One in a subordinate position

3. What can the reader infer from the following text?

> I would sometimes lie down, and let five or six of them dance on my hand; and at last the boys and girls would venture to come and play at hide-and-seek in my hair.

a. The children tortured Gulliver.
b. Gulliver traveled because he wanted to meet new people.
c. Gulliver is considerably larger than the children who are playing around him.
d. Gulliver has a genuine love and enthusiasm for people of all sizes.

4. What is the significance of the word *mind* in the following passage?

> The emperor had a mind one day to entertain me with several of the country shows, wherein they exceed all nations I have known, both for dexterity and magnificence.

a. The ability to think
b. A collective vote
c. A definitive decision
d. A mythological question

5. Which of the following assertions does not support the fact that games are a commonplace event in this culture?
a. My gentlest and good behavior . . . short time.
b. They are trained in this art from their youth . . . liberal education.
c. Very often the chief ministers themselves are commanded to show their skill . . . not lost their faculty.
d. Flimnap, the treasurer, is allowed to cut a caper on the straight rope . . . higher than any other lord in the whole empire.

6. How does Gulliver's description of Flimnap's, the treasurer's, ability to *cut a caper on the straight rope*, and Reldresal, principal secretary for private affairs, being the *second to the treasurer,* serve as evidence of the community's emphasis in regards to the correlation between physical strength and leadership abilities?
a. Only children used Gulliver's hands as a playground.
b. The two men who exhibited superior abilities held prominent positions in the community.
c. Only common townspeople, not leaders, walk the straight rope.
d. No one could jump higher than Gulliver.

Questions 7–12 are based upon the following passage:

"Did you ever come across a protégé of his—one Hyde?" He asked.

"Hyde?" repeated Lanyon. "No. Never heard of him. Since my time."

That was the amount of information that the lawyer carried back with him to the great, dark bed on which he tossed to and fro until the small hours of the morning began to grow large. It was a night of little ease to his toiling mind, toiling in mere darkness and besieged by questions.

Six o'clock struck on the bells of the church that was so conveniently near to Mr. Utterson's dwelling, and still he was digging at the problem. Hitherto it had touched him on the intellectual side alone; but now his imagination also was engaged, or rather enslaved; and as he lay and tossed in the gross darkness of the night in the curtained room, Mr. Enfield's tale went by before his mind in a scroll of lighted pictures. He would be aware of the great field of lamps in a nocturnal city; then of the figure of a man walking swiftly; then of a child running from the doctor's; and then these met, and that human Juggernaut trod the child down and passed on regardless of her screams. Or else he would see a room in a rich house, where his friend lay asleep, dreaming and smiling at his dreams; and then the door of that room would be opened, the curtains of the bed plucked apart, the sleeper recalled, and, lo! There would stand by his side a figure to whom power was given, and even at that dead hour he must rise and do its bidding. The figure in these two phases haunted the lawyer all night; and if at any time he dozed over, it was but to see it glide more stealthily through sleeping houses, or move the more swiftly, and still the more smoothly, even to dizziness, through wider labyrinths of lamplighted city, and at every street corner crush a child and leave her screaming. And still the figure had no face by which he might know it; even in his dreams it had no face, or one that baffled him and melted before his eyes; and thus it was that there sprung up and grew apace in the lawyer's mind a singularly strong, almost an inordinate, curiosity to behold the features of the real Mr. Hyde. If he could but once set eyes on him, he thought the mystery would lighten and perhaps roll altogether away, as was the habit of mysterious things when well examined. He might see a reason for his friend's strange preference or bondage, and even for the startling clauses of the will. And at least it would be a face worth seeing: the face of a man who was without bowels of mercy: a face which had but to show itself to raise up, in the mind of the unimpressionable Enfield, a spirit of enduring hatred.

From that time forward, Mr. Utterson began to haunt the door in the by-street of shops. In the morning before office hours, at noon when business was plenty and time scarce, at night under the face of the fogged city moon, by all lights and at all hours of solitude or concourse, the lawyer was to be found on his chosen post.

"If he be Mr. Hyde," he had thought, "I should be Mr. Seek."

Excerpt from Robert Louis Stevenson's The Strange Case of Dr. Jekyll and Mr. Hyde

7. What is the purpose of the use of repetition in the following passage?

> It was a night of little ease to his toiling mind, toiling in mere darkness and besieged by questions.

a. It serves as a demonstration of the mental state of Mr. Lanyon.
b. It is reminiscent of the church bells that are mentioned in the story.
c. It mimics Mr. Utterson's ambivalence.
d. It emphasizes Mr. Utterson's anguish in failing to identify Hyde's whereabouts.

8. What is the setting of the story in this passage?
a. In the city
b. On the countryside
c. In a jail
d. In a mental health facility

9. What can one infer about the meaning of the word *Juggernaut* from the author's use of it in the passage?
a. It is an apparition that appears at daybreak.
b. It scares children.
c. It is associated with space travel.
d. Mr. Utterson finds it soothing.

10. What is the definition of the word *haunt* in the following passage?

> From that time forward, Mr. Utterson began to haunt the door in the by-street of shops. In the morning before office hours, at noon when business was plenty and time scarce, at night under the face of the fogged city moon, by all lights and at all hours of solitude or concourse, the lawyer was to be found on his chosen post.

a. To levitate
b. To constantly visit
c. To terrorize
d. To daunt

11. The phrase *labyrinths of lamplighted city* contains an example of what?
a. Hyperbole
b. Simile
c. Metaphor
d. Alliteration

12. What can one reasonably conclude from the final comment of this passage?

> "If he be Mr. Hyde," he had thought, "I should be Mr. Seek."

a. The speaker is considering a name change.
b. The speaker is experiencing an identity crisis.
c. The speaker has mistakenly been looking for the wrong person.
d. The speaker intends to continue to look for Hyde.

Questions 13–18 are based upon the following passage:

Fellow-citizens, pardon me, allow me to ask, why am I called upon to speak here to-day? What have I, or those I represent, to do with your national independence? Are the great principles of political freedom and of natural justice, embodied in that Declaration of Independence, extended to us? and am I, therefore, called upon to bring our humble offering to the national altar, and to confess the benefits and express devout gratitude for the blessings resulting from your independence to us?

Would to God, both for your sakes and ours, ours that an affirmative answer could be truthfully returned to these questions! Then would my task be light, and my burden easy and delightful. For who is there so cold, that a nation's sympathy could not warm him? Who so obdurate and dead to the claims of gratitude, that would not thankfully acknowledge such priceless benefits? Who so stolid and selfish, that would not give his voice to swell the hallelujahs of a nation's jubilee, when the chains of servitude had been torn from his limbs? I am not that man. In a case like that, the dumb may eloquently speak, and the lame man leap as an hart.

But, such is not the state of the case. I say it with a sad sense of the disparity between us. I am not included within the pale of this glorious anniversary. Oh pity! Your high independence only reveals the immeasurable distance between us. The blessings in which you, this day, rejoice, are not enjoyed in common. – The rich inheritance of justice, liberty, prosperity and independence, bequeathed by your fathers, is shared by you, not by me. The sunlight that brought life and healing to you, as brought stripes and death to me. This Fourth [of] July is yours, not mine. You may rejoice, I must mourn. To drag a man in fetters into the grand illuminated temple of liberty, and call upon him to join you in joyous anthems, were inhuman mockery and sacrilegious irony. Do you mean, citizens, to mock me, by asking me to speak to-day? If so, there is a parallel to your conduct. And let me warn you that it is dangerous to copy the example of a nation whose crimes, lowering up to heaven, were thrown down by the breath of the Almighty, burying that nation in irrecoverable ruin! I can to-day take up the plaintive lament of a peeled and woe-smitten people!

"By the rivers of Babylon, there we sat down Yea! we wept when we remembered Zion. We hanged our harps upon the willows in the midst thereof. For there, they that carried us away captive, required of us a song; and they who wasted us required of us mirth, saying, Sing us one of the songs of Zion. How can we sing the Lord's song in a strange land? If I forget thee, O Jerusalem, let my right hand forget her cunning. If I do not remember thee, let my tongue cleave to the roof of my mouth."

Excerpt from "What to the Slave is the Fourth of July?" by Frederick Douglass; Rochester, New York; July 5, 1852

13. What is the tone of the first paragraph of this passage?
    a. Incredulous
    b. Inclusive
    c. Contemplative
    d. Nonchalant

14. Which word CANNOT be used synonymously with the term *obdurate* as it is conveyed in the text below?

> Who so obdurate and dead to the claims of gratitude, that would not thankfully acknowledge such priceless benefits?

a. Steadfast
b. Stubborn
c. Contented
d. Unwavering

15. What is the central purpose of this text?
a. To demonstrate the author's extensive knowledge of the Bible
b. To address the feelings of exclusion expressed by Black Americans after the establishment of the Fourth of July holiday
c. To convince wealthy landowners to adopt new holiday rituals
d. To explain why minorities often relished the notion of segregation in government institutions

16. Which statement serves as evidence of the question above?
a. By the rivers of Babylon . . . down.
b. Fellow citizens . . . today.
c. I can . . . woe-smitten people.
d. The rich inheritance of justice . . . *not by me*.

17. The statement below features an example of which of the following literary devices?

> Your high independence only reveals the immeasurable distance between us.

a. Assonance
b. Parallelism
c. Amplification
d. Hyperbole

18. The speaker's use of biblical references, such as "rivers of Babylon" and the "songs of Zion," helps the reader to do all of the following EXCEPT:
a. Identify with the speaker through the use of common text.
b. Draw a connection between another group of people who have been affected by slavery and American slaves.
c. Recognize the equivocation of the speaker and those that he represents.
d. Appeal to the listener's sense of humanity.

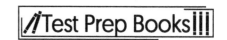

Questions 19–24 are based upon the following passage:

Four score and seven years ago our fathers brought forth on this continent, a new nation, conceived in Liberty, and dedicated to the proposition that all men are created equal.

Now we are engaged in a great civil war, testing whether that nation, or any nation so conceived and so dedicated, can long endure We are met on a great battle-field of that war. We have come to dedicate a portion of that field, as a final resting place for those who here gave their lives that that nation might live. It is altogether fitting and proper that we should do this.

But, in a larger sense, we can not dedicate—we can not consecrate—we cannot hallow—this ground. The brave men, living and dead, who struggled here, have consecrated it, far above our poor power to add or detract. The world will little note, nor long remember what we say here, but it can never forget what they did here. It is for us the living, rather, to be dedicated here to the unfinished work which they who fought here have thus far so nobly advanced. It is rather for us to be here dedicated to the great task remaining before us—that from these honored dead we take increased devotion to that cause for which they gave the last full measure of devotion—that we here highly resolve that these dead shall not have died in vain—that these this nation, under God, shall have a new birth of freedom —and that government of the people, by the people, for the people, shall not perish from the earth.

Excerpt from Abraham Lincoln's Address Delivered at the Dedication of the Cemetery at Gettysburg, November 19, 1863

19. The best description for the phrase *four score and seven years ago* is which of the following?
    a. A unit of measurement
    b. A period of time
    c. A literary movement
    d. A statement of political reform

20. What is the setting of this text?
    a. A battleship off of the coast of France
    b. A desert plain on the Sahara Desert
    c. A battlefield in North America
    d. The residence of Abraham Lincoln

21. Which war is Abraham Lincoln referring to in the following passage?

> Now we are engaged in a great civil war, testing whether that nation, or any nation so conceived and so dedicated, can long endure.

 a. World War I
 b. The War of the Spanish Succession
 c. World War II
 d. The American Civil War

22. What message is the author trying to convey through this address?

 a. The audience should consider the death of the people that fought in the war as an example and perpetuate the ideals of freedom that the soldiers died fighting for.
 b. The audience should honor the dead by establishing an annual memorial service.
 c. The audience should form a militia that would overturn the current political structure.
 d. The audience should forget the lives that were lost and discredit the soldiers.

23. Which rhetorical device is being used in the following passage?

> . . . we here highly resolve that these dead shall not have died in vain—that these this nation, under God, shall have a new birth of freedom —and that government of people, by the people, for the people, shall not perish from the earth.

 a. Antimetabole
 b. Antiphrasis
 c. Anaphora
 d. Epiphora

24. What is the effect of Lincoln's statement in the following passage?

> But, in a larger sense, we can not dedicate—we can not consecrate—we cannot hallow—this ground. The brave men, living and dead, who struggled here, have consecrated it, far above our poor power to add or detract.

 a. His comparison emphasizes the great sacrifice of the soldiers who fought in the war.
 b. His comparison serves as a remainder of the inadequacies of his audience.
 c. His comparison serves as a catalyst for guilt and shame among audience members.
 d. His comparison attempts to illuminate the great differences between soldiers and civilians.

Questions 25–30 are based upon the following passage:

> My Good Friends,—When I first imparted to the committee of the projected Institute my particular wish that on one of the evenings of my readings here the main body of my audience should be composed of working men and their families, I was animated by two desires; first, by the wish to have the great pleasure of meeting you face to face at this Christmas time, and accompany you myself through one of my little Christmas books; and second, by the wish to have an opportunity of stating publicly in your presence, and in the presence of the committee, my earnest hope that the Institute will, from the beginning, recognise one great principle—strong in reason and justice—which I believe to be essential to the very life of such an Institution. It is, that the working man shall, from the first unto the last, have a share in the management of an Institution which is designed for his benefit, and which calls itself by his name.

I have no fear here of being misunderstood—of being supposed to mean too much in this. If there ever was a time when any one class could of itself do much for its own good, and for the welfare of society—which I greatly doubt—that time is unquestionably past. It is in the fusion of different classes, without confusion; in the bringing together of employers and employed; in the creating of a better common understanding among those whose interests are identical, who depend upon each other, who are vitally essential to each other, and who never can be in unnatural antagonism without deplorable results, that one of the chief principles of a Mechanics' Institution should consist. In this world a great deal of the bitterness among us arises from an imperfect understanding of one another. Erect in Birmingham a great Educational Institution, properly educational; educational of the feelings as well as of the reason; to which all orders of Birmingham men contribute; in which all orders of Birmingham men meet; wherein all orders of Birmingham men are faithfully represented—and you will erect a Temple of Concord here which will be a model edifice to the whole of England.

Contemplating as I do the existence of the Artisans' Committee, which not long ago considered the establishment of the Institute so sensibly, and supported it so heartily, I earnestly entreat the gentlemen—earnest I know in the good work, and who are now among us,—by all means to avoid the great shortcoming of similar institutions; and in asking the working man for his confidence, to set him the great example and give him theirs in return. You will judge for yourselves if I promise too much for the working man, when I say that he will stand by such an enterprise with the utmost of his patience, his perseverance, sense, and support; that I am sure he will need no charitable aid or condescending patronage; but will readily and cheerfully pay for the advantages which it confers; that he will prepare himself in individual cases where he feels that the adverse circumstances around him have rendered it necessary; in a word, that he will feel his responsibility like an honest man, and will most honestly and manfully discharge it. I now proceed to the pleasant task to which I assure you I have looked forward for a long time.

Excerpt from Charles Dickens' speech in Birmingham in England on December 30, 1853 on behalf of the Birmingham and Midland Institute

25. Which word is most closely synonymous with the word *patronage* as it appears in the following statement?
    . . . that I am sure he will need no charitable aid or condescending patronage

   a. Auspices
   b. Aberration
   c . Acerbic
   d. Adulation

26. Which term is most closely aligned with the definition of the term *working man* as it is defined in the following passage?

> You will judge for yourselves if I promise too much for the working man, when I say that he will stand by such an enterprise with the utmost of his patience, his perseverance, sense, and support . . .

a. Plebian
b. Viscount
c. Entrepreneur
d. Bourgeois

27. Which of the following statements most closely correlates with the definition of the term *working man* as it is defined in Question 26?

a. A working man is not someone who works for institutions or corporations, but someone who is well versed in the workings of the soul.
b. A working man is someone who is probably not involved in social activities because the physical demand for work is too high.
c. A working man is someone who works for wages among the middle class.
d. The working man has historically taken to the field, to the factory, and now to the screen.

28. Based upon the contextual evidence provided in the passage above, what is the meaning of the term *enterprise* in the third paragraph?

a. Company
b. Courage
c. Game
d. Cause

29. The speaker addresses his audience as *My Good Friends*—what kind of credibility does this salutation give to the speaker?

a. The speaker is an employer addressing his employees, so the salutation is a way for the boss to bridge the gap between himself and his employees.
b. The speaker's salutation is one from an entertainer to his audience and uses the friendly language to connect to his audience before a serious speech.
c. The salutation gives the serious speech that follows a somber tone, as it is used ironically.
d. The speech is one from a politician to the public, so the salutation is used to grab the audience's attention.

30. According to the aforementioned passage, what is the speaker's second desire for his time in front of the audience?

a. To read a Christmas story
b. For the working man to have a say in his institution which is designed for his benefit.
c. To have an opportunity to stand in their presence
d. For the life of the institution to be essential to the audience as a whole

Questions 31–36 are based upon the following passage:

Three years ago, I think there were not many bird-lovers in the United States, who believed it possible to prevent the total extinction of both egrets from our fauna. All the known rookeries accessible to plume-hunters had been totally destroyed. Two years ago, the secret discovery of several small, hidden colonies prompted William Dutcher, President of the National Association of Audubon Societies, and Mr. T. Gilbert Pearson, Secretary, to attempt the protection of those colonies. With a fund contributed for the purpose, wardens were hired and duly commissioned. As previously stated, one of those wardens was shot dead in cold blood by a plume hunter. The task of guarding swamp rookeries from the attacks of money-hungry desperadoes to whom the accursed plumes were worth their weight in gold, is a very chancy proceeding. There is now one warden in Florida who says that "before they get my rookery they will first have to get me."

Thus far the protective work of the Audubon Association has been successful. Now there are twenty colonies, which contain all told, about 5,000 egrets and about 120,000 herons and ibises which are guarded by the Audubon wardens. One of the most important is on Bird Island, a mile out in Orange Lake, central Florida, and it is ably defended by Oscar E. Baynard. To-day, the plume hunters who do not dare to raid the guarded rookeries are trying to study out the lines of flight of the birds, to and from their feeding-grounds, and shoot them in transit. Their motto is—"Anything to beat the law, and get the plumes." It is there that the state of Florida should take part in the war.

The success of this campaign is attested by the fact that last year a number of egrets were seen in eastern Massachusetts—for the first time in many years. And so to-day the question is, can the wardens continue to hold the plume-hunters at bay?

Excerpt from Our Vanishing Wildlife, by William T. Hornaday

31. The author's use of first person pronoun in the following text does NOT have which of the following effects?

Three years ago, I think there were not many bird-lovers in the United States, who believed it possible to prevent the total extinction of both egrets from our fauna.

a. The phrase *I think* acts as a sort of hedging, where the author's tone is less direct and/or absolute.
b. It allows the reader to more easily connect with the author.
c. It encourages the reader to empathize with the egrets.
d. It distances the reader from the text by overemphasizing the story.

32. What purpose does the quote serve at the end of the first paragraph?
a. The quote shows proof of a hunter threatening one of the wardens.
b. The quote lightens the mood by illustrating the colloquial language of the region.
c. The quote provides an example of a warden protecting one of the colonies.
d. The quote provides much needed comic relief in the form of a joke.

33. What is the meaning of the word *rookeries* in the following text?

   To-day, the plume hunters who do not dare to raid the guarded rookeries are trying to study out the lines of flight of the birds, to and from their feeding-grounds, and shoot them in transit.

   a. Houses in a slum area
   b. A place where hunters gather to trade tools
   c. A place where wardens go to trade stories
   d. A colony of breeding birds

34. What is on Bird Island?
   a. Hunters selling plumes
   b. An important bird colony
   c. Bird Island Battle between the hunters and the wardens
   d. An important egret with unique plumes

35. What is the main purpose of the passage?
   a. To persuade the audience to act in preservation of the bird colonies
   b. To show the effect hunting egrets has had on the environment
   c. To argue that the preservation of bird colonies has had a negative impact on the environment
   d. To demonstrate the success of the protective work of the Audubon Association

36. Why are hunters trying to study the lines of flight of the birds?
   a. To study ornithology, one must know the lines of flight that birds take.
   b. To help wardens preserve the lives of the birds
   c. To have a better opportunity to hunt the birds
   d. To build their homes under the lines of flight because they believe it brings good luck

Questions 37–42 are based upon the following passage:

   Insects as a whole are preeminently creatures of the land and the air. This is shown not only by the possession of wings by a vast majority of the class, but by the mode of breathing to which reference has already been made, a system of branching air-tubes carrying atmospheric air with its combustion-supporting oxygen to all the insect's tissues. The air gains access to these tubes through a number of paired air-holes or spiracles, arranged segmentally in series.

   It is of great interest to find that, nevertheless, a number of insects spend much of their time under water. This is true of not a few in the perfect winged state, as for example aquatic beetles and water-bugs ('boatmen' and 'scorpions') which have some way of protecting their spiracles when submerged, and, possessing usually the power of flight, can pass on occasion from pond or stream to upper air. But it is advisable in connection with our present subject to dwell especially on some insects that remain continually under water till they are ready to undergo their final moult and attain the winged state, which they pass entirely in the air. The preparatory instars of such insects are aquatic; the adult instar is aerial. All may-flies, dragon-flies, and caddis-flies, many beetles and two-winged flies, and a few moths thus divide their life-story between the water and the air. For the present we confine attention to the Stone-flies, the May-flies, and the Dragon-flies, three well-known orders of insects respectively called by systematists the Plecoptera, the Ephemeroptera, and the Odonata.

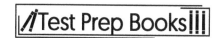

In the case of many insects that have aquatic larvae, the latter are provided with some arrangement for enabling them to reach atmospheric air through the surface-film of the water. But the larva of a stone-fly, a dragon-fly, or a may-fly is adapted more completely than these for aquatic life; it can, by means of gills of some kind, breathe the air dissolved in water.

Excerpt from The Life-Story of Insects, by Geo H. Carpenter

37. Which statement best details the central idea in this passage?
   a. It introduces certain insects that transition from water to air.
   b. It delves into entomology, especially where gills are concerned.
   c. It defines what constitutes insects' breathing.
   d. It invites readers to have a hand in the preservation of insects.

38. Which definition most closely relates to the usage of the word *moult* in the passage?
   a. An adventure of sorts, especially underwater
   b. Mating act between two insects
   c. The act of shedding part or all of the outer shell
   d. Death of an organism that ends in a revival of life

39. What is the purpose of the first paragraph in relation to the second paragraph?
   a. The first paragraph serves as a cause and the second paragraph serves as an effect.
   b. The first paragraph serves as a contrast to the second.
   c. The first paragraph is a description for the argument in the second paragraph.
   d. The first and second paragraphs are merely presented in a sequence.

40. What does the following sentence most nearly mean?
   The preparatory instars of such insects are aquatic; the adult instar is aerial.

   a. The volume of water is necessary to prep the insect for transition rather than the volume of the air.
   b. The abdomen of the insect is designed like a star in the water as well as the air.
   c. The early stages in between periods of molting are acted out in the water, while the last stage is in the air.
   d. These insects breathe first in the water through gills, yet continue to use the same organs to breathe in the air.

41. Which of the statements reflect information that one could reasonably infer based on the author's tone?
   a. The author's tone is persuasive and attempts to call the audience to action.
   b. The author's tone is passionate due to excitement over the subject and personal narrative.
   c. The author's tone is informative and exhibits interest in the subject of the study.
   d. The author's tone is somber, depicting some anger at the state of insect larvae.

42. Which statement best describes stoneflies, mayflies, and dragonflies?
   a. They are creatures of the land and the air.
   b. They have a way of protecting their spiracles when submerged.
   c. Their larvae can breathe the air dissolved in water through gills of some kind.
   d. The preparatory instars of these insects are aerial.

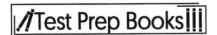
Listening

Directions: The Listening section measures your ability to understand conversations and lectures in English. In this test, you will listen to several pieces of content and answer questions after each one. The questions typically ask about the main idea and supporting details. Some questions ask about a speaker's purpose or attitude. Answer the questions based on what is stated or implied by the speakers.

Listen to all of these passages by going to testprepbooks.com/toefl or by scanning the QR code below:

Note that on the actual test, you can take notes while you listen and use your notes to help you answer the questions. Your notes will not be scored.

For your convenience, the transcripts of all of the audio passages are provided after the answer explanations. However, on the actual test, no such transcripts will be provided.

Passage #1: Conversation

43. What was Greg looking for help with?
    a. Biology class material
    b. Studying economics
    c. Getting off campus to run errands
    d. Finding the administration building

44. How does a student replace their campus ID according to Deborah? Mark all that apply.
    a. Go to the library by the encyclopedias
    b. Go to the administration building
    c. Fill out a form and show a picture ID
    d. Pay a replacement fee

45. Where did Greg lose his ID?
    a. At the movies
    b. In biology class
    c. Grocery shopping
    d. At the basketball game

46. Where is the library?
    a. Next to the dining hall on the main quad
    b. Across from the dining hall on the main quad
    c. Away from the main quad near the administration building
    d. Next to the dorms on the main quad

47. Read the following statement from the conversation and then answer the question:
Male student: I haven't really gotten into a study rhythm yet this semester. That may be part of my problem. I guess I study in my room, when my roommate and I aren't playing video games, that is.

What does the male student mean when he says he has not really gotten into "a study rhythm yet"?

    a. He has not yet studied with music
    b. He needs to study with video games
    c. He has not yet established a study routine or habit
    d. He only studies in the library after class

48. Why does the female student say: "Well, I've got to run to Economics class now"?
    a. She is preparing to end the conversation
    b. She enjoys running for the school's track team
    c. She is trying to change the topic of conversation
    d. She wants a ride to class because she has to get there quickly

Passage #2: Lecture

49. What is the main topic of the lecture?
    a. The range of learning disabilities that future teachers should be aware of
    b. The ways in which Executive Functioning Disorder impacts students
    c. The cures for Executive Functioning Disorder
    d. How to teach students who are interested in psychology

50. What is the role of the executive function of the brain?
    a. To make business decisions for the brain and body
    b. To plan, organize, and manage tasks, processes, and deadlines
    c. To prevent learning disabilities
    d. To help take notes, listen to lectures, and perform well on exams

51. Why does the professor explain in detail how teachers can modify their instruction to help students with Executive Functioning Disorder?
    a. Because many of the students listening to the lecture want to become teachers
    b. Because many of the students listening to the lecture have Executive Functioning Disorder
    c. Because Executive Functioning Disorder only affects students in school
    d. Because the students listening to the lecture are teachers

52. What does the professor mean by: While executive functioning issues alone can have a significant impact on an individual, I want you to think about how it often um...appears concurrently with other learning disorders like ADHD or dyslexia.
  a. Executive Function Disorder is worse than ADHD or dyslexia
  b. Executive Functioning Disorder is discussed in the same lecture as ADHD and dyslexia
  c. People with Executive Functioning Disorder visually look a certain way
  d. People with Executive Function Disorders often have other learning disabilities too

53. Why does the professor add the clause "Like in our class" to the beginning of the sentence: "Like in our class, teachers should review prior material briefly before building upon it in the new lesson"?
  a. To help students connect the lesson with their own experience
  b. To remind students of their learning disabilities
  c. To show students that he is a good professor
  d. To persuade students to become teachers

54. Read the following sentences from the lecture and then answer the question:
"They also may find analyzing ideas and identifying when and how to seek help to be a challenge. Let's see...heeding attention to and remembering details is also encumbered."

Encumbered most nearly means which of the following?

  a. Hindered
  b. Enticing
  c. Important
  d. Recognized

55. Based on the information in the lecture, which of the following would someone with Executive Functioning Disorder likely struggle with?
  a. Reading a fantasy novel
  b. Playing sports on a team
  c. Remembering what to buy in the grocery store without a list
  d. Painting or drawing realistic landscapes

Passage #3: Lecture

56. What was the main topic addressed in the lecture?
  a. The contributions of various historical astronomers to our understanding of modern astronomy
  b. The importance of the telescope in our understanding of the Universe
  c. The history of how the Universe and Solar System formed billions of years ago
  d. The geocentric model of the Solar System

57. According to the professor, what was Copernicus' main contribution to our understanding?
  a. He proposed the geocentric model of the Solar System
  b. He invented the telescope, which we have used to make more discoveries
  c. He proposed the three laws of motion
  d. He developed the idea that Earth, and the other planets, rotate around the Sun

58. How was the information in the lecture organized?
  a. In order of importance of each scientist's discoveries
  b. In chronological order of the scientists' work
  c. In the order presented in the course textbook
  d. In the order of how many discoveries each scientist made

59. What does the professor imply about the scientists discussed in the lecture?
  a. That only their accurate discoveries or proposals were important to our understanding
  b. That they made a lot of mistakes in their discoveries
  c. That they did not know very much about the Universe
  d. That their contributions, even when inaccurate, helped shape our current understanding

60. Which of the following are attributed to Galileo? Pick two answers.
  a. He proposed the three laws of motion
  b. He said the Sun was a star
  c. He invented the telescope
  d. He lay the foundation for scientific thought and experimentation

61. Read the sentences about Brahe and then answer the question.
"He thought the Earth was not moving and that the Sun and Moon revolved around the stationary planet, so we know now that this part was off-base but he's still a key player in our evolution."

What does the professor imply about Brahe in this sentence?

  a. That his ideas were wrong and not important in the discussion of astronomy
  b. That other scientists and other humans continued to evolve from his DNA
  c. That he made a bunch of discoveries we have verified as correct
  d. That he is important in any discussion of the history of astronomy, even if some of his ideas were incorrect

Passage #4: Lecture and Discussion

62. What is the main topic of the lecture?
  a. The scientific method and how to conduct experiments
  b. How gemstones are used for jewelry
  c. Why rubies are rare and how they form
  d. How to read articles in *Discover* magazine

63. Why did Penn State University Geosciences professor Peter Heaney refer to rubies as a "minor geological miracle"?
  a. Because conditions must be perfect for them to form and this is rare
  b. Because they are important gemstones that contribute to our economy
  c. Because they can be discovered through scientific experiments
  d. Because they are red

64. According to the professor, how do gemstones get their colors?
   a. By the different temperature under which they form
   b. By forming in volcanoes or in the Himalayas, areas that have lots of color
   c. By various elemental substitutions to the normal arrangement of aluminum and oxygen atoms.
   d. By jewelers looking to design beautiful, ornate designs that consumers will buy

65. Based on what the professor says about conducting scientific experiments, which of the following experiments would he likely recommend for making the best chocolate chip cookies?
   a. An experiment that manipulates baking conditions by cooking batches at different temperatures and for different lengths of time
   b. An experiment that adds different amounts of sugar and bakes them for different lengths of time
   c. An experiment that adds different proportions of whole wheat and white flower, different amounts of sugar, and bakes them for different lengths of time
   d. An experiment that uses the same exact recipe but bakes them for different lengths of time

66. According to the lecture, where are rubies formed?
   a. At the boundaries of different plates, where sedimentary rock gets pushed under the other plate and gets metamorphosed
   b. In magma percolating under a volcano
   c. Abundantly in the Himalayas
   d. Where aluminum and oxygen come together in a Venn diagram

67. According to the discussion, which of the following are true about rubies? Select two correct answers.
   a. They are gemstones
   b. They readily form
   c. They are a variety of corundum
   d. We have no idea how old they are

Passage #5: Conversation

68. What is the main problem the student is having?
   a. She does not know which classes to register for
   b. She needs to get a job on campus
   c. Her bill is higher than she predicted
   d. She is looking for financial aid forms

69. Which of the following are ways that students can receive financial assistance with their school bills?
   a. Scholarships
   b. Loans
   c. Work-study
   d. Tuition

70. When would be the best time for students to speak to a financial aid officer?
   a. At 12:30pm on a Tuesday
   b. Saturday mornings
   c. At 4:15pm on Monday
   d. At 2:00pm on Wednesday

71. Which of the following were components of the student's bill? Select all that apply.
    a. Tuition
    b. Technology fee
    c. Meal plan and housing
    d. Activities fee

72. The financial aid officer explains to the student what she needs to do to fill out her FASFA, apply for a work-study, and fix the hold on her account. In what order does he list the steps?

A. Register for classes
B. Apply for a campus job
C. Wait for evaluation of financial aid package
D. Pay balance on the account
E. Register to fill out the FAFSA
F. Input prior year's tax information
G. Ask for tuition reduction

1	
2	
3	
4	
5	
6	

73. Based on the conversation, which job is the student most likely to apply for?
    a. A job at the financial aid office
    b. A job at the computer lab
    c. A job at the sports center
    d. A job at the library

Passage #6: Lecture Discussion

74. What was the main topic of the discussion between the professor and her students?
    a. The importance of literature
    b. The themes in *Gulliver's Travels*
    c. The literal meaning in Swift's book
    d. The reasons that Gulliver travels

75. What does the professor mean when she says, "I want to dig deeper into this thought…"
   a. She needs to uncover a time capsule that she has buried
   b. She needs to unearth her copy of the book on her desk
   c. She wants to bury the conversation
   d. She wants to explore this topic more

76. Why might the professor say, "Name-dropping is our modern equivalent to Gulliver's boasting about his close relationships with Kings and Queens!"
   a. To help students remember the names of all of the characters in the book
   b. To help students understand things in the book by relating it to things they are familiar with
   c. To remind students that everyone forgets names, so not to worry
   d. To show empathy towards Gulliver

77. What does the professor argue is the value of reading *Gulliver's Travels?*
   a. For entertainment value
   b. To consider human nature and its imperfections
   c. To persuade readers to travel more, even though it is expensive
   d. To teach readers about all the kings and queens and faraway lands

78. According to the participants in the discussion, what would Swift's reaction be to humans being called "social animals"?
   a. Swift would disagree because he thinks humans are antisocial
   b. Swift would disagree because humans have high self-esteem
   c. Swift would agree because humans want to preserve their self-esteem
   d. Swift would agree because he thinks humans are very antisocial

Speaking

79. Imagine that you are selected to be a tour guide for an exchange student for an afternoon. Talk about your favorite places in your city, town, or campus. Describe these places and explain why you like them.

   - Preparation Time: 15 seconds
   - Response Time: 45 seconds

80. Some people think it's smarter for people to set realistic goals that they are confident they can achieve, while others argue it's better to set ambitious goals that one may fail to achieve. What is your opinion? Explain why.

   - Preparation Time: 15 seconds
   - Response Time: 45 seconds

81. Read the following passage and then the conversation. Lastly, answer the question that follows them.

   The following text was reported by the University administrators to all students and their parents. Read the announcement. (The allotted reading time on the exam would be 45–60 seconds).

   Students are likely aware of the General Education requirements at the University. All students must take a handful of classes distributed across all major academic disciplines in addition to the specific

course requirements dictated by their major. This design exposes students to a variety of fields in the social and physical sciences, the arts, and mathematics so that all of our graduates have a well-rounded liberal arts education in addition to the advanced studies in their field of choice. Upon reviewing the requirements and the surveys from our department heads about student benchmarks and achievements, the University's Academic Advisory Committee has decided to implement an additional writing requirement. This decision was based on the collective feeling among faculty members that the ability to communicate effectively in an academic tone is paramount to students' future career success. Beginning in the next academic year, in addition to the writing requirement that freshmen must satisfy, all students must take an additional academic writing course during their degree program. This new policy will apply to all current and incoming students.

(Female student) I think the Academic Advisory Committee has made a bad decision. I'm mad.

(Male student) Really? Why do you think it's a bad decision?

(Female student) We already have to take a bunch of distribution requirements and they're boring. If we know what we want to study, why should we have to take courses in other departments?

(Male student) Well, I think some students haven't fully decided what they want to major in, so the general education requirements expose them to all sorts of topics, so they can think about different careers, maybe even ones they didn't consider.

(Female student) Yeah, but they are free to dabble in whatever. I've known I want to major in biology and do the pre-med track since I was young. I've always wanted to be a doctor. The last thing I need is another writing class!

(Male student) I see your point but the ability to write well is so important in all fields, even medicine. Imagine if you conduct important research that will help patients improve their health. If you are unable to communicate it effectively and professionally in writing, your research won't be published and the patients won't benefit from your work.

(Female student) I think that's a stretch. We have been writing our whole lives and the one freshmen writing class requirement is plenty. There's no way we need a whole additional writing course to be decent academic writers. It's a waste of time and we'd be better suited to take another class in our major that we're actually interested in.

Question: The female student expresses her opinion about the University's new writing requirement. State and explain her opinion and compare it with the Academic Advisory Committee's opinion.

- Preparation Time: 30 seconds
- Response Time: 60 seconds

82. Read the passage from a sports psychology textbook and the lecture that follows it. Then, answer the question. (Reading time in an actual test would be 45–50 seconds.)

The Inverted-U Theory of Arousal

The Inverted-U Theory posits that too little or too much arousal negatively impacts athletic performance, and there is an optimal level of arousal that facilitates optimal performance. The inverted-U graphically shows this (x-axis is level of arousal; y-axis is performance), as the shape demonstrates that low levels or high levels beyond the optimal level of arousal result in worse

performance, and somewhere between low and high arousal is the range of arousal associated with optimal performance (the top of the inverted-U). At this point, the internal and external stimuli experienced by the athlete generate the optimal amount of arousal required to enhance performance. Some anticipation, anxiety, and arousal leads to increased levels of epinephrine, which prepares the body for increased athletic performance. On the other hand, too much stress and arousal can flood the system with epinephrine and increase heart rate and blood pressure beyond helpful levels. This can lead to a detrimental state where the exercise, on top of the increased sympathetic nervous system response, drives these physiologic variables too high, resulting in the body reducing its physical output during the exercise.

Professor: Arousal is an important concept in sports psychology and there are several theories that have been developed to model the optimal arousal for performance. As your textbook mentions, the "inverted U" visually shows the optimal point on the arousal-relaxation curve, for best performance. For example, if an athlete is too relaxed and unfocused, their heart rate will be slow and the body will not be ready to perform well athletically. These athletes may need cheering, motivation, verbal "pumping up," and some small stimulus of external pressure to increase their arousal. I used to coach an athlete that was overly anxious. She would get so worked up before basketball games that her heart would be racing, her palms would be sweaty, and she would start to fatigue before the game even started, which negatively impacted her performance. She sometimes was so jittery that she missed easy shots and could barely run down the court without being winded.

Question: Explain the Inverted-U Theory and how the professor's example illustrates how the concept can be applied.

- Preparation Time: 30 seconds
- Response Time: 60 seconds

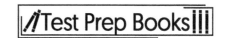

First Essay

1. First read the article below. Then click the link below the article and watch the Ted Talk video. Then review the prompt and write an essay synthesizing the two sources.

Caloric Intake From Fast Food Among Adults: United States, 2007–2010

by Cheryl D. Fryar, M.S.P.H., and R. Bethene Ervin, Ph.D., R.D.

Key findings

Data from the National Health and Nutrition Examination Survey

- During 2007–2010, adults consumed, on average, 11.3% of their total daily calories from fast food.

- The consumption of calories from fast food significantly decreased with age.

- Non-Hispanic black adults consumed a higher percentage of calories from fast food compared with non-Hispanic white and Hispanic adults.

- No difference was observed by income status in the percentage of calories consumed from fast food among all adults. Among young adults, however, as income increased, the percentage of calories from fast food decreased.

- The percentage of total daily calories from fast food increased as weight status increased.

As lifestyles become more hectic, fast-food consumption has become a growing part of the American diet (1,2). Fast food is food usually sold at eating establishments for quick availability or takeout (3). More than one-third of U.S. adults are obese (4), and frequent fast-food consumption has been shown to contribute to weight gain (1–6). This report presents the percentage of calories consumed from fast food by adults in the United States, including differences by sociodemographic characteristics and weight status.

What percentage of calories consumed by adults comes from fast food?

During 2007–2010, adults consumed an average 11.3% of their total daily calories from fast food (Figure 1), a decrease from 12.8% for 2003–2006 (data not shown). The percentage of calories consumed from fast food did not differ significantly between men (11.8%) and women (10.9%). The percentage of calories consumed from fast food decreased with age, with adults aged 60 and over (6.0%) consuming the lowest percentage of their daily calories from fast foods. This decrease with age was found among both men and women.

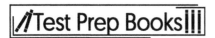

Figure 1. Percentage of calories from fast food among adults aged 20 and over, by sex and age: United States, 2007–2010

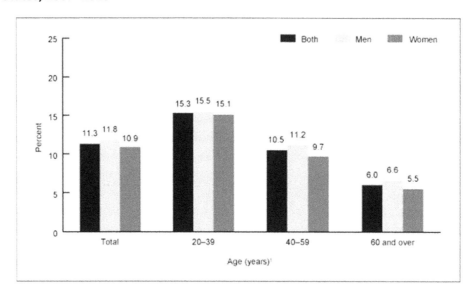

[1]Significant linear trend by age ($p < 0.05$).
NOTE: Total estimates are age adjusted to the 2000 projected U.S. standard population using three age groups: 20–39, 40–59, and 60 and over.
SOURCE: National Health and Nutrition Examination Survey, 2007–2010.

Does the percentage of calories consumed from fast food differ by race and ethnicity?

No significant differences were found between non-Hispanic white and Hispanic adults in the percentage of calories consumed from fast food. The lack of difference, in the percentage of calories consumed from fast food, between non-Hispanic white and Hispanic adults was observed among all age groups. However, among adults aged 20 and over, consumption of calories from fast food was higher among non-Hispanic black adults than non-Hispanic white and Hispanic adults (Figure 2). This disparity was found for young adults aged 20–39, where non-Hispanic black adults consumed more than one-fifth of their percentage of calories from fast food. Among middle-aged adults in the 40–59 age group, the pattern was similar, but the difference between non-Hispanic black and Hispanic persons did not reach statistical significance. No race or ethnic differences were found among adults aged 60 and over.

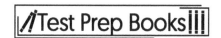

Figure 2. Percentage of calories from fast food among adults aged 20 and over, by age and race and ethnicity: United States, 2007–2010

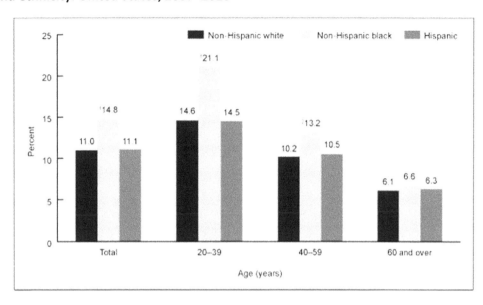

[1]Statistically different from non-Hispanic white and Hispanic adults (p < 0.05).
[2]Statistically different from non-Hispanic white adults (p < 0.05).
NOTE: Total estimates are age adjusted to the 2000 projected U.S. standard population using three age groups: 20–39, 40–59, and 60 and over.
SOURCE: National Health and Nutrition Examination Survey, 2007–2010.

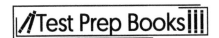
Does the percentage of calories consumed from fast food differ by income?

Overall, no difference was observed by income status in the percentage of calories consumed from fast food (Figure 3). However, in the youngest age group, 20–39, the percentage of calories consumed from fast food significantly decreased with increasing income level.

Figure 3. Percentage of calories from fast food among adults aged 20 and over, by age and income: United States, 2007–2010

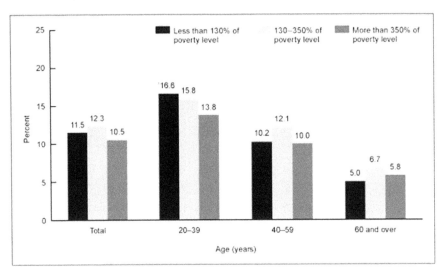

[1]Significant decreasing linear trend ($p < 0.05$).
NOTE: Total estimates are age adjusted to the 2000 projected U.S. standard population using three age groups: 20–39, 40–59, and 60 and over.
SOURCE: National Health and Nutrition Examination Survey, 2007–2010.

Does the percentage of calories consumed from fast food differ by weight status?

Among adults, the percentage of calories consumed from fast food varied by weight status (Figure 4). The percentage of total daily calories from fast food increased as weight status increased. For each age group, obese adults consumed the highest percentage of their calories from fast food.

Figure 4. Percentage of calories from fast food among adults aged 20 and over, by age and weight status: United States, 2007–2010

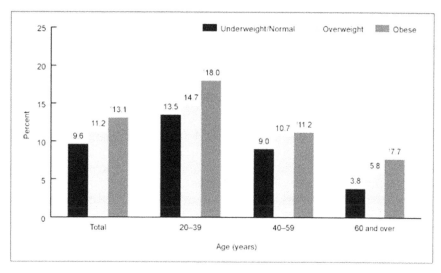

[1]Significant increasing linear trend ($p < 0.05$).
NOTES: Underweight/Normal weight is body mass index (BMI) less than 25.0; overweight is BMI of 25.0–29.9; and obese is BMI greater than or equal to 30.0. Total estimates are age adjusted to the 2000 projected U.S. standard population using three age groups: 20–39, 40–59, and 60 and over.
SOURCE: National Health and Nutrition Examination Survey, 2007–2010.

Summary

An earlier report by the U.S. Department of Agriculture found that the percentage of adults eating fast food increased from the early 1990s to the mid-1990s ([1]). Moreover, previous studies have reported that more frequent fast-food consumption is associated with higher energy and fat intake and lower intake of healthful nutrients ([1,2]). This report indicates that for 2007–2010, on average, adults consumed just over one-tenth of their percentage of calories from fast food, which represents a decrease from 2003–2006 when approximately 13% of calories were consumed from fast food.

During 2007–2010, the highest percentage of calories from fast food was consumed among adults who were aged 20–39 or non-Hispanic black or obese. Among young non-Hispanic black adults, more than one-fifth of their calories were consumed from fast food.

From https://www.cdc.gov/nchs/products/databriefs/db114.htm

2. Listen to the following lecture: goo.gl/sfqQv4

3. Prompt: Summarize the points presented in the lecture. Explain how they relate to specific points in the reading passage.

Second Essay

Prepare an essay of about 300–600 words on the topic below.

Some people feel that sharing their lives on social media sites such as Facebook, Instagram, and Snapchat is fine. They share every aspect of their lives, including pictures of themselves and their families, what they ate for lunch, who they are dating, and when they are going on vacation. They even say that if it's not on social media, it didn't happen. Other people believe that sharing so much personal information is an invasion of privacy and could prove dangerous. They think sharing personal pictures and details invites predators, cyberbullying, and identity theft.

Write an essay to someone who is considering whether to participate in social media. Take a side on the issue and argue whether or not he/she should join a social media network. Use specific examples to support your argument.

Answer Explanations #1

Reading

1. C: *C* is the correct answer because it most extensively summarizes the entire passage. While Choices *A* and *B* are reasonable possibilities, they reference portions of Gulliver's experiences, not the whole. Choice *D* is incorrect because Gulliver doesn't express repentance or sorrow in this particular passage.

2. A: Principal refers to *chief* or *primary* within the context of this text. Choice *A* is the answer that most closely aligns with this answer. Choices *B* and *D* make reference to a helper or followers while Choice *C* doesn't meet the description of Gulliver from the passage.

3. C: One can reasonably infer that Gulliver is considerably larger than the children who were playing around him because multiple children could fit into his hand. Choice *A* is incorrect because there is no indication of stress in Gulliver's tone. Choices *B* and *D* aren't the best answer because though Gulliver seems fond of his new acquaintances, he didn't travel there with the intentions of meeting new people, nor does he express a definite love for them in this particular portion of the text.

4. C: The emperor made a *definitive decision* to expose Gulliver to their native customs. In this instance, the word *mind* was not related to a vote, question, or cognitive ability.

5. A: Choice *A* is correct. This assertion does *not* support the fact that games are a commonplace event in this culture because it mentions conduct, not games. Choices *B*, *C*, and *D* are incorrect because these do support the fact that games were a commonplace event.

6. B: Choice *B* is the only option that mentions the correlation between physical ability and leadership positions. Choices *A* and *D* are unrelated to physical strength and leadership abilities. Choice *C* does not make a deduction that would lead to the correct answer—it only comments upon the abilities of common townspeople.

7. D: It emphasizes Mr. Utterson's anguish in failing to identify Hyde's whereabouts. Context clues indicate that Choice *D* is correct because the passage provides great detail of Mr. Utterson's feelings about locating Hyde. Choice *A* does not fit because there is no mention of Mr. Lanyon's mental state. Choice *B* is incorrect; although the text does make mention of bells, Choice *B* is not the *best* answer overall. Choice *C* is incorrect because the passage clearly states that Mr. Utterson was determined, not unsure.

8. A: The word *city* appears in the passage several times, thus establishing the location for the reader.

9. B: The passage states that the Juggernaut causes the children to scream. Choices *A* and *D* don't apply because the text doesn't mention either of these instances specifically. Choice *C* is incorrect because there is nothing in the text that mentions space travel.

10. B: The mention of *morning, noon,* and *night* make it clear that the word *haunt* refers to frequent appearances at various locations. Choice *A* doesn't work because the text makes no mention of levitating. Choices *C* and *D* are not correct because the text makes mention of Mr. Utterson's anguish and disheartenment because of his failure to find Hyde but does not make mention of Mr. Utterson's feelings negatively affecting anyone else.

11. D: This is an example of alliteration. Choice *D* is the correct answer because of the repetition of the *L*-words. Hyperbole is an exaggeration, so Choice *A* doesn't work. No comparison is being made, so no simile or metaphor is being used, thus eliminating Choices *B* and *C*.

12. D: Choices *A* and *B* are not possible answers because the text doesn't refer to any name changes or an identity crisis, despite Mr. Utterson's extreme obsession with finding Hyde. The text also makes no mention of a mistaken identity when referring to Hyde, so Choice *C* is also incorrect.

13. A: The tone is *incredulous*. While contemplative is an option because of the inquisitive nature of the text, Choice *A* is correct because Frederick Douglass is astonished that he, a former slave, would be called upon to celebrate liberty that was not extended to him or to others of his race. Choice *B* is incorrect because Frederick Douglass is drawing contrasts between two groups of people rather than being inclusive. Choice *C* is incorrect because Frederick Douglass is expressing strong emotion, incredulity, rather than contemplation. Choice *D* is incorrect because Frederick Douglass is not nonchalant, nor accepting of the circumstances which he describes.

14. C: Choice *C*, *contented*, is the only word that has the opposite meaning of *obdurate*. Therefore, Choices *A*, *B*, and *D* are incorrect.

15. B: To address the feelings of exclusion expressed by Black Americans after the establishment of the Fourth of July holiday. While the speaker makes biblical references, it is not the main focus of the passage, thus eliminating Choice *A* as an answer. The passage also makes no mention of wealthy landowners and doesn't speak of any positive response to the historical events, so Choices *C* and *D* are not correct.

16. D: Choice *D* is the correct answer because it clearly references the disparity between slaves and free men in the United States. Choice *A* is incorrect because it demonstrates Frederick Douglass's knowledge of the Bible. Choice *B* is incorrect because it demonstrates his incredulity at his invitation to speak. Choice *C* is incorrect because Frederick Douglass is highlighting the terrible situation of slaves, but he is not highlighting the disparity between slaves and free men.

17. D: Choices *A* and *B* are unrelated. Assonance is the repetition of sounds and commonly occurs in poetry. Parallelism refers to two statements that correlate in some manner. Choice *C* is incorrect because amplification normally refers to clarification of meaning by broadening the sentence structure, while hyperbole refers to a phrase or statement that is being exaggerated.

18. C: Recognize the equivocation of the speaker and those that he represents. Choice *C* is correct because the speaker is clear about his intention and stance throughout the text; he does not equivocate, so this answer choice is the only one that biblical references do not help the reader to do. Choice *A* is incorrect because quotations from the Bible would have been common at the time, creating a common ground between Frederick Douglass and his audience. Choice *B* is incorrect because another group of people affected by slavery are being referenced, and Frederick Douglass is clearly drawing a connection between that group of people and American slaves. Choice *D* is incorrect because Frederick Douglass's speech is designed to appeal to the listener's sense of humanity and create an abhorrence for slavery.

19. B: It is apparent that Lincoln is referring to a period of time within the context of the passage because of how the sentence is structured with the word *ago*.

20. C: Lincoln's reference to *the brave men, living and dead, who struggled here,* proves that he is referring to a battlefield. Choices *A* and *B* are incorrect, as a *civil war* is mentioned and not a war with

France or a war in the Sahara Desert. Choice *D* is incorrect because it does not make sense to consecrate a President's ground instead of a battlefield ground for soldiers who died during the American Civil War.

21. D: Abraham Lincoln is the former president of the United States, and he references a "civil war" during his address.

22. A: The audience should consider the death of the people that fought in the war as an example and perpetuate the ideals of freedom that the soldiers died fighting for. Lincoln doesn't address any of the topics outlined in Choices *B*, *C*, or *D*. Therefore, Choice *A* is the correct answer.

23. D: Choice *D* is the correct answer because of the repetition of the word *people* at the end of the passage. Choice *A*, *antimetatabole*, is the repetition of words in a succession. Choice *B*, *antiphrasis*, is a form of denial of an assertion in a text. Choice *C*, *anaphora*, is the repetition that occurs at the beginning of sentences.

24. A: Choice *A* is correct because Lincoln's intention was to memorialize the soldiers who had fallen as a result of war as well as celebrate those who had put their lives in danger for the sake of their country. Choices *B*, *C*, and *D* are incorrect because Lincoln's speech was supposed to foster a sense of pride among the members of the audience while connecting them to the soldiers' experiences.

25. A: The word *patronage* most nearly means *auspices*, which means *protection* or *support*. Choice *B*, *aberration*, means *deformity* and does not make sense within the context of the sentence. Choice *C*, *acerbic,* means *bitter* and also does not make sense in the sentence. Choice *D*, *adulation*, is a positive word meaning *praise*, and thus does not fit with the word *condescending* in the sentence.

26. D: *Working man* is most closely aligned with Choice *D*, *bourgeois.* In the context of the speech, the word *bourgeois* means *working* or *middle class*. Choice *A*, *plebian*, does suggest *common people*; however, this is a term that is specific to ancient Rome. Choice *B*, *viscount*, is a European title used to describe a specific degree of nobility. Choice *C*, *entrepreneur*, is a person who operates their own business.

27. C: In the context of the speech, the term *working man* most closely correlates with Choice *C*, *a working man is someone who works for wages among the middle class*. Choice *A* is not mentioned in the passage and is off-topic. Choice *B* may be true in some cases, but it does not reflect the sentiment described for the term *working man* in the passage. Choice *D* may also be arguably true. However, it is not given as a definition but as *acts* of the working man, and the topics of *field, factory,* and *screen* are not mentioned in the passage.

28. D: *Enterprise* most closely means *cause*. Choices *A, B,* and *C* are all related to the term *enterprise*. However, Dickens speaks of a *cause* here, not a company, courage, or a game. *He will stand by such an enterprise* is a call to stand by a cause to enable the working man to have a certain autonomy over his own economic standing. The very first paragraph ends with the statement that the working man *shall . . . have a share in the management of an institution which is designed for his benefit.*

29. B: The speaker's salutation is one from an entertainer to his audience and uses the friendly language to connect to his audience before a serious speech. Recall in the first paragraph that the speaker is there to "accompany [the audience] . . . through one of my little Christmas books," making him an author there to entertain the crowd with his own writing. The speech preceding the reading is the passage itself, and, as the tone indicates, a serious speech addressing the "working man." Although the passage speaks of employers and employees, the speaker himself is not an employer of the audience, so Choice

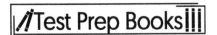

A is incorrect. Choice *C* is also incorrect, as the salutation is not used ironically, but sincerely, as the speech addresses the wellbeing of the crowd. Choice *D* is incorrect because the speech is not given by a politician, but by a writer.

30. B: Choice A is incorrect because that is the speaker's *first* desire, not his *second*. Choices C and D are tricky because the language of both of these is mentioned after the word *second.* However, the speaker doesn't get to the second wish until the next sentence. Choices C and D are merely preliminary remarks before the statement of the main clause, Choice *B*.

31. D: The use of "I" could have all of the effects for the reader; it could serve to have a "hedging" effect, allow the reader to connect with the author in a more personal way, and cause the reader to empathize more with the egrets. However, it doesn't distance the reader from the text, thus eliminating Choice *D*.

32. C: The quote provides an example of a warden protecting one of the colonies. Choice *A* is incorrect because the speaker of the quote is a warden, not a hunter. Choice *B* is incorrect because the quote does not lighten the mood, but shows the danger of the situation between the wardens and the hunters. Choice *D* is incorrect because there is no humor found in the quote.

33. D: A *rookery* is a colony of breeding birds. Although *rookery* could mean Choice *A*, houses in a slum area, it does not make sense in this context. Choices *B* and *C* are both incorrect, as this is not a place for hunters to trade tools or for wardens to trade stories.

34. B: An important bird colony. The previous sentence is describing "twenty colonies" of birds, so what follows should be a bird colony. Choice *A* may be true, but we have no evidence of this in the text. Choice *C* does touch on the tension between the hunters and wardens, but there is no official "Bird Island Battle" mentioned in the text. Choice *D* does not exist in the text.

35. D: To demonstrate the success of the protective work of the Audubon Association. The text mentions several different times how and why the association has been successful and gives examples to back this fact. Choice *A* is incorrect because although the article, in some instances, calls certain people to act, it is not the purpose of the entire passage. There is no way to tell if Choices *B* and *C* are correct, as they are not mentioned in the text.

36. C: To have a better opportunity to hunt the birds. Choice *A* might be true in a general sense, but it is not relevant to the context of the text. Choice *B* is incorrect because the hunters are not studying lines of flight to help wardens, but to hunt birds. Choice *D* is incorrect because nothing in the text mentions that hunters are trying to build homes underneath lines of flight of birds for good luck.

37. A: It introduces certain insects that transition from water to air. Choice *B* is incorrect because although the passage talks about gills, it is not the central idea of the passage. Choices *C* and *D* are incorrect because the passage does not "define" or "invite," but only serves as an introduction to stoneflies, dragonflies, and mayflies and their transition from water to air.

38. C: To *moult* is to shed part or all of the outer shell, as noted in Choice *C*. Choices *A*, *B*, and *D* are incorrect.

39. B: The first paragraph serves as a contrast to the second. Notice how the first paragraph goes into detail describing how insects are able to breathe air. The second paragraph acts as a contrast to the first by stating "[i]t is of great interest to find that, nevertheless, a number of insects spend much of their

time under water." Watch for transition words such as "nevertheless" to help find what type of passage you're dealing with.

40: C: *Instars* are the phases between two periods of molting, and the text explains when these transitions occur. The preparatory stages are acted out in the water while the last stage is in the air. Choices A, B, and D are all incorrect.

41. C: The author's tone is informative and exhibits interest in the subject of the study. Overall, the author presents us with information on the subject. One moment where personal interest is depicted is when the author states, "It is of great interest to find that, nevertheless, a number of insects spend much of their time under water."

42. C: Their larva can breathe the air dissolved in water through gills of some kind. This is stated in the last paragraph. Choice A is incorrect because the text mentions this in a general way at the beginning of the passage concerning "insects as a whole." Choice B is incorrect because this is stated of beetles and water-bugs, and not the insects in question. Choice D is incorrect because this is the opposite of what the text says of instars.

Listening

43. A: At the beginning of the conversation, listeners should recall that the male student, Greg, was asking the female student, Deborah, how she did on the biology exam. Deborah informs Greg that she did well, earning a 96, while Greg responds that he only got a 69. He says, "This stuff isn't making sense to me." *Stuff,* in this case, refers to the biology class material.

44. B, C, D: Deborah says that a student must go to the administration building with their student ID or another form of picture ID, pay a $15 replacement fee, and fill out a form. She mentions the encyclopedia section in the library in an earlier part of the conversation, referring to where she studies.

45. D: Greg says, "I lost my ID at the basketball game last weekend. Do you know where I can get a new one?"

46. B: Greg admits to Deborah that he's not honestly sure where the library is, and he asks her if it's over the dining hall on the main quad (the central square of a campus, which often has a grassy lawn and several main buildings surrounding it). Deborah's response confirms that Greg is in the ballpark, or close in his guess. She says, "Yes, it's over next to the administration building on the main quad, directly across from the dining hall." Test takers must carefully listen to select the correct answer. Choice A is incorrect because although the library is on the main quad, it is across from, rather than next to the dining hall, which is Choice B. Choice C is incorrect because although the library is next to the administration building, it is on the main quad. It is not near the dorms, so Choice D is incorrect.

47. C: When Greg says that he has not really gotten into "a study rhythm yet" he means that he has not yet established a study routine or habit.

48. A: Deborah says, "Well, I've got to run to Economics class now"" to signal that she is preparing to end the conversation. This is a common phrase used in casual conversation to convey that one person needs to leave and move on to the next thing and that he or she wants to end the conversation. She may not literally need to "run" to class, but she is wrapping up the conversation.

49. B: The main topic of the lecture is the ways in which Executive Functioning Disorder impacts students. Listeners hear about the symptoms of the disorder, how these symptoms play out in the classroom, and various techniques or accommodations that teachers may provide to assist a student with the disorder. Choice *A* is incorrect because while Executive Functioning Disorder is a learning disability and the professor mentions that the lecture is building upon previously discussed learning disabilities, the focus of the lecture is on the specific issue of Executive Functioning Disorder, not learning disabilities at large. Cures for the disorder are not mentioned, so Choice *C* is incorrect, and while the students listening to the lecture are in a psychology class, the lecture is not about how to teach them, so Choice *D* is incorrect.

50. B: The professor equates executive function of the brain to a CEO of a company because it is involved in the planning, organizing, and managing of tasks, processes, and deadlines. While it is helpful for the tasks in Choice *D* (taking notes, listening to lectures, and performing well on exams), these are examples of instances where it is used but does not refer to its general function overall.

51. A: The professor explains how teachers can modify their instruction to help students with Executive Functioning Disorder because many of the students listening to the lecture want to become teachers. This is evidenced by the fact that he says, "I know many of you have expressed an interest in teaching someday so uh...it's important to think about how this will affect students in your classrooms."

52. D: The professor ends the lecture clip by saying, "While executive functioning issues alone can have a significant impact on an individual, I want you to think about how it often um...appears concurrently with other learning disorders like ADHD or dyslexia." There are a few key words that indicate what this means. *While executive functioning issues alone can have a significant impact on an individual,* means that just having that single disorder can be challenging for a student. Then the next sentence uses the word *concurrently,* saying that it (executive functioning issues) often occurs "concurrently with other learning disorders like ADHD or dyslexia." This means that they occur at the same time, so that someone can have both or multiple learning disabilities at once. This idea is further confirmed by his last statement: "This can make it, uh...especially challenging."

53. A: The professor says, "Like in our class, teachers should review prior material briefly before building upon it in the new lesson" to help students connect the lesson with their own experience in his classroom. Listeners get a glimpse into the fact that he has done this at the very beginning of the lecture. "Today, we are going to pick up where we left off last class talking about learning disabilities. Now, we will turn our attention to another common learning disability known as Executive Functioning Disorder." Teachers often try to connect concepts in the classroom to students' own experiences so that new material makes more sense and is relatable.

54. A: Read the following sentences from the lecture and then answer the question: *Encumbered* most nearly means hindered or impeded. Even without knowing this vocabulary word, test takers can look for context clues to determine the meaning. The part of the passage in which that words appeared was mentioning difficulties or challenges faced by those with Executive Functioning Disorder. "They also may find analyzing ideas and identifying when and how to seek help to be a challenge. Let's see...heeding attention to and remembering details is also encumbered." It is clear that we are looking for a choice that signifies an issue, difficulty, or problem, making Choice *A* the only reasonable option.

55. C: Listeners learn that Executive Functioning Disorder causes difficulties with planning, organizing, and managing of tasks, processes, and deadlines. We also hear that they struggle to "memorize and

especially retrieve things from their memory" which would make remembering what to buy in the grocery store without a list quite difficult.

56. A: This lecture is mainly focused on the contributions of various historical astronomers to our understanding of modern astronomy. While the telescope's importance is mentioned (Choice *B*), this is not the main topic of the lecture. Choice *C* is incorrect because the history of how the Universe and Solar System formed billions of years ago is not mentioned at all. The history of advancements in astronomy is, instead. Lastly, while the geocentric model of the Solar System is briefly discussed, it is not the primary topic in the lecture, as a much more significant portion of the talk is about notable advancements and discoveries, making Choice *D* incorrect.

57. D: The professor says, "Copernicus, in many ways, can be thought of as the first in the modern astronomy scientists because he overturned the geocentric model of the solar system that had stood for over two thousand years, and instead, correctly (but shockingly at the time) suggested that the sun was the center of the solar system and the planets revolved around the sun. This was basically the birth of our present understanding of the solar system – the Heliocentric model." This means that Copernicus developed the idea that Earth, and the other planets, rotate around the Sun, which overturned the geocentric model of the Solar System, making Choice *A* incorrect. Galileo invented the telescope so Choice *B* is incorrect, and Newton proposed the three laws of motion, so Choice *C* is incorrect.

58. B: The professor structures the lecture in chronological order of the scientists' work. Although dates are not provided, listeners can answer this correctly based on what the professor says at the beginning of the lecture: "We are *continuing* our discussion today of the history of astronomers *from ancient times working up to the present day*. So, remember, we are talking about the key contributors that have helped build our understanding of astronomy today."

59. D: The professor implies that the contributions of the discussed scientists, even when inaccurate, helped shape our current understanding of astronomy. Perhaps the best evidence for this argument comes from when she is talking about Brahe's importance, even though some of his ideas were incorrect. "He thought the Earth was not moving and that the Sun and Moon revolved around the stationary planet, so we know now that this part was off-base, *but he's still a key player in our evolution*."

60. C & D: Galileo invented the telescope and lay the foundation for scientific thought and experimentation. Newton proposed the three laws of motion, making Choice *A* incorrect. Copernicus said the Sun was a star, which makes Choice *B* incorrect.

61. D: As mentioned, the selected statement implies that Brahe is important in any discussion of the history of astronomy, even if some of his ideas were incorrect. Choice *A* is incorrect because she said he *is* still important, Choice *C* is incorrect because she is confirming that some of his ideas were incorrect, and Choice *B* is incorrect because "evolution" in this context isn't referring to human evolution or genetics, but the evolution or growth of our understanding of astronomy and how it is has changed over time.

62. C: The main topic of the lecture is why rubies are rare and how they form. Choice *A,* the scientific method and how to conduct experiments, is discussed, but is not the main focus of the talk. Choices *B* and *D* are barely touched upon, and are therefore incorrect.

63. A: Penn State University Geosciences professor Peter Heaney referred to rubies as a "minor geological miracle" because the conditions must be perfect for them to form and this is rare. This is,

essentially, what the lecture discussion is all about. As the male student, Xavier, says, "Basically, he's saying um...that the formation of rubies is essentially a perfect storm and a rare occurrence. It's like a miracle that they ever form." The professor elaborates: "Corundum is rare, the elemental substitutions are rare, chromium itself is rare, and even *more* rare is the fact that this cannot occur in the presence of silica or large amounts of iron, and silica is one of the most abundant elements in the crust and iron is common too but must be in very low concentrations to form rubies. This can kind of be visualized as hmmm...like a Venn diagram of increasingly more rare occurrences and just a tiny overlapped center where the formation of this gemstone is actually possible."

64. C: The professor states: "Rubies are a specific type of the rare mineral corundum, which is composed of densely packed aluminum and oxygen atoms. These atoms are normally colorless, but when other atoms, like in this case chromium, are substituted for a some of the uh...aluminum ones, the deep red color of rubies is produced. Other substitutions cause the bright colors of other gemstones such as sapphire from the substitution of um, uh...from titanium and iron." This means that gemstones get their colors via the various elemental substitutions to the normal arrangement of aluminum and oxygen atoms.

65. D: Listeners should recall that the professor says the following: "Scientists typically only address one question at a time so that they can use the scientific method...By focusing on just one hypothesis, scientists should only manipulate a single variable at a time, called the independent variable, and then examine its results on the dependent variable." Using this information, test takers can review the proposed experiments in the answer choices and select the one that only manipulates one variable at a time, which is Choice *D:* An experiment that uses the same exact recipe but bakes them for different lengths of time. The other experiments were changing multiple factors at one time, which contradicts the premise of the scientific method.

66. A: According to the lecture, rubies are formed at the boundaries of different plates, such as in the Himalayas, where sedimentary rock gets pushed under the other plate and gets metamorphosed. Choice *C* is incorrect because although they are found near the Himalayas, they are not abundant. The whole lecture focuses on how rare they are, which is the opposite of abundant.

67. A & C: According to the discussion, rubies are gemstones and "are a specific type of the rare mineral corundum." Choice *B* is incorrect because they are not readily formed; in fact, they are rare. Choice *D* is incorrect because the professor says that "Geologists can even date the formation of these gemstones with the tectonic movements."

68. C: The student is having an issue with her bill. It is higher than she predicted. She starts the conversation by saying: "Hi. Is this the right place to ask about a problem with my bill?" Then she later says, "So, I received my bill for the semester and it says I owe $18,000. I thought I had a scholarship so there's no way I can pay this bill."

69. A, B & C: The financial aid offer says, "if you qualify for additional financial aid, we can set up a package for you. Some students get additional scholarships based on financial need, or there are loans, and work-study opportunities."

70. D: The financial aid officer tells the student, "The financial aid office is open Monday through Friday 9–4 but we close every day at noon for an hour for lunch." Therefore, all of the other choices would not be a good time to get help at the office because it would be closed.

71. A, B, & C: The financial aid officer says, "I see the tuition billed to your account is $8,500. Your meal plan and housing in the dorms is $7,000 this semester and there is a technology fee and other posted fees including your parking permit totaling $2,500." There is no mention of a specific activities fee (Choice *D*).

72. According to the advice from the financial aid officer, the necessary order is the following:

1	Register to fill out the FAFSA
2	Input prior year's tax information
3	Evaluate financial aid package
4	Apply for a campus job
5	Pay balance on the account
6	Register for classes

73. B: The student is most likely to apply for a job at the computer lab. Listeners can select this response based on the student's comment: "Back home I worked as a computer programmer at my mom's software company."

74. B: The main topic of the discussion between the professor and her students is the themes in *Gulliver's Travels*. They discuss the figurative, rather than literal, meaning in Swift's book, which makes Choice *C* incorrect. Choices *A* and *D* are not really discussed, and are certainly not the main focus.

75. D: When the professor says, "I want to dig deeper into this thought…" she is implying that she wants to explore this topic more. This is a figure of speech. She is not literally digging for something she buried, which makes the other choices incorrect.

76. B: The professor likely says, "Name-dropping is our modern equivalent to Gulliver's boasting about his close relationships with Kings and Queens" to help students understand things in the book by relating it to things they are familiar with. This will help the students understand something that may otherwise feel abstract or foreign. Name-dropping is a phrase used to refer to the act of casually mentioning famous people's names in conversation, as if indicating one has a personal connection or relationship to them, with the hope of impressing others. It isn't a way to remember names (Choice *A*) and doesn't refer to forgetting names (Choice *C*). She is not directly showing empathy towards Gilliver, although she is saying his actions, even if in poor choice, are still something people do today.

77. B: The professor argues that the value of reading *Gulliver's Travels* is to consider human nature and its imperfections. She says, "Gulliver's Travels" can be read simply for entertainment value, but the true worth of Swift's story is his comment on human nature and its imperfections."

78. A: According to the participants in the discussion, Swift would disagree because he thinks humans are antisocial. Natasha says, "I think Swift would disagree (that humans are "social animals") because he kind of calls readers' attention to our own antisocial behaviors that we try to gloss over or ignore entirely to preserve our self-esteem."

Listening Transcripts

Passage #1

(Narrator) Listen to the following conversation between two students and then answer the following questions.

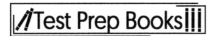

(Greg) Hi Deborah, how did you do on the biology exam?

(Deborah) Pretty well! I got a 96. How about you?

(Greg) Wow. I'm jealous. I got a 69. This stuff isn't making sense to me.

(Deborah) Oh no, I'm sorry to hear that, Greg. I could help you study if you'd like. I usually go to the library after my classes for a couple hours. We could work together on the practice questions and tackle this week's assignment if you want.

(Greg) Actually, that would be great. Are you sure you don't mind?

(Deborah) No, not at all. I have to go to my economics class right now, but I'm usually at the library around 4:00pm. I sit in the back by the reference section. Do you know where the encyclopedias are?

(Greg) Uh, to be honest, I've never been to the library here. I don't even know where on campus it is. Is it over by the dining hall on the main quad?

(Deborah) Oh wow! You've never been?! Where do you study? Yes, it's over next to the administration building on the main quad, directly across from the dining hall. You need to make sure you have your college ID with you to get in.

(Greg) I haven't really gotten into a study rhythm yet this semester. That may be part of my problem. I guess I study in my room, when my roommate and I aren't playing video games, that is. I lost my ID at the basketball game last weekend. Do you know where I can get a new one?

(Deborah) Oh Greg! We need to get you organized. But yes, go to the administration building with another form of picture ID, and you'll need to pay a $15 replacement fee, and fill out a form.

(Greg) Does a driver's license work?

(Deborah) Yes. Do you drive?

(Greg) Yes, I have a Honda Civic parked over by my dorm. I go off campus a lot to buy things at the grocery store or to go to the movies.

(Deborah) That's awesome. I would love to get off campus once in a while and get a breath of "real-world" air, if you know what I mean.

(Greg) Yeah, absolutely. Hey, how about I take you with me when I go shopping tomorrow afternoon in exchange for you tutoring me with the biology stuff?

(Deborah) Sounds perfect! Well, I've got to run to Economics class now. I'll see you at the library at 4:00pm. Let's just meet on the front steps and then we will go in together and find somewhere to work.

Passage #2

(Narrator) Listen to the following part of a lecture on Executive Functioning Disorder from a psychology class.

(Professor) Today, we are going to pick up where we left off last class talking about learning disabilities. Now, we will turn our attention to another common learning disability known as Executive Functioning Disorder. Some people um…equate executive function with the CEO of the brain because the role of

executive function is to plan, organize, and manage tasks, processes, and deadlines. Let's see...essentially, it is the sum total of mental processes that enable an individual to connect their past experiences with current and future situations. Individuals with executive functioning disorder may struggle with time management, organization, planning and forethought, um...follow through, memory, prioritizing, and getting started on tasks, among other challenges. Many students with executive functioning difficulties also struggle to apply previously learned ideas and information to new concepts or to solve problems. They also may find analyzing ideas and identifying when and how to seek help to be a challenge. Let's see...heeding attention to and remembering details is also encumbered. These difficulties can greatly impact a child or adult in school, work, and even with daily tasks that involve time management or multiple steps. Uh...students may lack the ability to plan work or change their plans, wait to be called on or to hear directions before proceeding, manage their time and space, get started on projects, switch between tasks efficiently, ask for guidance when they are confused, memorize and especially retrieve things from their memory, and turn in assignments in a timely manner.

I know many of you have expressed an interest in teaching someday so uh...it's important to think about how this will affect students in your classrooms. Let's see...students may need accommodations for assessments and test taking. For example, they may be permitted to provide oral answers rather than circling or filling in bubbles or writing. They may be provided with the test format ahead of time so they can understand what will be asked of them and just focus on the content during studying. They may be allowed additional time during test taking or they may be provided with outlines of a lesson prior to sitting through it. This helps, uh...because then they only need to focus on listening rather than uh...writing and listening.

Now, there are also things that teachers can do. Because of the challenges planning and following steps, teachers are encouraged to uh...give step-by-step instructions that students should repeat back to demonstrate listening and understanding. Um, the number of steps should remain reasonable and simple instructions, uh like those given in written form, should be provided. Depending on the age of the students and their reading abilities, a written outline of the lesson and any directions can also be provided. This is particularly important to assist with note-taking during a lesson and uh...help key students into the main points versus the details. Using directed phrases like, "this is important because..." can also help students identify key points and begin making connections as to why something is important. Like in our class, teachers should review prior material briefly before building upon it in the new lesson. To help keep students on task and meeting deadlines, teachers can provide daily to do checklists, encourage an assignment notebook that parents must review with their child. Lastly, to optimize success with assessments, teachers should explain what an ideal assignment or test looks like and provide a model.

While executive functioning issues alone can have a significant impact on an individual, I want you to think about how it often um...appears concurrently with other learning disorders like ADHD or dyslexia. Remember? We talked about these last class. This can make it, uh...especially challenging.

Passage #3

(Narrator) Listen to part of a lecture from astronomy class and then answer the questions.

(Professor) We are continuing our discussion today of the history of astronomers from ancient times working up to the present day. So, remember, we are talking about the key contributors that have helped build our understanding of astronomy today. Let's pick up now with Nicolaus Copernicus. Copernicus, in many ways, can be thought of as the first in the modern astronomy scientists because he overturned the geocentric model of the solar system that had stood for over two thousand years, and

instead, correctly (but shockingly at the time) suggested that the sun was the center of the solar system and the planets revolved around the sun. This was basically the birth of our present understanding of the solar system – the Heliocentric model. Before we go on, I want to remind you about the geocentric model we talked about last class. Remember, the ancient Greeks believed in a geocentric model of the universe, such that the planets and stars rotated around the central, stationary Earth. But Copernicus recognized that the uh...that the moon rotated around the Earth and that the Earth is just one of several planets revolving around the Sun. He also noted that the Sun is a star, the closest star, and other stars are much further away, that Earth rotates around its axis every day in addition to its yearly revolution, and that closer planets have shorter "years." Pretty important discoveries, huh?

Then we have Tycho Brahe. Now, Brahe was instrumental in determining the positions of fixed stars, unaided by telescopes, which were not yet invented. He made astronomical tools to help with mapping and understanding the "heavens" and the Solar System. He thought the Earth was not moving and that the Sun and Moon revolved around the stationary planet, so we know now that this part was off-base, but he's still a key player in our evolution.

Johannes Kepler was interested in math and astronomy and felt that geometric figures influenced the universe. He built upon Copernicus' heliocentric model and you've probably heard of his three Laws of Planetary Motion. The first law states that planetary orbits are elliptical, not circular, and the Sun is at one of the foci and not the center. The second law says that the planetary speed is faster near the sun and slower when it is more distant. The third law is somewhat similar. This one states that um...that the larger the orbit of a planet, the slower its average velocity.

Next, we have Galileo Galilei. That's a fun name to say. Well, Galileo made many advancements to our thinking and to our ability to make further discoveries, like he invented the telescope. He used it to observe sunspots and discovered that the lunar surface, like Earth, had mountains and valleys. Let's see...he also noted that the Milky Way galaxy had separate stars, he discovered moons around Jupiter, and designed instruments such as a compass and this neat little calculating device. These discoveries helped prove the universe was dynamic and changing. Perhaps most importantly, he lay the foundations for scientific thought and process, the importance of logic and reason, and how to do experiments.

Lastly, Sir Isaac Newton. Remember, Newton was the one that proposed the three laws of motion that I'm sure you've heard in physics class: an object in motion stays in motion and an object at rest stays at rest unless acted on by an external force, force equals mass times acceleration, and every action has an equal and opposite reaction. He also proposed the Universal Law of Gravitation, which states that gravity is a force and that every object in the Universe is attracted to every other object. The magnitude of this force is directly proportional to the product of the masses of the objects and inversely proportional to the square of the distances between them.

Passage #4
(Narrator) Listen to the following portion of a lecture and discussion from a geology class.

(Professor) So now I want to turn our discussion to your homework assignment, Anne Sasso's article in *Discover* magazine called "The Geology of...Rubies." This article discussed how rubies are formed, why they have been so enamored throughout history, and what causes their brilliant red color, which, as I hope you read, is due to the ultraviolet light from the Sun causing the chromium in rubies to glow. Geologists are still searching for reasons as to how the existence of rubies came to be. Do you remember how Penn State University Geosciences professor Peter Heaney referred to rubies as a "minor geological miracle"? Can anyone tell me why Dr. Heaney says this?

(Student #1) Basically, he's saying um...that the formation of rubies is essentially a perfect storm and a rare occurrence. It's like a miracle that they ever form.

(Professor) Exactly, Xavier. Rubies are a specific type of the rare mineral corundum, which is composed of densely packed aluminum and oxygen atoms. These atoms are normally colorless, but when other atoms, like in this case chromium, are substituted for a some of the uh...aluminum ones, the deep red color of rubies is produced. Other substitutions cause the bright colors of other gemstones such as sapphire from the substitution of um, uh...from titanium and iron. Corundum is rare, the elemental substitutions are rare, chromium itself is rare, and even *more* rare is the fact that this cannot occur in the presence of silica or large amounts of iron, and silica is one of the most abundant elements in the crust and iron is common too but must be in very low concentrations to form rubies. This can kind of be visualized as hmmm...like a Venn diagram of increasingly more rare occurrences and just a tiny overlapped center where the formation of this geode is actually possible.

Does anyone remember from the article how rubies form?

(Student #2) Was that the part about how they are used for jewelry and even people centuries ago marveled at their beauty?

(Professor) Well that's more about their importance or our interest in them. I'm looking for how they are created geologically.

(Student #2) Oh! Oops. Yeah, they form through plate tectonics, particularly at the boundary by the um, um...Himalayas, where deposits of the sedimentary rock limestone get pushed under the other plate and metamorphosed into the marble.

(Professor) Exactly Claudia! Molten granite in magma percolates in and infiltrates the forming marble. This limestone and granite interaction contains the chemical elements we now know are present in rubies. Importantly, this process removes the silica but left the aluminum. Geologist can even date the formation of these gemstones with the tectonic movements. Even more recently, teams of scientists have found that salt played an integral role in the formation of the rubies because it allowed the aluminum atoms to be fluid enough to get displaced occasionally by chromium.

Does anyone have any questions?... Yes, Xavier.

(Student #1) Have geologists done experiments to try to recreate all these conditions at once to make all different kinds of gemstones in the lab?

(Professor) Well, kind of. Remember...scientists typically only address one question at a time so that they can use the scientific method. This method establishes a rigorous process of investigation so that it can be uh...replicated by other scientists to verify results. By focusing on just one hypothesis, scientists should only manipulate a single variable at a time, called the independent variable, and then examine its results on the dependent variable. What would happen if scientists didn't carefully isolate variables?

(Student #2) Well, if scientists were to manipulate multiple variables, it would be impossible to know which change resulted in the observed effects.

(Professor) You got it! If scientists were to work to investigate multiple questions or change more than one variable when conducting an experiment, the research would be scattered, unfocused, and unable to prove anything.

Passage #5

(Narrator) Listen to the following conversation between a student and the school's financial aid officer.

(Student) Hi. Is this the right place to ask about a problem with my bill?

(Officer) Yes. This is the financial aid office so I can assist you with any tuition and billing questions.

(Student) Great. So, I received my bill for the semester and it says I owe $18,000. I thought I had a scholarship so there's no way I can pay this bill, plus now there's a hold on my account so I can't seem to register for classes and I'm worried they are going to fill up.

(Officer) Ok let's see. Do you have a copy of your bill with you?

(Student) No. I left it in my dorm by accident.

(Officer) No problem. Can I see your student ID? I can pull it up in our system.

(Student) Yes. Here it is. Don't mind the picture. I didn't know I was going to be photographed that day!

(Officer) Oh, don't be silly...you look nice! Ok. Let me just take a look here at your bill and see what's going on. Hmm...Yes, I see the tuition billed to your account is $8,500. Your meal plan and housing in the dorms is $7,000 this semester and there is a technology fee and other posted fees including your parking permit totaling $2,500. The total amount posted to your account is $18,000.

(Student) What about my scholarship?

(Officer) Well, it looks like you have a scholarship that is pending in your account for the amount of tuition, the $8500. It has not been applied because we are waiting on your financial aid application. Did you fill out the FAFSA? We need a current copy of that on file.

(Student) No. I didn't know I needed to do that.

(Officer) You'll definitely want to get that in as soon as possible. That way we can process your scholarship and also if you qualify for additional financial aid, we can set up a package for you. Some students get additional scholarships based on financial need, or there are loans, and work-study opportunities.

(Student) Oh, that sounds helpful. What is work-study?

(Officer) Work study refers to campus-based jobs where the compensation for you comes directly off of your bill. There are a variety of available positions for students around campus like in the library, at the sports center, or even in one of the administrative offices.

(Student) Ok cool. Back home I worked as a computer programmer at my mom's software company.

(Officer) Well we have lots of office positions too. So, what you need to do first is register to fill out FASFA on the website. You'll need to put in last year's tax information, so make sure you have that as well. Then, they will evaluate your financial aid package to determine what your needs are. If you want to do a work-study you can apply for a campus job. Lastly, make sure you pay the remaining balance on your account so that you can register for classes.

(Student) Ok thanks. I better get going on this!

Passage #6

(Narrator) Listen to the short lecture discussion in a literature class and then answer the questions.

(Professor) So, we've finally finished "Gulliver's Travels" by Jonathan Swift. As we've been discussing, this work is the expression of Swifts view of humanity hidden within the plot of a shipwrecked antihero's adventures. Gulliver is Swift's "everyman" and he represents, you know, like the English population in general. Although during his adventures Gulliver comments on the various creatures he encounters, those comments unknowingly reveal more information about Gulliver himself than their intended subjects. Through Gulliver, Swift argues that some of the forces that motivate human nature are quite unpleasant and embarrassing to admit.

Why do you think Swift presents his argument about humankind this way? Through Gulliver as a vehicle, I mean?

(Student #1) Maybe because readers would otherwise deny these charges if Swift's argument wasn't presented in such a convincing manner?

(Professor) That's a great point, Alex. It helps the argument feel less personal as well. Swift shows how Gulliver's pride can take control of his actions and words. Gulliver cannot recognize his own faults even while notifying the reader of the same faults he sees in others. Remember how Swift shows Gulliver's tendency to lie, to project his self-hatred onto those around him, and to depend greatly on others to take care of him? Swift makes it clear that he views the general population to behave in much the same way. He suggests humans should behave more like the rational Houyhnhnm race created within the text. "Gulliver's Travels" can be read simply for entertainment value, but the true worth of Swift's story is his comment on human nature and its imperfections. Based on Swift's attitude as portrayed in this story, how do you think he'd respond to the fact that humans are often called "social animals"?

(Student #2) I think Swift would disagree because he kind of calls the readers' attention to our own antisocial behaviors that we try to gloss over or ignore entirely to preserve our self-esteem.

(Professor) Natasha, that's a fabulous point. One of Swift's prevailing opinions on human personality is that we are creatures driven by our excessive pride. Humans like to consider themselves to be more important than they actually are. Remember how Gulliver is always telling his readers that he was of the most importance to his various masters and their rulers? Like in Lilliput, the Imperial Majesty decides to have dinner with Gulliver. The rhetoric that Gulliver uses while relating this to the reader makes the occasion appear more momentous.

(Student #2) Yeah, he like glamorizes the situation and reveals that Gulliver considers himself to be of great concern to the powerful people of Lilliput.

(Professor) Right! And his experiences in Brobdingnag include a similar occurrence. Hearing Gulliver tell us how important he is to the rulers of these foreign lands helps us realize how petty some of our own actions are. Name-dropping is our modern equivalent to Gulliver's boasting about his close relationships with Kings and Queens!

(Student #1) It seems Swift thinks that Humans are content to follow their mistakes through to the end rather than admit to making a mistake regardless of the consequences of unwavering persistence.

(Professor) Wow, that's such a good point. What textual evidence do you have to support that thought?

(Student #1) Well, Gulliver stands by his convictions even after the reasonable king he respects greatly presents a profound argument against the usage of such a violent weapon.

(Professor) I want to dig deeper into this thought but we have to end here today because of the time. Let's pick this back up on Thursday.

Speaking

79. I live in New York City and I love it here. There are a lot of interesting places where I would enjoy taking an exchange student. I think I would choose sites that are less well-known, because they attract fewer tourists and are less crowded. General Grant's tomb is situated next to Riverside Park and has beautiful views of the Hudson river and George Washington Bridge. The architecture of the tomb and the bridge are striking and it is very lovely walking along the pathways. There is an interesting museum dedicated to this history of General Grant and New York City there as well. I would also take the student to the Natural History Museum, which is on the west side of Central Park. Although this museum does attract a lot of tourists, it does rightfully so because it has a fascinating amount of rocks, minerals, historic natural specimens, and exhibits about animals, biomes, and the evolution of different cultures and societies. I saw a fantastic exhibit about the biodiversity and ecology of Cuba and saw an interesting planetarium show about the night sky. Nearby, there is a great rooftop bar where you can enjoy drinks and appetizers in the open air above the city.

80. I think it is better to set ambitious goals even if there is a chance of failure. When people set goals that are too easy, they are denying themselves the chance to really push themselves and grow. If someone doesn't set their sights high and just stays within their comfort zone, they'll never know what they can achieve and they might limit their potential. If instead, they set a big, lofty goal, they may fall short and not fully achieve it but they will likely still exceed where they would have landed with a low-level goal. For example, if an athlete wants to run a 5k race and get a fast time, she will be motivated to train really hard and stay disciplined if she sets a big goal that excites her. If she sets an easy goal that she is pretty confident she can achieve without putting in much work, she will probably not push herself as hard in workouts and might get a slower time.

81. The female student thinks that the new additional writing course requirement at the University is unnecessary and she's not happy about the Academic Advisory Committee's decision to implement it. She thinks that because college students have been writing their whole lives, the one freshmen writing class requirement they already have is plenty. She thinks any additional writing class would be a waste of time, especially for students who know what they want to study. Those students would do better taking an additional course in their major, particularly if their focus doesn't relate too directly to writing, in her opinion. The University's Academic Advisory Committee, on the other hand, has implemented the additional writing course because the University's faculty feels that students' ability to communicate effectively in an academic tone is critical for future success in jobs and life.

82. The Inverted-U Theory is used in sports psychology to describe ideal levels of arousal for optimal athletic performance. The theory gets its name from its characteristic shape. It is graphed as an upside-down "U" with arousal versus performance. Being too relaxed or too stressed about an athletic event can be detrimental to performance because the body reacts physiologically to the stress itself, by influencing heart rate and levels of hormones, like epinephrine. Instead, being moderately stressed and somewhat relaxed at the same time is ideal for success. The professor talks about the anxious basketball player he coached. She would get so wound up for games that she would get winded and tired, miss easy shots, and play worse. As a coach, he could apply these concepts of the Inverted-U Theory by

working with the athlete on meditation and relaxation exercises in practices and games to help calm her down before she would need to play. This could help prevent her from getting overly anxious and keep her more in the optimal level. This is the opposite approach that he'd have to take with overly relaxed athletes. He mentioned that these athletes may need cheering or pumping up, and a little bit of pressure to bring them up to more ideal levels of arousal for success.

Practice Test #2

Reading

Reading *Questions 1–6 are based on the following passage:*

Dana Gioia argues in his article that poetry is dying, now little more than a limited art form confined to academic and college settings. Of course, poetry remains healthy in the academic setting, but the idea of poetry being limited to this academic subculture is a stretch. New technology and social networking alone have contributed to poets and other writers' work being shared across the world. YouTube has emerged to be a major asset to poets, allowing live performances to be streamed to billions of users. Even now, poetry continues to grow and voice topics that are relevant to the culture of our time. Poetry is not in the spotlight as it may have been in earlier times, but it's still a relevant art form that continues to expand in scope and appeal.

Furthermore, Gioia's argument does not account for live performances of poetry. Not everyone has taken a poetry class or enrolled in university—but most everyone is online. The Internet is a perfect launching point to get all creative work out there. An example of this was the performance of Buddy Wakefield's *Hurling Crowbirds at Mockingbars*. Wakefield is a well-known poet who has published several collections of contemporary poetry. One of my favorite works by Wakefield is *Crowbirds*, specifically his performance at New York University in 2009. Although his reading was a campus event, views of his performance online number in the thousands. His poetry attracted people outside of the university setting.

Naturally, the poem's popularity can be attributed both to Wakefield's performance and the quality of his writing. *Crowbirds* touches on themes of core human concepts such as faith, personal loss, and growth. These are not ideas that only poets or students of literature understand, but all human beings: "You acted like I was hurling crowbirds at mockingbars / and abandoned me for not making sense. / Evidently, I don't experience things as rationally as you do" (Wakefield 15–17). Wakefield weaves together a complex description of the perplexed and hurt emotions of the speaker undergoing a separation from a romantic interest. The line "You acted like I was hurling crowbirds at mockingbars" conjures up an image of someone confused, seemingly out of their mind . . . or in the case of the speaker, passionately trying to grasp at a relationship that is fading. The speaker is looking back and finding the words that described how he wasn't making sense. This poem is particularly human and gripping in its message, but the entire effect of the poem is enhanced through the physical performance.

At its core, poetry is about addressing issues/ideas in the world. Part of this is also addressing the perspectives that are exiguously considered. Although the platform may look different, poetry continues to have a steady audience due to the emotional connection the poet shares with the audience.

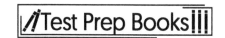

1. Which one of the following best explains how the passage is organized?
    a. The author begins with a long definition of the main topic, and then proceeds to prove how that definition has changed over the course of modernity.
    b. The author presents a puzzling phenomenon and uses the rest of the passage to showcase personal experiences in order to explain it.
    c. The author contrasts two different viewpoints, then builds a case showing preference for one over the other.
    d. The passage is an analysis of another theory in which the author has no stake in.

2. The author of the passage would likely agree most with which of the following?
    a. Buddy Wakefield is a genius and is considered at the forefront of modern poetry.
    b. Poetry is not irrelevant; it is an art form that adapts to the changing time while containing its core elements.
    c. Spoken word is the zenith of poetic forms and the premier style of poetry in this decade.
    d. Poetry is on the verge of vanishing from our cultural consciousness.

3. Which one of the following words, if substituted for the word *exiguously* in the last paragraph, would LEAST change the meaning of the sentence?
    a. Indolently
    b. Inaudibly
    c. Interminably
    d. Infrequently

4. Which of the following is most closely analogous to the author's opinion of Buddy Wakefield's performance in relation to modern poetry?
    a. Someone's refusal to accept that the Higgs Boson will validate the Standard Model.
    b. An individual's belief that soccer will lose popularity within the next fifty years.
    c. A professor's opinion that poetry contains the language of the heart, while fiction contains the language of the mind.
    d. A student's insistence that psychoanalysis is a subset of modern psychology.

5. What is the primary purpose of the passage?
    a. To educate readers on the development of poetry and describe the historical implications of poetry in media.
    b. To disprove Dana Gioia's stance that poetry is becoming irrelevant and is only appreciated in academia.
    c. To inform readers of the brilliance of Buddy Wakefield and to introduce them to other poets that have influence in contemporary poetry.
    d. To prove that Gioia's article does have some truth to it and to shed light on its relevance to modern poetry.

6. What is the author's main reason for including the quote in the passage?
    a. The quote opens up opportunity to disprove Gioia's views.
    b. To demonstrate that people are still writing poetry even if the medium has changed in current times.
    c. To prove that poets still have an audience to write for even if the audience looks different than it did centuries ago.
    d. The quote illustrates the complex themes poets continue to address, which still draws listeners and appreciation.

Questions 7–14 are based on the following passage:

In the quest to understand existence, modern philosophers must question if humans can fully comprehend the world. Classical western approaches to philosophy tend to hold that one can understand something, be it an event or object, by standing outside of the phenomena and observing it. It is then by unbiased observation that one can grasp the details of the world. This seems to hold true for many things. Scientists conduct experiments and record their findings, and thus many natural phenomena become comprehendible. However, several of these observations were possible because humans used tools in order to make these discoveries.

This may seem like an extraneous matter. After all, people invented things like microscopes and telescopes in order to enhance their capacity to view cells or the movement of stars. While humans are still capable of seeing things, the question remains if human beings have the capacity to fully observe and see the world in order to understand it. It would not be an impossible stretch to argue that what humans see through a microscope is not the exact thing itself, but a human interpretation of it.

This would seem to be the case in the "Business of the Holes" experiment conducted by Richard Feynman. To study the way electrons behave, Feynman set up a barrier with two holes and a plate. The plate was there to indicate how many times the electrons would pass through the hole(s). Rather than casually observe the electrons acting under normal circumstances, Feynman discovered that electrons behave in two totally different ways depending on whether or not they are observed. The electrons that were observed had passed through either one of the holes or were caught on the plate as particles. However, electrons that weren't observed acted as waves instead of particles and passed through both holes. This indicated that electrons have a dual nature. Electrons seen by the human eye act like particles, while unseen electrons act like waves of energy.

This dual nature of the electrons presents a conundrum. While humans now have a better understanding of electrons, the fact remains that people cannot entirely perceive how electrons behave without the use of instruments. We can only observe one of the mentioned behaviors, which only provides a partial understanding of the entire function of electrons. Therefore, we're forced to ask ourselves whether the world we observe is objective or if it is subjectively perceived by humans. Or, an alternative question: can man understand the world only through machines that will allow them to observe natural phenomena?

Both questions humble man's capacity to grasp the world. However, those ideas don't consider that many phenomena have been proven by human beings without the use of machines, such as the discovery of gravity. Like all philosophical questions, whether man's reason and observation alone can understand the universe can be approached from many angles.

7. The word *extraneous* in paragraph two can be best interpreted as referring to which one of the following?

    a. Indispensable

    b. Bewildering

    c. Superfluous

    d. Exuberant

8. What is the author's motivation for writing the passage?

    a. To bring to light an alternative view on human perception by examining the role of technology in human understanding.

    b. To educate the reader on the latest astroparticle physics discovery and offer terms that may be unfamiliar to the reader.

    c. To argue that humans are totally blind to the realities of the world by presenting an experiment that proves that electrons are not what they seem on the surface.

    d. To reflect on opposing views of human understanding.

9. Which of the following most closely resembles the way in which paragraph four is structured?

    a. It offers one solution, questions the solution, and then ends with an alternative solution.

    b. It presents an inquiry, explains the details of that inquiry, and then offers a solution.

    c. It presents a problem, explains the details of that problem, and then ends with more inquiry.

    d. It gives a definition, offers an explanation, and then ends with an inquiry.

10. For the classical approach of understanding to hold true, which of the following must be required?

    a. A telescope

    b. A recording device

    c. Multiple witnesses present

    d. The person observing must be unbiased

11. Which best describes how the electrons in the experiment behaved like waves?

    a. The electrons moved up and down like actual waves.

    b. The electrons passed through both holes and then onto the plate.

    c. The electrons converted to photons upon touching the plate.

    d. Electrons were seen passing through one hole or the other.

12. The author mentions "gravity" in the last paragraph in order to do what?

    a. To show that different natural phenomena test man's ability to grasp the world.

    b. To prove that since man has not measured it with the use of tools or machines, humans cannot know the true nature of gravity.

    c. To demonstrate an example of natural phenomena humans discovered and understand without the use of tools or machines.

    d. To show an alternative solution to the nature of electrons that humans have not thought of yet.

13. Which situation best parallels the revelation of the dual nature of electrons discovered in Feynman's experiment?
    a. A man is born color-blind and grows up observing everything in lighter or darker shades. With the invention of special goggles he puts on, he discovers that there are other colors in addition to different shades.
    b. The coelacanth was thought to be extinct, but a live specimen was just recently discovered. There are now two living species of coelacanth known to man, and both are believed to be endangered.
    c. In the Middle Ages, blacksmiths added carbon to iron, thus inventing steel. The consequences of this important discovery would have its biggest effects during the industrial revolution.
    d. In order to better examine and treat broken bones, the x-ray machine was invented and put to use in hospitals and medical centers.

14. Which statement about technology would the author likely disagree with?
    a. Technology can help expand the field of human vision.
    b. Technology renders human observation irrelevant.
    c. Developing tools used in observation and research indicates growing understanding of our world itself.
    d. Studying certain phenomena necessitates the use of tools and machines.

Questions 15–19 are based on the following passage:

> The Middle Ages were a time of great superstition and theological debate. Many beliefs were developed and practiced, while some died out or were listed as heresy. Boethianism is a Medieval theological philosophy that attributes sin to gratification and righteousness with virtue and God's providence. Boethianism holds that sin, greed, and corruption are means to attain temporary pleasure, but that they inherently harm the person's soul as well as other human beings.

> In *The Canterbury Tales,* we observe more instances of bad actions punished than goodness being rewarded. This would appear to be some reflection of Boethianism. In the "Pardoner's Tale," all three thieves wind up dead, which is a result of their desire for wealth. Each wrong doer pays with their life, and they are unable to enjoy the wealth they worked to steal. Within his tales, Chaucer gives reprieve to people undergoing struggle, but also interweaves stories of contemptible individuals being cosmically punished for their wickedness. The thieves idolize physical wealth, which leads to their downfall. This same theme and ideological principle of Boethianism is repeated in the "Friar's Tale," whose summoner character attempts to gain further wealth by partnering with a demon. The summoner's refusal to repent for his avarice and corruption leads to the demon dragging his soul to Hell. Again, we see the theme of the individual who puts faith and morality aside in favor for a physical prize. The result, of course, is that the summoner loses everything.

> The examples of the righteous being rewarded tend to appear in a spiritual context within the *Canterbury Tales*. However, there are a few instances where we see goodness resulting in physical reward. In the Prioress' Tale, we see corporal punishment for barbarism *and* a reward for goodness. While the boy does die, he is granted a lasting reward by being able to sing even after his death, a miracle that marks that the murdered youth led a pure life. Here, the miracle represents eternal favor with God.

Again, we see the theological philosophy of Boethianism in Chaucer's *The Canterbury Tales* through acts of sin and righteousness and the consequences that follow. When pleasures of the world are sought instead of God's favor, we see characters being punished in tragic ways. However, the absence of worldly lust has its own set of consequences for the characters seeking to obtain God's favor.

15. What would be a potential reward for living a good life, as described in Boethianism?
    a. A long life sustained by the good deeds one has done over a lifetime
    b. Wealth and fertility for oneself and the extension of one's family line
    c. Vengeance for those who have been persecuted by others who have a capacity for committing wrongdoing
    d. God's divine favor for one's righteousness

16. What might be the main reason why the author chose to discuss Boethianism through examining The Canterbury Tales?
    a. *The Canterbury Tales* is a well-known text.
    b. *The Canterbury Tales* is the only known fictional text that contains use of Boethianism.
    c. *The Canterbury Tales* presents a manuscript written in the medieval period that can help illustrate Boethianism through stories and show how people of the time might have responded to the idea.
    d. Within each individual tale in *The Canterbury Tales*, the reader can read about different levels of Boethianism and how each level leads to greater enlightenment.

17. What "ideological principle" is the author referring to in the middle of the second paragraph when talking about the "Friar's Tale"?
    a. The principle that the act of ravaging another's possessions is the same as ravaging one's soul.
    b. The principle that thieves who idolize physical wealth will be punished in an earthly sense as well as eternally.
    c. The principle that fraternization with a demon will result in one losing everything, including their life.
    d. The principle that a desire for material goods leads to moral malfeasance punishable by a higher being.

18. Which of the following words, if substituted for the word *avarice* in paragraph two, would LEAST change the meaning of the sentence?
    a. Perniciousness
    b. Pithiness
    c. Parsimoniousness
    d. Precariousness

19. Based on the passage, what view does Boethianism take on desire?
    a. Desire does not exist in the context of Boethianism
    b. Desire is a virtue and should be welcomed
    c. Having desire is evidence of demonic possession
    d. Desire for pleasure can lead toward sin

Questions 20–27 are based on the following passages:

Passage I

Lethal force, or deadly force, is defined as the physical means to cause death or serious harm to another individual. The law holds that lethal force is only accepted when you or another person are in immediate and unavoidable danger of death or severe bodily harm. For example, a person could be beating someone in such a way that the victim is suffering severe trauma that could result in death or serious harm. This would be an instance where lethal force would be acceptable and possibly the only way to save the victim from irrevocable damage.

Another example of when to use lethal force would be when someone enters your home with a deadly weapon. The intruder's presence and possession of the weapon indicate mal-intent and the ability to inflict death or severe injury to you and your loved ones. Again, lethal force can be used in this situation. Lethal force can also be applied to prevent the harm of another individual. If a woman is being brutally assaulted and is unable to fend off an attacker, lethal force can be used to defend her as a last-ditch effort. If she is in immediate jeopardy of rape, harm, and/or death, lethal force could be the only response that could effectively deter the assailant.

The key to understanding the concept of lethal force is the term *last resort*. Deadly force cannot be taken back; it should be used only to prevent severe harm or death. The law does distinguish whether the means of one's self-defense is fully warranted, or if the individual goes out of control in the process. If you continually attack the assailant after they are rendered incapacitated, this would be causing unnecessary harm, and the law can bring charges against you. Likewise, if you kill an attacker unnecessarily after defending yourself, you can be charged with murder. This would move lethal force beyond necessary defense, making it no longer a last resort but rather a use of excessive force.

Passage II

Assault is the unlawful attempt of one person to apply apprehension on another individual by an imminent threat or by initiating offensive contact. Assaults can vary, encompassing physical strikes, threatening body language, and even provocative language. In the case of the latter, even if a hand has not been laid, it is still considered an assault because of its threatening nature.

Let's look at an example: A homeowner is angered because his neighbor blows fallen leaves into his freshly mowed lawn. Irate, the homeowner gestures a fist to his neighbor and threatens to bash his head in for littering on his lawn. The homeowner's physical motions and verbal threats herald a physical threat against the other neighbor. These factors classify the homeowner's reaction as an assault. If the angry neighbor hits the threatening homeowner in retaliation, that would constitute an assault as well because he physically hit the homeowner.

Assault also centers on the involvement of weapons in a conflict. If someone fires a gun at another person, this could be interpreted as an assault unless the shooter acted in self-defense. If an individual drew a gun or a knife on someone with the intent to harm

them, that would be considered assault. However, it's also considered an assault if someone simply aimed a weapon, loaded or not, at another person in a threatening manner.

20. What is the purpose of the second passage?
    a. To inform the reader about what assault is and how it is committed
    b. To inform the reader about how assault is a minor example of lethal force
    c. To disprove the previous passage concerning lethal force
    d. The author is recounting an incident in which they were assaulted

21. Which of the following situations, according to the passages, would not constitute an illegal use of lethal force?
    a. A disgruntled cashier yells obscenities at a customer.
    b. A thief is seen running away with stolen cash.
    c. A man is attacked in an alley by another man with a knife.
    d. A woman punches another woman in a bar.

22. Given the information in the passages, which of the following must be true about assault?
    a. Assault charges are more severe than unnecessary use of force charges.
    b. There are various forms of assault.
    c. Smaller, weaker people cannot commit assaults.
    d. Assault is justified only as a last resort.

23. Which of the following, if true, would most seriously undermine the explanation proposed by the author in Passage I in the third paragraph?
    a. An instance of lethal force in self-defense is not absolutely absolved from blame. The law considers the necessary use of force at the time it is committed.
    b. An individual who uses lethal force under necessary defense is in direct compliance of the law under most circumstances.
    c. Lethal force in self-defense should be forgiven in all cases for the peace of mind of the primary victim.
    d. The use of lethal force is not evaluated on the intent of the user, but rather the severity of the primary attack that warranted self-defense.

24. Based on the passages, what can be inferred about the relationship between assault and lethal force?
    a. An act of lethal force always leads to a type of assault.
    b. An assault will result in someone using lethal force.
    c. An assault with deadly intent can lead to an individual using lethal force to preserve their well-being.
    d. If someone uses self-defense in a conflict, it is called deadly force; if actions or threats are intended, it is called assault.

25. Which of the following best describes the way the passages are structured?
    a. Both passages open by defining a legal concept and then continue to describe situations that further explain the concept.
    b. Both passages begin with situations, introduce accepted definitions, and then cite legal ramifications.
    c. Passage I presents a long definition while the Passage II begins by showing an example of assault.
    d. Both cite specific legal doctrines, then proceed to explain the rulings.

26. What can be inferred about the role of intent in lethal force and assault?
    a. Intent is irrelevant. The law does not take intent into account.
    b. Intent is vital for determining the lawfulness of using lethal force.
    c. Intent is very important for determining both lethal force and assault; intent is examined in both parties and helps determine the severity of the issue.
    d. The intent of the assailant is the main focus for determining legal ramifications; it is used to determine if the defender was justified in using force to respond.

27. The author uses the example in the second paragraph of Passage II in order to do what?
    a. To demonstrate two different types of assault by showing how each specifically relates to the other
    b. To demonstrate a single example of two different types of assault, then adding in the third type of assault in the example's conclusion
    c. To prove that the definition of lethal force is altered when the victim in question is a homeowner and his property is threatened
    d. To suggest that verbal assault can be an exaggerated crime by the law and does not necessarily lead to physical violence

Questions 28–33 are based upon the following passage:

MANKIND being originally equals in the order of creation, the equality could only be destroyed by some subsequent circumstance; the distinctions of rich, and poor, may in a great measure be accounted for, and that without having recourse to the harsh, ill-sounding names of oppression and avarice. Oppression is often the CONSEQUENCE , but seldom or never the MEANS of riches; and though avarice will preserve a man from being necessitously poor, it generally makes him too timorous to be wealthy.

But there is another and greater distinction, for which no truly natural or religious reason can be assigned, and that is, the distinction of men into KINGS and SUBJECTS. Male and female are the distinctions of nature, good and bad the distinctions of heaven; but how a race of men came into the world so exalted above the rest, and distinguished like some new species, is worth enquiring into, and whether they are the means of happiness or of misery to mankind.

In the early ages of the world, according to the scripture chronology, there were no kings; the consequence of which was, there were no wars; it is the pride of kings which throw mankind into confusion. Holland without a king hath enjoyed more peace for this last century than any of the monarchical governments in Europe. Antiquity favors the same remark; for the quiet and rural lives of the first patriarchs hath a happy something in them, which vanishes away when we come to the history of Jewish royalty.

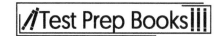

Government by kings was first introduced into the world by the Heathens, from whom the children of Israel copied the custom. It was the most prosperous invention the Devil ever set on foot for the promotion of idolatry. The Heathens paid divine honors to their deceased kings, and the Christian world hath improved on the plan, by doing the same to their living ones. How impious is the title of sacred majesty applied to a worm, who in the midst of his splendor is crumbling into dust!

As the exalting one man so greatly above the rest cannot be justified on the equal rights of nature, so neither can it be defended on the authority of scripture; for the will of the Almighty, as declared by Gideon and the prophet Samuel, expressly disapproves of government by kings. All anti-monarchical parts of scripture have been very smoothly glossed over in monarchical governments, but they undoubtedly merit the attention of countries which have their governments yet to form. RENDER UNTO CAESAR THE THINGS WHICH ARE CAESAR'S is the scripture doctrine of courts, yet it is no support of monarchical government, for the Jews at that time were without a king, and in a state of vassalage to the Romans.

Now three thousand years passed away from the Mosaic account of the creation, till the Jews under a national delusion requested a king. Till then their form of government (except in extraordinary cases, where the Almighty interposed) was a kind of republic administered by a judge and the elders of the tribes. Kings they had none, and it was held sinful to acknowledge any being under that title but the Lord of Hosts. And when a man seriously reflects on the idolatrous homage which is paid to the persons of kings, he need not wonder that the Almighty, ever jealous of his honor, should disapprove of a form of government which so impiously invades the prerogative of heaven.

Excerpt From "Common Sense" by Thomas Paine, 1775–1776

28. According to the passage, what role does avarice, or greed, play in poverty?
   a. Avarice makes a man poor.
   b. Avarice is the consequence of wealth.
   c. Avarice prevents a man from being poor, but makes him too fearful to be wealthy.
   d. Avarice is what drives a person to be wealthy.

29. Of these distinctions, which does the author believe to be beyond natural or religious reason?
   a. Good and bad
   b. Male and female
   c. Human and animal
   d. King and subjects

30. According to the passage, what are the Heathens responsible for?
   a. Government by kings
   b. Quiet and rural lives of patriarchs
   c. Paying divine honors to their living kings
   d. Equal rights of nature

31. Which of the following best states Paine's rationale for the denouncement of monarchy?
    a. It is against the laws of nature
    b. It is against the equal rights of nature and is denounced in scripture
    c. Despite scripture, a monarchal government is unlawful
    d. Neither the law nor scripture denounce monarchy

32. Based on the passage, what is the best definition of the word *idolatrous*?
    a. Worshipping kings
    b. Being deceitful
    c. Sinfulness
    d. Engaging in illegal activities

33. What is the essential meaning of lines 41–44?

> And when a man seriously reflects on the idolatrous homage which is paid to the persons of kings, he need not wonder that the Almighty, ever jealous of his honor, should disapprove of a form of government which so impiously invades the prerogative of heaven.

    a. God disapproves of the irreverence of a monarchical government.
    b. With careful reflection, men should realize that heaven is not promised.
    c. God will punish those that follow a monarchical government.
    d. Belief in a monarchical government cannot coexist with belief in God.

Questions 34–39 are based on the following passage:

As long ago as 1860 it was the proper thing to be born at home. At present, so I am told, the high gods of medicine have decreed that the first cries of the young shall be uttered upon the anesthetic air of a hospital, preferably a fashionable one. So young Mr. and Mrs. Roger Button were fifty years ahead of style when they decided, one day in the summer of 1860, that their first baby should be born in a hospital. Whether this anachronism had any bearing upon the astonishing history I am about to set down will never be known.

I shall tell you what occurred, and let you judge for yourself.

The Roger Buttons held an enviable position, both social and financial, in ante-bellum Baltimore. They were related to the This Family and the That Family, which, as every Southerner knew, entitled them to membership in that enormous peerage which largely populated the Confederacy. This was their first experience with the charming old custom of having babies— Mr. Button was naturally nervous. He hoped it would be a boy so that he could be sent to Yale College in Connecticut, at which institution Mr. Button himself had been known for four years by the somewhat obvious nickname of "Cuff."

On the September morning <u>consecrated</u> to the enormous event he arose nervously at six o'clock dressed himself, adjusted an impeccable stock, and hurried forth through the streets of Baltimore to the hospital, to determine whether the darkness of the night had borne in new life upon its bosom.

When he was approximately a hundred yards from the Maryland Private Hospital for Ladies and Gentlemen he saw Doctor Keene, the family physician, descending the front steps, rubbing his hands together with a washing movement—as all doctors are required to do by the unwritten ethics of their profession.

Mr. Roger Button, the president of Roger Button & Co., Wholesale Hardware, began to run toward Doctor Keene with much less dignity than was expected from a Southern gentleman of that picturesque period. "Doctor Keene!" he called. "Oh, Doctor Keene!"

The doctor heard him, faced around, and stood waiting, a curious expression settling on his harsh, medicinal face as Mr. Button drew near.

"What happened?" demanded Mr. Button, as he came up in a gasping rush. "What was it? How is she? A boy? Who is it? What—"

"Talk sense!" said Doctor Keene sharply. He appeared somewhat irritated.

"Is the child born?" begged Mr. Button.

Doctor Keene frowned. "Why, yes, I suppose so—after a fashion." Again he threw a curious glance at Mr. Button.

Excerpt from The Curious Case of Benjamin Button, F.S. Fitzgerald, 1922

34. What major event is about to happen in this story?
    a. Mr. Button is about to go to a funeral.
    b. Mr. Button's wife is about to have a baby.
    c. Mr. Button is getting ready to go to the doctor's office.
    d. Mr. Button is about to go shopping for new clothes.

35. What kind of tone does the above passage have?
    a. Nervous and Excited
    b. Sad and Angry
    c. Shameful and Confused
    d. Grateful and Joyous

36. What is the meaning of the word "consecrated" in paragraph 4?
    a. Numbed
    b. Chained
    c. Dedicated
    d. Moved

37. What does the author mean to do by adding the following statement?
    "rubbing his hands together with a washing movement—as all doctors are required to do by the unwritten ethics of their profession."

    a. Suggesting that Mr. Button is tired of the doctor.
    b. Trying to explain the detail of the doctor's profession.
    c. Hinting to readers that the doctor is an unethical man.
    d. Giving readers a visual picture of what the doctor is doing.

38. Which of the following best describes the development of this passage?
    a. It starts in the middle of a narrative in order to transition smoothly to a conclusion.
    b. It is a chronological narrative from beginning to end.
    c. The sequence of events is backwards—we go from future events to past events.
    d. To introduce the setting of the story and its characters.

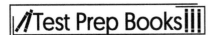

39. Which of the following is an example of an imperative sentence?
    a. "Oh, Doctor Keene!"
    b. "Talk sense!"
    c. "Is the child born?"
    d. "Why, yes, I suppose so—"

Questions 40–45 are based on the following passage:

Knowing that Mrs. Mallard was afflicted with heart trouble, great care was taken to break to her as gently as possible the news of her husband's death.

It was her sister Josephine who told her, in broken sentences; veiled hints that revealed in half concealing. Her husband's friend Richards was there, too, near her. It was he who had been in the newspaper office when intelligence of the railroad disaster was received, with Brently Mallard's name leading the list of "killed." He had only taken the time to assure himself of its truth by a second telegram, and had hastened to forestall any less careful, less tender friend in bearing the sad message.

She did not hear the story as many women have heard the same, with a paralyzed inability to accept its significance. She wept at once, with sudden, wild abandonment, in her sister's arms. When the storm of grief had spent itself she went away to her room alone. She would have no one follow her.

There stood, facing the open window, a comfortable, roomy armchair. Into this she sank, pressed down by a physical exhaustion that haunted her body and seemed to reach into her soul.

She could see in the open square before her house the tops of trees that were all aquiver with the new spring life. The delicious breath of rain was in the air. In the street below a peddler was crying his wares. The notes of a distant song which some one was singing reached her faintly, and countless sparrows were twittering in the eaves.

There were patches of blue sky showing here and there through the clouds that had met and piled one above the other in the west facing her window.

She sat with her head thrown back upon the cushion of the chair, quite motionless, except when a sob came up into her throat and shook her, as a child who has cried itself to sleep continues to sob in its dreams.

She was young, with a fair, calm face, whose lines bespoke repression and even a certain strength. But now here was a dull stare in her eyes, whose gaze was fixed away off yonder on one of those patches of blue sky. It was not a glance of reflection, but rather indicated a suspension of intelligent thought.

There was something coming to her and she was waiting for it, fearfully. What was it? She did not know; it was too subtle and elusive to name. But she felt it, creeping out of the sky, reaching toward her through the sounds, the scents, and color that filled the air.

Now her bosom rose and fell tumultuously. She was beginning to recognize this thing that was approaching to possess her, and she was striving to beat it back with her will—as powerless as her two white slender hands would have been. When she abandoned herself a little whispered

word escaped her slightly parted lips. She said it over and over under her breath: "free, free, free!" The vacant stare and the look of terror that had followed it went from her eyes. They stayed keen and bright. Her pulses beat fast, and the coursing blood warmed and relaxed every inch of her body.

She did not stop to ask if it were or were not a monstrous joy that held her. A clear and exalted perception enabled her to dismiss the suggestion as trivial. She knew that she would weep again when she saw the kind, tender hands folded in death; the face that had never looked save with love upon her, fixed and gray and dead. But she saw beyond that bitter moment a long procession of years to come that would belong to her absolutely. And she opened and spread her arms out to them in welcome.

Excerpt from "The Story of An Hour," Kate Chopin, 1894

40. What point of view is the above passage told in?
    a. First person
    b. Second person
    c. Third person omniscient
    d. Third person limited

41. What kind of irony are we presented with in this story?
    a. The way Mrs. Mallard reacted to her husband's death.
    b. The way in which Mr. Mallard died.
    c. The way in which the news of her husband's death was presented to Mrs. Mallard.
    d. The way in which nature is compared with death in the story.

42. What is the meaning of the word "elusive" in paragraph 9?
    a. Horrible
    b. Indefinable
    c. Quiet
    d. Joyful

43. What is the best summary of the passage above?
    a. Mr. Mallard, a soldier during World War I, is killed by the enemy and leaves his wife widowed.
    b. Mrs. Mallard understands the value of friendship when her friends show up for her after her husband's death.
    c. Mrs. Mallard combats mental illness daily and will perhaps be sent to a mental institution soon.
    d. Mrs. Mallard, a newly widowed woman, finds unexpected relief in her husband's death.

44. What is the tone of this story?
    a. Confused
    b. Joyful
    c. Depressive
    d. All of the above

45. What is the meaning of the word "tumultuously" in paragraph 10?
    a. Orderly
    b. Unashamedly
    c. Violently
    d. Calmly

Questions 46–47 are based on the following passage:

When researchers and engineers undertake a large-scale scientific project, they may end up making discoveries and developing technologies that have far wider uses than originally intended. This is especially true in NASA, one of the most influential and innovative scientific organizations in America. NASA spinoff technology refers to innovations originally developed for NASA space projects that are now used in a wide range of different commercial fields. Many consumers are unaware that products they are buying are based on NASA research! Spinoff technology proves that it is worthwhile to invest in science research because it could enrich people's lives in unexpected ways.

The first spinoff technology worth mentioning is baby food. In space, where astronauts have limited access to fresh food and fewer options with their daily meals, malnutrition is a serious concern. Consequently, NASA researchers were looking for ways to enhance the nutritional value of astronauts' food. Scientists found that a certain type of algae could be added to food, improving the food's neurological benefits. When experts in the commercial food industry learned of this algae's potential to boost brain health, they were quick to begin their own research. The nutritional substance from algae then developed into a product called life's DHA, which can be found in over 90 percent of infant food sold in America.

Another intriguing example of a spinoff technology can be found in fashion. People who are always dropping their sunglasses may have invested in a pair of sunglasses with scratch resistant lenses—that is, it's impossible to scratch the glass, even if the glasses are dropped on an abrasive surface. This innovation is incredibly advantageous for people who are clumsy, but most shoppers don't know that this technology was originally developed by NASA. Scientists first created scratch resistant glass to help protect costly and crucial equipment from getting scratched in space, especially the helmet visors in space suits. However, sunglass companies later realized that this technology could be profitable for their products, and they licensed the technology from NASA.

46. What is the main purpose of this article?
   a. To advise consumers to do more research before making a purchase
   b. To persuade readers to support NASA research
   c. To tell a narrative about the history of space technology
   d. To define and describe instances of spinoff technology

47. What is the organizational structure of this article?
   a. A general definition followed by more specific examples
   b. A general opinion followed by supporting evidence
   c. An important moment in history followed by chronological details
   d. A popular misconception followed by counterevidence

Listening

Directions: The Listening section measures your ability to understand conversations and lectures in English. In this test, you will listen to several pieces of content and answer questions after each one. The questions typically ask about the main idea and supporting details. Some questions ask about a speaker's purpose or attitude. Answer the questions based on what is stated or implied by the speakers.

Listen to all of these passages by going to testprepbooks.com/toefl or by scanning the QR code below:

Note that on the actual test, you can take notes while you listen and use your notes to help you answer the questions. Your notes will not be scored.

For your convenience, the transcripts of all of the audio passages are provided after the answer explanations. However, on the actual test, no such transcripts will be provided.

Passage #1: Conversation

Questions 48–52: Complete the sentences below.

> Write NO MORE THAN TWO WORDS for each answer.
>
> 48. The colors of the bug on Tom's arm are ___ and _____.
>
> 49. Tom thinks if the bug bites him he is going to ___.
>
> 50. Suzie says that red and yellow _____ are poisonous.
>
> 51. Suzie's cousin got bit by a _____ once and he had to go to the hospital.
>
> 52. What is the emergency number Suzie mentioned? ___

Passage #2: Conversation

Questions 53–57: Complete the summary below using NO MORE THAN ONE WORD per space.

> There are lots of free parks in Houston. Memorial park has 53._____ and 54._____ trails. Discovery green offers ice skating in the winter and sessions of outdoor 55. _____ during the warmer months. At Herman Park , take a 56. _____ to go around the pond or play on the 57._____.

Passage #3: Lecture

Questions 58–63: Complete the sentences below.

> Write NO MORE THAN TWO WORDS for each answer.
>
> 58. This passage is about _____.

59. What discovery was made by William Dutcher? _____

60. Who was shot dead by a plume hunter? _____

61. What association works to protect the bird colonies? _____

62. One of the most important colonies is on _____ _____.

63. What type of bird was seen in eastern Massachusetts? _____

Passage #4: Conversation

For Questions 64–66, complete the summary provided below.

In a paper, the 64._____ is like a road map for readers. It should be one sentence long and placed in the 65._____. It's important to provide sufficient supporting 66._____.

a. Assignment

b. Body paragraph

c. Conclusion

d. Evidence

e. Introduction

f. Presentation

g. Summary

h. Thesis statement

i. Topic sentence

67. Which statement most accurately characterizes the teaching assistant's attitude toward the student?
  a. The teaching assistant is seeking to establish a strong rapport with the student.
  b. The teaching assistant is trying to remain impartial while still being helpful.
  c. The teaching assistant is behaving more like a friend than a supervisor.
  d. The teaching assistant is expressing frustration with the student.

68. After speaking with the teaching assistant, the student will likely select the _____ as their topic.
  a. Cold War
  b. Cuban Missile Crisis
  c. Korean War
  d. Iran-Contra Affair

Passage #5

For Question 69, complete the diagram below.

POLITICAL ASSOCIATIONS

Electoral Body

Political Party

69. Which of the following best completes the diagram?
    a. Legislature
    b. Partisan
    c. President
    d. Representative

70. Which constitutional amendment is the class currently discussing?
    a. First Amendment
    b. Second Amendment
    c. Third Amendment
    d. Fourth Amendment

71. Political associations require both assent and _____.
    a. Capital
    b. Deviation
    c. Engagement
    d. License

72. According to the professor, opinions appear in their most exact and explicit forms when widely held across the _____.
    a. Center of action
    b. Government
    c. Society
    d. Universe

For Questions 73–74, complete the notes below.

    <u>Notes on the Second Degree of Association</u>

- Lies in the power of 73._____.

- Involves establishing centers of action.

- The centers of action 74._____ influence and enthusiasm.

a. Amplify

b. Condense

c. Discord

d. Dissent

e. Meeting

f. Truth

g. Wither

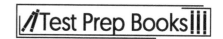

Passage #6

For Questions 75–77, complete the summary below.

The lecture mentions yellow fever epidemics in the United States, Cuba,
75._____, Spain, and the West Indies. One of the worst epidemics killed 10,000
people in Philadelphia over a three-month period. Several epidemics of yellow fever caused
intense 76._____. However, once scientists discovered that
77._____ were the vector of transmission, the epidemics became much less
severe.

a. Boston

b. Brazil

c. Fleas

d. Jamaica

e. Mosquitos

f. Organisms

g. Panic

h. Zeal

78. Which country was occupying Cuba during the spring of 1900?
   a. Netherlands
   b. Jamaica
   c. Spain
   d. United States

79. Which fact can be properly inferred from the data about yellow fever's average mortality rate?
   a. Yellow fever was less transmissible than the average disease.
   b. Yellow fever killed more people than more common diseases.
   c. Yellow fever spread fast because it didn't require a vector for transmission.
   d. Yellow fever declined dramatically due to its average mortality rate.

80. During the next class, students will make presentations on _____.
   a. Famous epidemiologists
   b. Insect-borne diseases
   c. Pioneers of modern medicine
   d. Tropical diseases

Passage #7

For Questions 81– 82, use the map to answer the questions below.

United Colonies (1775)

81. Which area was the Continental Army besieging when it was adopted by the Continental Congress?
    a. Boston
    b. Philadelphia
    c. Ticonderoga
    d. Virginia

82. Which direction did Thomas Jefferson travel in to reach the Continental Congress?
    a. North
    b. East
    c. South
    d. West

For Questions 83–84, match the correct job title to each individual.

83. John Hancock

84. George Washington

a. Chief diplomat to Great Britain

b. Commander-in-Chief of the Continental Army

c. Garrison commander at Ticonderoga

d. Governor of Massachusetts

e. Governor of Virginia

f. President of the Continental Congress

g. State legislature

85. Who did NOT attend the Continental Congress?
   a. Benjamin Harrison
   b. John Adams
   c. Rutherford B. Hayes
   d. Samuel Adams

86. Which fact can be properly inferred from the lecture?
   a. John Hancock was plotting to seize dictatorial control over the United Colonies.
   b. Fewer Southerners would've enlisted in the Continental Army if it was led by a New Englander.
   c. The replacement of Peyton Randolph with Thomas Jefferson was critical to the success of the Continental Congress.
   d. The Continental Congress valued garrisoning troops at Ticonderoga more than besieging Boston.

Speaking

87. Read the passage from the textbook and then answer the question.

Physical activity comprises a set of behaviors that appears to play a unique role in health and well-being due to a wide range of benefits. Physical activity is a strong protective factor from premature mortality, most of the leading chronic diseases, risk factors for chronic diseases, and common mental health problems, such as depression and anxiety and Alzheimer's disease. Possibly because physical activity requires integrated and coordinated functioning of the whole body, it appears to benefit many biological systems. Throughout human history, physical activity has been required for obtaining food, working, getting from one place to another (transportation), and performing household chores. Dance and sports were developed in virtually every culture for pleasure and cultural expression.

Mechanization started during the Industrial Revolution and replaced many types of labor, both at work and at home. Activity is no longer required to obtain food. Automobiles have largely replaced walking for transportation in recent decades. Dance and leisure have become mostly spectator activities, while the ever-increasing options for electronic entertainment have become the dominant form of leisure activity. These long-term trends have helped produce inactive lifestyles in most of the world's

populations, and the profoundly negative consequences for health have been extensively documented. Physical inactivity has become one of the biggest threats to worldwide health.

A recent analysis revealed that physical inactivity is responsible for over 5 million deaths annually worldwide, which is similar to the death toll of tobacco smoking. The World Health Organization estimates that physical inactivity is the fourth leading cause of death globally; lower than hypertension and tobacco smoking, similar to obesity, and higher than dietary patterns and hyperglycemia. Most of the inactivity-related deaths are in low- and middle-income countries, so this is not just a concern in high-income countries. Some consider physical inactivity to be a global pandemic. Physical inactivity also is the fourth underlying cause of death in the United States, with an estimated 200,000 deaths per year. This is about half the deaths attributable to tobacco smoking but twice the deaths attributable to alcohol use and low intake of fruits and vegetables.

Physical activity affects health and disease through many pathways and systems. The Report of the Physical Activity Guidelines Advisory Committee consisted of almost 700 pages of systematic literature reviews. They found strong evidence that physical activity reduces risk of premature mortality, coronary heart disease, high blood pressure, stroke, metabolic syndrome, type 2 diabetes, breast cancer, colon cancer, depression, and falling, and it is associated with improved body composition, bone health, functional health, and cognitive health. It is likely that physical activity provides a broader range of documented health benefits than any other factor (e.g., behavior, medication, or medical procedure).

The strength of the effects of physical activity on leading chronic diseases is notable. In a recent review, I-Min Lee and colleagues conservatively calculated that physical inactivity accounts for 5.8 percent of deaths from coronary heart disease, 7.2 percent from type 2 diabetes, 10.1 percent from breast cancer, and 10.4 percent from colon cancer. These calculations, while impressive, are almost certainly underestimated because they were adjusted for risk factors that are affected by physical activity such as obesity, lipids, and glucose. A U.S. study indicated that inactive adults would gain 1.3 to 3.7 years of life expectancy by becoming active at age 50. This result compares favorably to 2.3 to 2.5 years gained among smokers who quit at age 50 and 0.5 to 0.7 years gained by all obese people becoming normal weight at age 50. A recent study using national U.S. data estimated that 9–11 percent of aggregate U.S. health care expenditures were associated with physical inactivity.

Though many evidence-based interventions are available to increase physical activity, they have not been widely implemented; the prevalence of sufficient physical activity in the United States remains low, with few signs of improvement. Thus, there is a compelling need for increased attention to and investment in physical activity interventions.

The need for improving physical activity is urgent, given the burden of disease, low prevalence rate, and at (leisure time activities) or declining (active transportation) trends in both adults and adolescents. The tools for increasing physical activity are available in the form of numerous evidence-based and cost-effective interventions. Thus, the physical activity research field has had dramatic successes in building evidence in several critical areas, though many questions remain. The biggest problem in the physical activity field is the failure to act on the evidence and make serious and well-funded efforts to implement evidence-based interventions. Increased commitment to physical activity promotion is needed in the government, non-profit, and private sectors.

Source: Population Health: Behavioral and Social Science Insights, edited by Robert M. Kaplan et al. (2015), published by the Agency for Healthcare Research and Quality (National Institutes of Health), "Physical Activity: Numerous Benefits and Effective Interventions" by James F. Sallis and Jordan A. Carlson, found at https://www.ahrq.gov/sites/default/files/publications/files/population-health.pdf

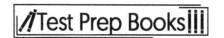

Question: Define physical activity, explain how technological changes impacted physical activity, and discuss the harm associated with physical inactivity.

- Reading Time: 50 seconds
- Response Time: 45 seconds

88. You are a member of the local school board. The board is voting to decide on a budget issue for the upcoming school year. There's only enough money to add artificial turf to the field or renovate the auditorium. Both improvements would benefit a lot of kids. The football, lacrosse, track, and soccer teams all play on the field. School plays, musicals, and concerts are all performed in the auditorium.

Question: How would you vote? Discuss how both projects would benefit the students, and why you chose one over the other. Compare some of the likely problems and consequences associated with leaving the auditorium and field as they currently are.

- Preparation Time: 20 seconds
- Response Time: 45 seconds

89. Imagine a close friend is visiting your favorite city in the world. Give your friend recommendations about what they should see and where they should eat. Explain your recommendations with specific examples.

- Preparation Time: 15 seconds
- Response Time: 45 seconds

90. Read the public service announcement and then answer the question that follows.

Vaccines are safe and effective. Because vaccines are given to millions of healthy people—including children—to prevent serious diseases, they're held to very high safety standards.

Every licensed and recommended vaccine goes through years of safety testing including:

- Testing and evaluation of the vaccine before it's licensed by the Food and Drug Administration (FDA) and recommended for use by the Centers for Disease Control and Prevention (CDC)

- Monitoring the vaccine's safety after it is recommended for infants, children, or adults

Before a vaccine is ever recommended for use, it's tested in labs. This process can take several years. FDA uses the information from these tests to decide whether to test the vaccine with people.

During a clinical trial, a vaccine is tested on people who volunteer to get vaccinated. Clinical trials start with 20 to 100 volunteers, but eventually include thousands of volunteers. These tests take several years and answer important questions like:

- Is the vaccine safe?
- What dose works best?
- How does the immune system react to it?

Throughout the process, FDA works closely with the company producing the vaccine to evaluate the vaccine's safety and effectiveness. All safety concerns must be addressed before FDA licenses a vaccine.

Once a vaccine is approved, it continues to be tested. The company that makes the vaccine tests batches to make sure the vaccine is:

- Potent, meaning it works like it's supposed to
- Pure, meaning certain ingredients used during production have been removed
- Sterile, meaning it doesn't have any outside germs

Once a vaccine is licensed and recommended for use, FDA, CDC, and other federal agencies continue to monitor its safety.

Source: "Vaccine Safety," published by the U.S. Department of Health and Human Services (2017), found at https://www.vaccines.gov/basics/safety/index.html.

Question: Summarize why vaccines are safe. Talk about each step in the process.

- Reading Time: 30 seconds
- Response Time: 45 seconds

First Essay

1. First read the article below. Then click the link below the article and watch the TED Talk video. Then review the prompt and write an essay synthesizing the two sources.

"Progress Cleaning the Air and Improving People's Health"

By the U.S. Environmental Protection Agency

[1] For more than forty-five years the Clean Air Act has cut pollution as the U.S. economy has grown. Experience with the Clean Air Act since 1970 has shown that protecting public health and building the economy can go hand in hand. Clean Air Act programs have lowered levels of six common pollutants—particles, ozone, lead, carbon monoxide, nitrogen dioxide and sulfur dioxide—as well as numerous toxic pollutants.

[2] From 1970 to 2015, aggregate national emissions of the six common pollutants alone dropped an average of 70 percent while gross domestic product grew by 246 percent. This progress reflects efforts by state, local and tribal governments; EPA; private sector companies; environmental groups and others.

[3] The emissions reductions have led to dramatic improvements in the quality of the air that we breathe. Between 1990 and 2015, national concentrations of air pollutants improved 85 percent for lead, 84 percent for carbon monoxide, 67 percent for sulfur dioxide (1-hour), 60 percent for nitrogen dioxide (annual), and 3 percent for ozone. Fine particle concentrations (24-hour) improved 37 percent and coarse particle concentrations (24-hour) improved 69 percent between 2000, when trends data begins for fine particles, and 2015.

[4] These air quality improvements have enabled many areas of the country to meet national air quality standards set to protect public health and the environment. For example, all of the 41 areas that had unhealthy levels of carbon monoxide in 1991 now have levels that meet the health-based national air quality standard. A key reason is that the motor vehicle fleet is much cleaner because of Clean Air Act emissions standards for new motor vehicles.

[5] Airborne lead pollution, a widespread health concern before EPA phased out lead in motor vehicle gasoline under Clean Air Act authority, now meets national air quality standards in most areas of the country.

[6] State emission control measures to implement the Act, as well as EPA's national emissions standards, have contributed to air quality improvements.

[7] Lower air pollution levels mean less damage to the health of ecosystems. Environmental effects of air pollution include damage to plants and long-term forest health, soil nutrient deterioration, accumulation of toxics in the food chain, damage to fish and other aquatic life in lakes and streams, and nitrogen enrichment of coastal estuaries causing oxygen depletion and resulting harm to fish and other aquatic animal populations.

[8] Reducing air pollution also improves crop and timber yields, a benefit worth an estimated $5.5 billion to those industries' welfare in 2010, according to the peer-reviewed March 2011 EPA study. Better visibility conditions in 2010 from improved air quality in selected national parks and metropolitan areas had an estimated value of $34 billion.

[9] EPA's peer-reviewed 2011 study found that clean air programs established by the 1990 CAA amendments are expected to yield direct benefits to the American people which vastly exceed compliance costs. The study's central benefits estimate of $2 trillion in 2020 exceeds costs by a factor of more than 30-to-1, and the high benefits estimate exceeds costs by 90 times. Even the low benefits estimate exceeds costs by about 3-to-1.

[10] In addition to direct benefits vastly exceeding direct costs, economy-wide modeling conducted for the study found that the economic welfare of American households is better with post-1990 clean air programs than without them. Economic welfare and economic growth rates are improved because cleaner air means fewer air-pollution-related illnesses, which in turn means less money spent on medical treatments and lower absenteeism among American workers. The study projects that the beneficial economic effects of these two improvements alone more than offset the expenditures for pollution control.

From https://www.epa.gov/clean-air-act-overview/progress-cleaning-air-and-improving-peoples-health

2. Listen to the following lecture:
https://www.ted.com/talks/jennifer_wilcox_a_new_way_to_remove_co2_from_the_atmosphere

3. Prompt: Summarize the points presented in the lecture and then use the information contained in the article to describe how the environment and the country could benefit from the technological breakthroughs discussed in the lecture.

Cite evidence found in the passage by placing the relevant paragraph number in parentheses at the end of the sentence.

Second Essay

Prepare an essay of about 300–600 words on the topic below.

Albert Einstein said that "Everybody is a genius. But if you judge a fish by its ability to climb a tree, it will live its whole life believing that it is stupid." What do you think Einstein meant by this statement? Support your answer with details and observations.

Answer Explanations #2

Reading

1. C: The author contrasts two different viewpoints, then builds a case showing preference for one over the other. Choice *A* is incorrect because the introduction does not contain an impartial definition, but rather, an opinion. Choice *B* is incorrect. There is no puzzling phenomenon given, as the author doesn't mention any peculiar cause or effect that is in question regarding poetry. Choice *D* does contain another's viewpoint at the beginning of the passage; however, to say that the author has no stake in this argument is incorrect; the author uses personal experiences to build their case.

2. B: Choice *B* accurately describes the author's argument in the text: that poetry is not irrelevant. While the author does praise, and even value, Buddy Wakefield as a poet, the author never heralds him as a genius. Eliminate Choice *A*, as it is an exaggeration. Not only is Choice *C* an exaggerated statement, but the author never mentions spoken word poetry in the text. Choice *D* is incorrect because this statement contradicts the writer's argument.

3. D: *Exiguously* means not occurring often, or occurring rarely, so Choice *D* would LEAST change the meaning of the sentence. Choice *A*, *indolently*, means unhurriedly, or slow, and does not fit the context of the sentence. Choice *B*, *inaudibly*, means quietly or silently. Choice *C*, *interminably*, means endlessly, or all the time, and is the opposite of the word *exiguously*.

4. D: A student's insistence that psychoanalysis is a subset of modern psychology is the most analogous option. The author of the passage tries to insist that performance poetry is a subset of modern poetry, and therefore, tries to prove that modern poetry is not "dying," but thriving on social media for the masses. Choice *A* is incorrect, as the author is not refusing any kind of validation. Choice *B* is incorrect; the author's insistence is that poetry will *not* lose popularity. Choice *C* mimics the topic but compares two different genres, while the author does no comparison in this passage.

5. B: The author's purpose is to disprove Gioia's article claiming that poetry is a dying art form that only survives in academic settings. In order to prove his argument, the author educates the reader about new developments in poetry (Choice *A*) and describes the brilliance of a specific modern poet (Choice *C*), but these serve as examples of a growing poetry trend that counters Gioia's argument. Choice *D* is incorrect because it contradicts the author's argument.

6. D: This question is difficult because the choices offer real reasons as to why the author includes the quote. However, the question specifically asks for the *main reason* for including the quote. The quote from a recently written poem shows that people are indeed writing, publishing, and performing poetry (Choice *B*). The quote also shows that people are still listening to poetry (Choice *C*). These things are true, and by their nature, serve to disprove Gioia's views (Choice *A*), which is the author's goal. However, Choice *D* is the most direct reason for including the quote, because the article analyzes the quote for its "complex themes" that "draws listeners and appreciation" right after it's given.

7. C: *Extraneous* most nearly means *superfluous*, or *trivial*. Choice *A*, *indispensable*, is incorrect because it means the opposite of *extraneous*. Choice *B*, *bewildering*, means *confusing* and is not relevant to the context of the sentence. Finally, Choice *D* is incorrect because although the prefix of the word is the same, *ex-*, the word *exuberant* means *elated* or *enthusiastic*, and is irrelevant to the context of the sentence.

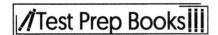

8. A: The author's purpose is to bring to light an alternative view on human perception by examining the role of technology in human understanding. This is a challenging question because the author's purpose is somewhat open-ended. The author concludes by stating that the questions regarding human perception and observation can be approached from many angles. Thus, the author does not seem to be attempting to prove one thing or another. Choice *B* is incorrect because we cannot know for certain whether the electron experiment is the latest discovery in astroparticle physics because no date is given. Choice *C* is a broad generalization that does not reflect accurately on the writer's views. While the author does appear to reflect on opposing views of human understanding (Choice *D*), the best answer is Choice *A*.

9. C: It presents a problem, explains the details of that problem, and then ends with more inquiry. The beginning of this paragraph literally "presents a conundrum," explains the problem of partial understanding, and then ends with more questions, or inquiry. There is no solution offered in this paragraph, making Choices *A* and *B* incorrect. Choice *D* is incorrect because the paragraph does not begin with a definition.

10. D: Looking back in the text, the author describes that classical philosophy holds that understanding can be reached by careful observation. This will not work if they are overly invested or biased in their pursuit. Choices *A*, *B*, and *C* are in no way related and are completely unnecessary. A specific theory is not necessary to understanding, according to classical philosophy mentioned by the author.

11. B: The electrons passed through both holes and then onto the plate. Choices *A* and *C* are incorrect because such movement is not mentioned at all in the text. In the passage the author says that electrons that were physically observed appeared to pass through one hole or another. Remember, the electrons that were observed doing this were described as acting like particles. Therefore, Choice *D* is incorrect. Recall that the plate actually recorded electrons passing through both holes simultaneously and hitting the plate. This behavior, the electron activity that wasn't seen by humans, was characteristic of waves. Thus, Choice *B* is the correct answer.

12. C: The author mentions "gravity" to demonstrate an example of natural phenomena humans discovered and understand without the use of tools or machines. Choice *A* mirrors the language in the beginning of the paragraph but is incorrect in its intent. Choice *B* is incorrect; the paragraph mentions nothing of "not knowing the true nature of gravity." Choice *D* and *E* is incorrect as well. There is no mention of an "alternative solution" in this paragraph.

13. A: The important thing to keep in mind is that we must choose a scenario that best parallels, or is most similar to, the discovery of the experiment mentioned in the passage. The important aspects of the experiment can be summed up like so: humans directly observed one behavior of electrons and then through analyzing a tool (the plate that recorded electron hits), discovered that there was another electron behavior that could not be physically seen by human eyes. This summary best parallels the scenario in Choice *A*. Like Feynman, the colorblind person can observe one aspect of the world but through the special goggles (a tool), he is able to see a natural phenomenon that he could not physically see on his own. While Choice *D* is compelling, the x-ray helps humans see the broken bone, but it does not necessarily reveal that the bone is broken in the first place. The other choices do not parallel the scenario in question. Therefore, Choice *A* is the best choice.

14. B: The author would not agree that technology renders human observation irrelevant. Choice *A* is incorrect because much of the passage discusses how technology helps humans observe what cannot be seen with the naked eye; therefore, the author would agree with this statement. This line of reasoning is

also why the author would agree with Choice *D*, making it incorrect as well. As indicated in the second paragraph, the author seems to think that humans create inventions and tools with the goal of studying phenomena more precisely. This indicates increased understanding as people recognize limitations and develop items to help bypass the limitations and learn. Therefore, Choice *C* is incorrect as well. Again, the author doesn't attempt to disprove or dismiss classical philosophy.

15. D: The author explains that Boethianism is a Medieval theological philosophy that attributes sin to temporary pleasure and righteousness with virtue and God's providence. Besides Choice *D*, the choices listed are all physical things. While these could still be divine rewards, Boethianism holds that the true reward for being virtuous is in God's favor. It is also stressed in the article that physical pleasures cannot be taken into the afterlife. Therefore, the best choice is *D*, God's favor.

16. C: *The Canterbury Tales* presents a manuscript written in the medieval period that can help illustrate Boethianism through stories and show how people of the time might have responded to the idea. Choices *A* and *B* are generalized statements, and we have no evidence to support Choice *B*. Choice *D* is very compelling, but it looks at Boethianism in a way that the author does not. The author does not mention "different levels of Boethianism" when discussing the tales, only that the concept appears differently in different tales. Boethianism also doesn't focus on enlightenment.

17. D: The author is referring to the principle that a desire for material goods leads to moral malfeasance punishable by a higher being. Choice *A* is incorrect; while the text does mention thieves ravaging others' possessions, it is only meant as an example and not as the principle itself. Choice *B* is incorrect for the same reason as *A*. Choice *C* is mentioned in the text and is part of the example that proves the principle, and also not the principle itself.

18. C: The word *avarice* most nearly means *parsimoniousness*, or an unwillingness to spend money. Choice *A* means *evil* or *mischief* and does not relate to the context of the sentence. Choice *B* is also incorrect, because *pithiness* means *shortness* or *conciseness*. Choice *D* is close because *precariousness* means dangerous or instability, which goes well with the context. However, we are told of the summoner's specific characteristic of greed, which makes Choice *C* the best answer.

19. D: Desire for pleasure can lead toward sin. Boethianism acknowledges desire as something that leads out of holiness, so Choice *A* is incorrect. Choice *B* is incorrect because in the passage, Boethianism is depicted as being wary of desire and anything that binds people to the physical world. Choice *C* can be eliminated because the author never says that desire indicates demonic possession.

20. A: The purpose is to inform the reader about what assault is and how it is committed. Choice *B* is incorrect because the passage does not state that assault is a lesser form of lethal force, only that an assault can use lethal force, or alternatively, lethal force can be utilized to counter a dangerous assault. Choice *C* is incorrect because the passage is informative and does not have a set agenda. Finally, Choice *D* is incorrect because although the author uses an example in order to explain assault, it is not indicated that this is the author's personal account.

21. C: If the man being attacked in an alley by another man with a knife used self-defense by lethal force, it would not be considered illegal. The presence of a deadly weapon indicates mal-intent and because the individual is isolated in an alley, lethal force in self-defense may be the only way to preserve his life. Choices *A* and *B* can be ruled out because in these situations, no one is in danger of immediate death or bodily harm by someone else. Choice *D* is an assault and does exhibit intent to harm, but this situation isn't severe enough to merit lethal force; there is no intent to kill.

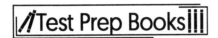

22. B: As discussed in the second passage, there are several forms of assault, like assault with a deadly weapon, verbal assault, or threatening posture or language. Choice *A* is incorrect because the author does mention what the charges are on assaults; therefore, we cannot assume that they are more or less than unnecessary use of force charges. Choice *C* is incorrect because anyone is capable of assault; the author does not state that one group of people cannot commit assault. Choice *D* is incorrect because assault is never justified. Self-defense resulting in lethal force can be justified.

23. D: The use of lethal force is not evaluated on the intent of the user, but rather on the severity of the primary attack that warranted self-defense. This statement most undermines the last part of the passage because it directly contradicts how the law evaluates the use of lethal force. Choices *A* and *B* are stated in the paragraph, so they do not undermine the explanation from the author. Choice *C* does not necessarily undermine the passage, but it does not support the passage either. It is more of an opinion that does not offer strength or weakness to the explanation.

24. C: An assault with deadly intent can lead to an individual using lethal force to preserve their well-being. Choice *C* is correct because it clearly establishes what both assault and lethal force are and gives the specific way in which the two concepts meet. Choice *A* is incorrect because lethal force doesn't necessarily result in assault. This is also why Choice *B* is incorrect. Not all assaults would necessarily be life-threatening to the point where lethal force is needed for self-defense. Choice *D* is compelling but ultimately too vague; the statement touches on aspects of the two ideas but fails to present the concrete way in which the two are connected to each other.

25. A: Both passages open by defining a legal concept and then continue to describe situations in order to further explain the concept. Choice *D* is incorrect because while the passages utilize examples to help explain the concepts discussed, the author doesn't indicate that they are specific court cases. It's also clear that the passages don't open with examples, but instead, they begin by defining the terms addressed in each passage. This eliminates Choice *B,* and ultimately reveals Choice *A* to be the correct answer. Choice *A* accurately outlines the way both passages are structured. Because the passages follow a nearly identical structure, the Choice *C* can easily be ruled out.

26. C: Intent is very important for determining both lethal force and assault; intent is examined in both parties and helps determine the severity of the issue. Choices *A* and *B* are incorrect because it is clear in both passages that intent is a prevailing theme in both lethal force and assault. Choice *D* is compelling, but if a person uses lethal force to defend himself or herself, the intent of the defender is also examined in order to help determine if there was excessive force used. Choice *C* is correct because it states that intent is important for determining both lethal force and assault, and that intent is used to gauge the severity of the issues. Remember, just as lethal force can escalate to excessive use of force, there are different kinds of assault. Intent dictates several different forms of assault.

27. B: The example is used to demonstrate a single example of two different types of assault, then adding in a third type of assault to the example's conclusion. The example mainly provides an instance of "threatening body language" and "provocative language" with the homeowner gesturing threats to his neighbor. It ends the example by adding a third type of assault: physical strikes. This example is used to show the variant nature of assaults. Choice *A* is incorrect because it doesn't mention the "physical strike" assault at the end and is not specific enough. Choice *C* is incorrect because the example does not say anything about the definition of lethal force or how it might be altered. Choice *D* is incorrect, as the example mentions nothing about cause and effect.

28. C: In lines 6 and 7, it is stated that avarice can prevent a man from being necessitously poor, but too timorous, or fearful, to achieve real wealth. According to the passage, avarice does tend to make a person very wealthy. The passage states that oppression, not avarice, is the consequence of wealth. The passage does not state that avarice drives a person's desire to be wealthy.

29. D: Paine believes that the distinction that is beyond a natural or religious reason is between king and subjects. Choice *A* is incorrect because he states that the distinction between good and bad is made in heaven. Choice *B* is incorrect because he states that the distinction between male and female is natural. Choice *C* is incorrect because he does not mention anything about the distinction between humans and animals.

30. A: The passage states that the Heathens were the first to introduce government by kings into the world. Choice *B* is incorrect because the quiet lives of patriarchs came before the Heathens introduced this type of government and Paine puts it in opposition to government by kings. Choice *C* is incorrect because it was Christians, not Heathens, who paid divine honors to living kings. Heathens honored deceased kings. Choice *D* is incorrect because, while equal rights of nature are mentioned in the paragraph, they are not mentioned in relation to the Heathens.

31. B: Paine asserts that a monarchy is against the equal rights of nature and cites several parts of scripture that also denounce it. He doesn't say it is against the laws of nature. Because he uses scripture to further his argument, it is not despite scripture that he denounces the monarchy. Paine addresses the law by saying the courts also do not support a monarchical government.

32. A: To be *idolatrous* is to worship someone or something other than God, in this case, kings. Choice *B* is incorrect because it is not defined as being deceitful. Choice *C* is incorrect because, while idolatry is considered a sin, it is an example of a sin, not a synonym for it. Choice *D* is incorrect because, while idolatry may have been considered illegal in some cultures, it is not a definition for the term.

33. A: The essential meaning of the passage is that the Almighty, God, disapproves of this type of government. Choice *B* is incorrect because, while heaven is mentioned, it is done so to suggest that the monarchical government is irreverent, not that heaven isn't promised. Choice *C* is incorrect because God's disapproval is mentioned, not his punishment. Choice *D* is incorrect because the passage refers to the Jewish monarchy, which required both belief in God and kings, and the tendency of monarchies to gloss over the anti-monarchical passages of scripture to support their form of government.

34. B: Mr. Button's wife is about to have a baby. The passage begins by giving the reader information about traditional birthing situations. Then, we are told that Mr. and Mrs. Button decide to go against tradition to have their baby in a hospital. The next few passages are dedicated to letting the reader know how Mr. Button dresses and goes to the hospital to welcome his new baby. There is a doctor in this excerpt, as Choice *C* indicates, and Mr. Button does put on clothes, as Choice *D* indicates. However, Mr. Button is not going to the doctor's office nor is he about to go shopping for new clothes.

35. A: The tone of the above passage is nervous and excited. We are told in the fourth paragraph that Mr. Button "arose nervously." We also see him running without caution to the doctor to find out about his wife and baby—this indicates his excitement. We also see him stuttering in a nervous yet excited fashion as he asks the doctor if it's a boy or girl. Though the doctor may seem a bit abrupt at the end, indicating a bit of anger or shame, neither of these choices is the overwhelming tone of the entire passage.

36. C: Dedicated. Mr. Button is dedicated to the task before him. Choice *A*, numbed, Choice *B*, chained, and Choice *D*, moved, all could grammatically fit in the sentence. However, they are not synonyms with *consecrated* like Choice *C* is.

37. D: Giving readers a visual picture of what the doctor is doing. The author describes a visual image—the doctor rubbing his hands together—first and foremost. The author may be trying to make a comment about the profession; however, the author does not "explain the detail of the doctor's profession" as Choice *B* suggests.

38. D: To introduce the setting of the story and its characters. We know we are being introduced to the setting because we are given the year in the very first paragraph along with the season: "one day in the summer of 1860." This is a classic structure of an introduction of the setting. We are also getting a long explanation of Mr. Button, what his work is, who is related to him, and what his life is like in the third paragraph.

39. B: "Talk sense!" is an example of an imperative sentence. An imperative sentence gives a command. The doctor is commanding Mr. Button to talk sense. Choice *A* is an example of an exclamatory sentence, which expresses excitement. Choice *C* is an example of an interrogative sentence—these types of sentences ask questions. Choice *D* is an example of a declarative sentence. This means that the character is simply making a statement.

40. C: The point of view is told in third person omniscient. We know this because the story starts out with us knowing something that the character does not know: that her husband has died. Mrs. Mallard eventually comes to know this, but we as readers know this information before it is broken to her. In third person limited, Choice *D*, we would only see and know what Mrs. Mallard herself knew, and we would find out the news of her husband's death when she found out the news, not before.

41. A: The way Mrs. Mallard reacted to her husband's death. The irony in this story is called situational irony, which means the situation that takes place is different than what the audience anticipated. At the beginning of the story, we see Mrs. Mallard react with a burst of grief to her husband's death. However, once she's alone, she begins to contemplate her future and says the word "free" over and over. This is quite a different reaction from Mrs. Mallard than what readers expected from the first of the story.

42. B: The word "elusive" most closely means "indefinable." Horrible, Choice *A*, doesn't quite fit with the tone of the word "subtle" that comes before it. Choice *C*, "quiet," is more closely related to the word "subtle." Choice *D*, "joyful," also doesn't quite fit the context here. "Indefinable" is the best option.

43. D: Mrs. Mallard, a newly widowed woman, finds unexpected relief in her husband's death. A summary is a brief explanation of the main point of a story. The story mostly focuses on Mrs. Mallard and her reaction to her husband's death, especially in the room when she's alone and contemplating the present and future. Choice *B* is briefly mentioned in the story; however it is not the main focus of the story.

44. D: The interesting thing about this story is that feelings that are confused, joyful, and depressive all play a unique and almost equal part of this story. There is no one right answer here, because the author seems to display all of these emotions through the character of Mrs. Mallard. She displays feelings of depressiveness by her grief at the beginning; then when she receives feelings of joy, she feels moments of confusion. We as readers cannot help but go through these feelings with the character. Thus, the author creates a tone of depression, joy, and confusion, all in one story.

45. C: The word "tumultuously" most nearly means "violently." Even if you don't know the word "tumultuously," look at the surrounding context to figure it out. The next few sentences we see Mrs. Mallard striving to "beat back" the "thing that was approaching to possess her." We see a fearful and almost violent reaction to the emotion that she's having. Thus, her chest would rise and fall turbulently, or violently.

46. D: To define and describe instances of spinoff technology. This is an example of a purpose question—*why* did the author write this? The article contains facts, definitions, and other objective information without telling a story or arguing an opinion. In this case, the purpose of the article is to inform the reader. Choices *A* and *B* are incorrect because they argue for an opinion or present a position. Choice *C* is incorrect because the focus of the article is spinoff technology, not the history of space technology.

47. B: A general opinion followed by supporting evidence. This organization question asks readers to analyze the structure of the essay. The topic of the essay is about spinoff technology, and the thesis statement at the end of the first paragraph offers the opinion, "Spinoff technology proves that it is worthwhile to invest in science research because it could enrich people's lives in unexpected ways." The next two paragraphs provide evidence to support this opinion. Choice *A* is the second-best option because the first paragraph gives a general definition of spinoff technology, while the following two paragraphs offer more detailed examples to help illustrate this idea. However, it is not the best answer because the main idea of the essay is that spinoff technology enriches people's lives in unexpected ways. Choice *C* is incorrect because the essay does not provide details of any specific moment in history. Choice *D* is incorrect because the essay does not discuss a popular misconception.

Listening

48. red, black

49. die

50. snakes

51. spider

52. 9-1-1

53. hiking

54. biking

55. yoga

56. paddleboat

57. playground

58. birds, or protecting birds

59. colonies

60. warden

61. Audubon, or Audubon Association

62. Bird Island

63. egret

64. H: The teaching assistant compares thesis statements to roadmaps at the beginning of the conversation. According to the teaching assistant, a thesis statements is like a roadmap because it describes how the writer will support their argument. Thus, Choice *H* is the correct answer. Introduction makes logical sense, but it doesn't fit grammatically. In addition, the conversation is much more focused on thesis statements than on introductions generally. Therefore, Choice *E* is incorrect. Topic sentences function as roadmaps for paragraphs; however, this topic isn't discussed, so Choice *I* is incorrect.

65. E: The teaching assistant mentions that thesis statements are placed in the introduction and often serve as the final sentence. Thus, Choice *E* is the correct answer. The assignment centers on thesis statements, but this part of the summary is about where the thesis statement goes in the essay. Therefore, Choice *A* is incorrect. Body paragraphs exist to support the thesis statement, so Choice *B* is incorrect. Conclusions and summaries are typically based on the thesis statement, but the thesis statement must first be placed in the introduction. Therefore, Choice *C* and Choice *G* are both incorrect.

66. D: According to the teaching assistant, the thesis statement must be supported by sufficient evidence. Thus, Choice *D* is the correct answer. Body paragraphs support thesis statements, but they do so by incorporating evidence. Furthermore, "supporting body paragraph" isn't as clean a grammatical fit as "supporting evidence." Normally, the adjective "sufficient" without an article like "a" or "an" would be followed by a plural noun phrase like "body *paragraphs*," or an uncountable noun like "evidence." So Choice *B* is incorrect. Choice *F* is incorrect because the presentation is about defending a thesis statement with evidence. So evidence is more directly related to this sentence's meaning than presentation.

67. A: Establishing rapport means to build a connection or relationship. The teaching assistant seeks to establish a rapport in two distinct ways. First, the teaching assistant tells the student about the professor's opinion of audiovisual components. Second, the teaching assistant asks the student about their other classes and offers to write a letter of recommendation. Thus, Choice *A* is the correct answer. The teaching assistant is not being strictly impartial. For example, telling the student about the professor's preferences for presentations provides an advantage over other students. So Choice *B* is incorrect. The teaching assistant is certainly being friendly, but they're still acting in a supervisory capacity. Therefore, Choice *C* is incorrect. Choice *D* is incorrect because the teaching assistant isn't frustrated with the student.

68. D: After the teaching assistant says the Cold War might be too broad, the student narrows down their topic to focus on the Iran-Contra Affair. Thus, Choice *D* is the correct answer. The Cold War is the student's initial topic, but the teaching assistant advises the student to focus on an individual event. So Choice *A* is incorrect. The Cuban Missile Crisis occurred during the Cold War, but it doesn't come up during the conversation. Therefore, Choice *B* is incorrect. Likewise, the Korean War isn't discussed during the conversation, so Choice *C* is incorrect.

69. D: The diagram's middle level is positioned between an electoral body and a political party. Additionally, the middle level is represented by one individual. A representative would be an individual chosen by a political party to serve in an electoral body. Thus, Choice *D* is the correct answer. A legislature is a type of electoral body, so Choice *A* is incorrect. Partisans are members of a political party,

and although a representative is often a partisan, representative is more directly on point. Therefore, Choice *B* is incorrect. A president is typically the head of an executive electoral body; therefore, Choice *C* is incorrect.

70. A: At the beginning of the lecture, the professor explains they're still working on their Bill of Rights unit, and they specifically discuss the right of association, which is provided for in the First Amendment. Thus, Choice *A* is the correct answer. None of the other answer choices are related to the right of association. The Second Amendment is the right to bear arms, so Choice *B* is incorrect. The Third Amendment prohibits soldiers from quartering in private homes except during wartime as prescribed by law, so Choice *C* is incorrect. The Fourth Amendment defines warrant requirements and prohibits unreasonable searches and seizures, so Choice *D* is incorrect.

71. C: Near the beginning of the lecture, the professor states that associations require both public assent and engagement to promote their doctrine. Throughout the rest of the lecture, the professor discusses the importance of engagement, especially in the centers of action. Thus, Choice *C* is the correct answer. Capital means financial assets, and while political associations would benefit from having capital available, the lecture doesn't address the financing of associations. Therefore, Choice *A* is incorrect. Choice *B* is incorrect because a deviation is the rejection of, or failure to reach, an agreed upon standard or course of action, which is antithetical to most associations. Some associations might issue licenses to provide authority or permission, but the professor doesn't state that licenses are a requirement for associations.

72. C: At the beginning of the lecture, the professor describes how associations gain exact and explicit form when they have assent and engagement across society. Thus, Choice *C* is the correct answer. Centers of action and governments both involve associations, and those associations often have exact and explicit forms. However, the professor directly ties exact and explicit forms of associations to society, and a society is broader than either a center of action or government. Therefore, Choice *A* and Choice *B* are both incorrect. Although a universe is broader than a society, the professor never addresses political associations formed across a universe. So Choice *D* is incorrect.

73. E: The first bullet point is best completed with a noun. The word *meeting* fits grammatically, and the professor defines the power of meeting as the second degree in the right of association. Thus, Choice *E* is the correct answer. *Discord* means conflict or dissonance, which would undermine associations. Therefore, Choice *C* is incorrect. Likewise, *dissent* means disagreement, so Choice *D* is incorrect. While the power of truth could benefit associations, the professor doesn't refer to truth during the lecture. Therefore, Choice *F* is incorrect. All of the other answer choices are verbs, so they are all also incorrect.

74. A: The correct answer must be a verb to properly complete the sentence. During the middle of the lecture, the professor discusses how centers of action amplify influence and activity by creating more opportunities for meetings, advanced means of execution, and enthusiastic opinions. Thus, Choice *A* is the correct answer. *Condense* means to make something more concentrated. While centers of actions could condense opinions, *amplify* more accurately reflects the relationship between centers of action, influence, and enthusiasm. Therefore, Choice *B* is incorrect. *Dissent* as a verb means to disagree with something, so Choice *D* is incorrect. Choice *G* is incorrect because *wither* means to decay or decline. The remaining answer choices are nouns, so they are also incorrect.

75. D: The professor describes a number of different epidemics during the lecture, including epidemics in the United States, Cuba, Spain, the West Indies, and Jamaica. According to the professor, the epidemic in Jamaica had an average mortality rate between 101 per 1,000 and 178 per 1,000. Thus,

Choice *D* is the correct answer. The professor doesn't mention Boston or Brazil. Therefore, Choice *A* and Choice *B* are both incorrect. None of the other answer choices are locations, so they cannot properly complete the sentence.

76. G: The correct answer must be a noun meaning something that can be described as intense. During the middle of the lecture, the professor describes how the epidemic in the United States caused a widespread panic and economic paralysis due to the appalling mortality rate. Thus, Choice *G* is the correct answer. *Zeal* fits grammatically, but it means enthusiastic passion, and that is not how the professor describes epidemics. Therefore, Choice *H* is incorrect. None of the other answer choices fit with the word *intense*, so they must be incorrect.

77. E: The professor opens the lecture discussing the importance of identifying vectors of transmission, and at the end of the lecture they explain how scientists made a major breakthrough when they discovered that mosquitoes were yellow fever's vector of transmission. Thus, Choice *E* is the correct answer. Fleas can be vectors of transmission, but the professor never associates fleas with yellow fever. So Choice *C* is incorrect. Most vectors of transmission are organisms, and mosquitos are organisms. However, the professor doesn't discuss the broad classification of organisms, so mosquito is a much more specific and accurate answer. Therefore, Choice *F* is incorrect. None of the other answers logically fit as vectors, so they must be incorrect.

78. D: At the end of the lecture, the professor states that the United States occupied Cuba during the spring of 1900, which is why Surgeon General Sternberg led the investigations into yellow fever. Thus, Choice *D* is the correct answer. The professor does not refer to Dutch colonies, so Choice *A* is incorrect. Similarly, the professor discusses epidemics in Jamaica, which aren't related to an occupation of Cuba. Spain occupied Cuba for centuries prior to the Spanish-American War (1898); however, this historical fact isn't mentioned in the passage, and the question specifically asks about the spring of 1900. Therefore, Choice *C* is incorrect.

79. B: The professor describes yellow fever's mortality rate as appalling and so devastating that it triggered widespread pandemics. Therefore, it can be inferred that yellow fever's average mortality rate is higher than common diseases. Thus, Choice *B* is the correct answer. The lecture is generally about how yellow fever was transmitted rapidly prior to the discovery of the mosquito theory, so Choice *A* is incorrect. The professor identifies mosquitoes as the vector for transmission; therefore, Choice *C* is incorrect. At the end of the lecture, the professor states that yellow fever dramatically declined after mosquitoes were identified as a vector of transmission, so the decline wasn't related to the disease's average mortality rate. Therefore, Choice *D* is incorrect.

80. A: At the very end of the lecture, the professor reminds student that their presentations on famous epidemiologists will be held during the next class. Thus, Choice *A* is the correct answer. The lecture is about an insect-borne disease, but the presentations are not about that. Therefore, Choice *B* is incorrect. Famous epidemiologists are likely pioneers of modern medicine, but not all pioneers of modern medicine are epidemiologists. So Choice *C* is incorrect. Lastly, yellow fever spreads in tropical areas, but the professor doesn't ask the students to make presentations on tropical diseases. Therefore, Choice *D* is incorrect.

81. A: During the middle of the lecture, the professor describes how the Congress adopted the army of New England as the Continental Army. At that time, the army was besieging Boston. Thus, Choice *A* is the correct answer. Philadelphia is where the Continental Congress met, not the site of a siege, so Choice *B* is incorrect. The professor mentions the Continental Congress's decision to garrison troops at

Ticonderoga, but they adopted the army besieging Boston. Therefore, Choice *C* is incorrect. Choice *D* is incorrect because Virginia is only mentioned in the discussion of Thomas Jefferson replacing Peyton Randolph as Virginia's representative at the Continental Congress.

82. A: According to the lecture, Thomas Jefferson traveled from Virginia to Philadelphia to take Peyton Randolph's seat at the Continental Congress. So, based on the map and compass, Thomas Jefferson must have traveled north from Virginia to reach Philadelphia. Thus, Choice *A* is the correct answer. If Jefferson traveled east, he would've reached the Atlantic coastline, so Choice *B* is incorrect. If Jefferson traveled south, he would've been traveling to North Carolina, so Choice *C* is incorrect. If Jefferson raveled west, he would've arrived in territory claimed by American Indian tribes, so Choice *D* is incorrect.

83. F: Following Peyton Randolph's departure from Philadelphia, the professor describes how the Continental Congress quickly chose John Hancock as Randolph's successor to the office of President of the Continental Congress. Thus, Choice *F* is the correct answer. The professor mentions that Hancock hoped to also be named the Commander-in-Chief of the Continental Army, but the Congress wanted a Southerner for unity purposes. So Choice *B* is incorrect. The professor briefly refers to the garrisoning of troops at Ticonderoga, but Hancock wasn't the garrison commander. Therefore, Choice *C* is incorrect. The professor never discusses the chief diplomat to Great Britain, governor of Massachusetts, governor of Virginia, or state legislatures. Therefore, Choice *A*, Choice *D*, Choice *E*, and Choice *G* are all incorrect.

84. B: At the end of the lecture, the professor recounts the Continental Congress's debate over who should command the Continental Army. Ultimately, the Congress selected George Washington to serve as the commander-in-chief of the Continental Army in order to better engage the Southern states in the struggle for independence. Thus, Choice *B* is the correct answer. None of the other answer choices are specifically mentioned in the lecture, so they cannot be correct.

85. C: In the first sentence, the professor lists the Adamses as delegates to the Continental Congress, and the lecture later specifically names John Adams and Samuel Adams. Therefore, Choice *B* and Choice *D* are both incorrect. Benjamin Harrison is mentioned in the middle of the lecture during the description of John Hancock becoming the President of the Continental Congress. So Choice *A* is incorrect. Rutherford B. Hayes was the nineteenth president of the United States (1877–1881), and the professor never refers him. Thus, Choice *C* is the correct answer.

86. B: The professor argues that naming a Southerner as the Commander-in-Chief of the Continental Army was a wise decision because it increased the Southern colonies' engagement. So it can be inferred that more Southerners enlisted to serve under George Washington than would have if a New Englander had assumed command. Thus, Choice *B* is the correct answer. The professor states that John Hancock was disappointed, but the professor doesn't accuse Hancock of trying to seize dictatorial control. Therefore, Choice *A* is incorrect. The professor describes how Thomas Jefferson replaced Peyton Randolph, but the professor never discusses Jefferson's role or value in the Continental Congress. So Choice *C* is incorrect. Similarly, the professor doesn't compare the value of the armies at Ticonderoga and Boston. In addition, the Continental Congress adopted the army besieging Boston as the Continental Army, so there's more evidence supporting the inference that the Congress valued the army of New England more. Therefore, Choice *D* is incorrect.

Listening Transcripts

Passage #1

(Narrator) Listen to the conversation and then answer the questions.

(Tom) ACK!

(Suzie) What's wrong?

(Tom) There's a bug on my arm!

(Suzie) Bug? What kind of bug?

(Tom) Don't touch it! If you make it mad, it might bite me. It's red and black. Don't the colors red and black mean an animal is poisonous? If it bites me, I'm going to die!

(Suzie) Don't be silly, Tom. You're thinking of snakes. Red and yellow snakes are poisonous. I don't think this bug is big enough to hurt you.

(Tom) I think you're wrong. I'm pretty sure the color red on its back means it's poisonous!

(Suzie) You're right! I think the spots are a bad sign. My cousin, Rob, got bitten by a spider once. It had spots on its back. His leg swelled up as big as a volleyball. My Aunt Becky had to take him to the hospital. The doctor had to use a needle to pop his leg like a balloon before it exploded. Don't cry, Tom. I'll go get Mrs. Henderson and tell her to call 9-1-1. They will send someone to get this bug. And they will send an ambulance in case it bites you.

(Tom) Don't get too close, Mrs. Henderson! If you make it mad, it might bite me!

(Mrs. Henderson) Why, Tom! Don't be afraid. I don't see any hospitals in your future. This innocuous little cutie is a ladybug!

Passage #2

(Narrator) Listen to the conversation and then answer the questions.

(Tourist) Hello, I was wondering if you could give me some information about Houston, Texas?

(Travel Agent) Sure! Houston, Texas, is a city with many exciting things to do and places to visit. Its museums and monuments provide a great historical background of the area. There are several amusement parks with plenty of games and rides to provide a day of fun for people of all ages. In addition, the city is home to many beautiful parks that host events year-round.

(Tourist) Can you tell me more about the museums and if they are worth checking out?

(Travel Agent) Houston's museums are worth checking out. The Natural Museum of Science showcases a variety of dinosaur skeletons, gemstones, and hand-carved artifacts. The Health Museum houses life-size animated organs to teach visitors about healthy lifestyles. Participants can also test their strength and play learning games at the museum. The Children's Museum is an interactive museum for children.

(Tourist) Can you tell me more about the entertainment side of the area?

(Travel Agent) If museums aren't exciting enough, visit one of Houston's nearby amusement parks. Spend the day at the Kemah Boardwalk riding a variety of rollercoasters, or ride the Bullet, a high-speed boat that makes a big splash. Pleasure Pier is located 45 miles away on Galveston Island. Carnival rides, games, and restaurants extend out over the water for a thrilling time. Typhoon Texas is an amusement park that offers only water rides. Splash in the wave pool, whoosh down slides, or relax by the pool.

(Tourist) Great, thanks! I'm working within a budget, so can you tell me more about activities that might be free of cost?

(Travel Agent) If cost is a concern, there are plenty of free parks to visit during a trip to Houston. Memorial Park is known for its miles of hiking and biking trails. Discovery Green is a park that offers seasonal citywide events. During the warmer months, enjoy a session of outdoor yoga. In the winter, a temporary ice-skating rink is built for all to enjoy. Herman Park is located in the Houston Medical Center. Take a paddleboat in the pond or hang around at the playground. You can also ride a miniature train around the park and enjoy the beautiful views.

(Tourist) Thanks so much for the information!

Passage #3

(Narrator) Listen to the lecture and then answer the questions.

(Professor and activist) Hello and welcome. Let's go into the history of the Audubon Association, specifically at a time when egrets were considered endangered. In 1910, I think there were not many bird-lovers in the United States who believed it possible to prevent the total extinction of both egrets from our fauna. All the known rookeries accessible to plume-hunters had been totally destroyed. In 1911, the secret discovery of several small, hidden colonies prompted William Dutcher, President of the National Association of Audubon Societies, and Mr. T. Gilbert Pearson, Secretary, to attempt the protection of those colonies. With a fund contributed for the purpose, wardens were hired and duly commissioned. As previously stated, one of those wardens was shot dead in cold blood by a plume hunter. The task of guarding swamp rookeries from the attacks of money-hungry desperadoes to whom the accursed plumes were worth their weight in gold, was a very chancy proceeding. There was even one warden in Florida who said that "before they get my rookery they will first have to get me."

The protective work of the Audubon Association was successful. In 1913 there were twenty colonies, which contain all told, about 5,000 egrets and about 120,000 herons and ibises which are guarded by the Audubon wardens. One of the most important was on Bird Island, a mile out in Orange Lake, central Florida, and it was ably defended by Oscar E. Baynard. In 1913, the plume hunters who did not dare to raid the guarded rookeries were trying to study out the lines of flight of the birds, to and from their feeding-grounds, and shoot them in transit. Their motto was—"Anything to beat the law, and get the plumes." It is there that the state of Florida should have taken part in the war.

The success of this campaign is attested by the fact that in 1912 a number of egrets were seen in eastern Massachusetts—for the first time in many years.

Excerpt is an adaptation from Our Vanishing Wildlife *by William T. Hornaday, 1913*

<u>Passage #4</u>

(Narrator) Listen to a conversation between a student and teaching assistant, and then answer the questions that follow.

(Student) Thank you for meeting with me. I have a couple of questions about the upcoming assignment.

(Teaching Assistant) Sure thing. Are you talking about the essay or presentation?

(Student) Both, I think; that's where I'm confused. Is the presentation supposed to be a summary of the essay? Or is the presentation allowed to primarily focus on one part of the essay?

(Teaching Assistant) That's a good question. The presentation is graded based on how well you defend your thesis. So it's similar to a summary of the essay, assuming you've followed the guidelines I provided. Have you written your thesis statement yet?

(Student) No, I've started writing the essay, but I'm confused about where the thesis statement should appear in the essay.

(Teaching Assistant) Your thesis statement functions like a road map because it explains to readers how you will be analyzing and interpreting the evidence that follows. Additionally, your thesis statement should directly answer the question that your essay is asking. So your thesis statement must be in the introduction, and it's typically the last sentence before the body paragraphs begin.

(Student) Gotcha. So it's a part of the introduction, not the whole thing, right?

(Teaching Assistant) Yeah, you should try to limit it to one sentence.

(Student) That makes sense.

(Teaching Assistant) Remind me, what's your topic?

(Student) I'm writing about the Cold War.

(Teaching Assistant) That's a little too broad for this assignment. Have you considered narrowing it down to a single event?

(Student) I've been very interested in the Iran-Contra Affair. Maybe I could write about that within the broader context of the Cold War?

(Teaching Assistant) Yeah, that sounds great. It also helps that that's a relatively recent event, so you could find some terrific audiovisual components into your presentation.

(Student) Is that a requirement?

(Teaching Assistant) No, but, between you and me, Professor Ramirez would love it. He's always talking about the persuasive power of video.

(Student) Wow, thanks for the tip. I've watched some of Oliver North's congressional testimony, and I'm sure I could find some short clips of it for the presentation.

(Teaching Assistant) That'd be phenomenal.

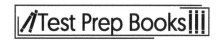

(Student) How long should the presentation be?

(Teaching Assistant) There's no time limit, but I think 10 minutes works best. You want to have enough time to defend your thesis without losing your audience's attention.

(Student) Got it.

(Teaching Assistant) How have your other classes been going? You're a history major, right?

(Student) No, I'm only minoring in history. My major is political science. Those classes have been a little abstract and dry.

(Teaching Assistant) I felt the same way in college, which is why I opted for history over political science for graduate school. Let me know if you're ever thinking about applying to the graduate program. I'd be more than happy to write you a recommendation.

(Student) Awesome, I might just take you up on that. Thanks for all your help.

(Teaching Assistant) No problem.

Passage #5

(Narrator) Listen to the lecture and then answer the questions.

(Professor) Good morning, it's great to see everyone after our long break. As a quick refresher, we're in the middle of our lessons on the Bill of Rights. Today we'll focus on freedom right of association. The First Amendment makes two references to associations—the right to assemble and the right to petition the government. In more recent years, the United States Supreme Court has interpreted these references to create a specific freedom of association.

An association consists simply in the public assent which a number of individuals give to certain doctrines, and in the engagement which they contract to promote the spread of those doctrines by their exertions. The right of association with these views is very analogous to the liberty of unlicensed writing; but societies thus formed possess more authority than the press. When an opinion is represented by a society, it necessarily assumes a more exact and explicit form. It numbers its partisans, and compromises their welfare in its cause: they, on the other hand, become acquainted with each other, and their zeal is increased by their number. An association unites the efforts of minds which have a tendency to diverge in one single channel, and urges them vigorously towards one single end which it points out.

The second degree in the right of association is the power of meeting. When an association is allowed to establish centers of action at certain important points in the country, its activity is increased and its influence extended. Men have the opportunity of seeing each other; means of execution are more readily combined, and opinions are maintained with a degree of warmth and energy which written language cannot approach.

Lastly, in the exercise of the right of political association, there is a third degree: the partisans of an opinion may unite in electoral bodies, and choose delegates to represent them in a central assembly. This is, properly speaking, the application of the representative system to a party.

Thus, in the first instance, a society is formed between individuals professing the same opinion, and the tie which keeps it together is of a purely intellectual nature; in the second case, small assemblies are

167

formed which only represent a fraction of the party. Lastly, in the third case, they constitute a separate nation in the midst of the nation, a government within the Government. Their delegates, like the real delegates of the majority, represent the entire collective force of their party; and they enjoy a certain degree of that national dignity and great influence which belong to the chosen representatives of the people. It is true that they have not the right of making the laws, but they have the power of attacking those which are in being, and of drawing up beforehand those which they may afterwards cause to be adopted.

Next class will be our final lesson on the Bill of Rights. Specifically, we'll be discussing the constitutional protections against criminal prosecution. Please review the text of the Fifth Amendment to prepare.

This lecture has been adapted from Democracy in America by Alexis de Tocqueville, translated by Henry Reeve, 1838, found at https://www.gutenberg.org/files/815/815-h/815-h.htm#link2HCH0017

Passage #6

(Narrator) Listen to the lecture and then answer the questions.

(Professor) Hello class, welcome back to the History of Modern Medicine 305. Today our goal is to finish our discussion on epidemiology. Scientists initially struggled to accurately identify the vectors of disease, which created serious obstacles in the fight to limit transmission. The history of yellow fever illustrates how epidemiology developed during the nineteenth century.

The story of yellow fever illustrates one of the greatest practical triumphs of scientific medicine; indeed, in view of its far-reaching commercial consequences, it may range as one of the first achievements of the race. Ever since the discovery of America, the disease has been one of its great scourges, permanently endemic in the Spanish Main, often extending to the Southern States, occasionally into the North, and not infrequently it has crossed the Atlantic. The records of the British Army in the West Indies show an appalling death rate, chiefly from this disease. In Jamaica, for the twenty years ending in 1836, the average mortality was 101 per 1,000, and in certain instances as high as 178. One of the most dreaded of all infections, the periods of epidemics in the Southern States have been the occasions of a widespread panic with complete paralysis of commerce. How appalling the mortality is may be judged from the outbreak in Philadelphia in 1793, when 10,000 people died in three months. The epidemics in Spain in the early part of the nineteenth century were of great severity. A glance through La Roche's great book on the subject soon gives one an idea of the enormous importance of the disease in the history of the Southern States. Havana, ever since its foundation, had been a hotbed of yellow fever. The best minds of the profession had been attracted to a solution of the problem, but all in vain. Commission after commission had been appointed, with negative results; various organisms had been described as the cause, and there were sad illustrations of the tragedy associated with investigations undertaken without proper training or proper technique. By the year 1900, not only had the ground been cleared, but the work on insect-borne disease by Manson and by Ross had given observers an important clue. It had repeatedly been suggested that some relation existed between the bites of mosquitoes and the tropical fevers, particularly by that remarkable student, Nott of Mobile, and the French physician, Beauperthuy. But the first to clearly announce the mosquito theory of the disease was Carlos Finlay of Havana. Early in the spring of 1900, during the occupation of Cuba by the United States, a commission appointed by Surgeon General Sternberg (himself one of the most energetic students of the disease) undertook fresh investigations.

Once the mosquito theory of the disease gained acceptance, incidents of yellow fever dramatically declined in the Western Hemisphere, demonstrating the importance of identifying and eliminating vectors of disease.

We'll be hitting pause on our lecture series next class to hold our presentations on famous epidemiologists. Please let me know if you have any questions about the format.

This lecture has been adapted from The History of Modern Medicine by William Osler, 1913, found at https://www.gutenberg.org/files/1566/1566-h/1566-h.htm#link2H_4_0032

Passage #7

(Narrator) Listen to the lecture and then answer the questions.

(Professor) Hello class, today we'll be learning about the early stages of the American Revolutionary War.

On the same day on which Ticonderoga surrendered, the Continental Congress met in Philadelphia. The Adamses and the Livingstons, Jay, Henry, Washington, and Lee were there, as also Franklin, just back from his long service in England. Of all the number, John Adams and Franklin had now, probably, come to agree with Samuel Adams that a political separation from Great Britain was inevitable; but all were fully agreed that any consideration of such a question was at present premature and uncalled for. The Congress was a body which wielded no technical legal authority; it was but a group of committees, assembled for the purpose of advising with each other regarding the public weal. Yet something very like a state of war existed in a part of the country, under conditions which intimately concerned the whole, and in the absence of any formally constituted government something must be done to provide for such a crisis. The spirit of the assembly was well shown in its choice of a president. Peyton Randolph was called back to Virginia to preside over the colonial assembly, so Thomas Jefferson was sent to the Congress instead; and it also became necessary for Congress to choose a president to succeed him. The proscribed John Hancock was at once chosen, and Benjamin Harrison, in conducting him to the chair, said, "We will show Great Britain how much we value her proscriptions." To the garrisoning of Ticonderoga and Crown Point by Connecticut, the Congress eventually consented, since the capture of these posts had been an act of offensive warfare. But without any serious opposition, in the name of the "United Colonies," the Congress adopted the army of New England men besieging Boston as the "Continental Army," and proceeded to appoint a commander-in-chief to direct its operations. Practically, this was the most important step taken in the whole course of the War of Independence. Nothing less than the whole issue of the struggle, for ultimate defeat or for ultimate victory, turned upon the selection to be made at this crisis. For nothing can be clearer than that in any other hands than those of George Washington the military result of the war must have been speedily disastrous to the Americans. In appointing a Virginian to the command of a New England army, the Congress showed rare wisdom. It would well have accorded with local prejudices had a New England general been appointed. John Hancock greatly desired the appointment, and seems to have been chagrined at not receiving it. But it was wisely decided that the common interest of all Americans could in no way be more thoroughly engaged in the war than by putting the New England army in charge of a general who represented in his own person the greatest of the Southern colonies.

Next class we'll look at how Washington's military strategy ultimately secured independence. Please read Chapter 6 and answer the discussion questions.

This lecture has been adapted from American Revolution by John Fiske, 1919, found at https://www.gutenberg.org/files/41266/41266-h/41266-h.htm

Speaking

87. Physical activity is a set of behaviors that appears to play a unique role in health and well-being since it provides a wide range of benefits. Plus, it's easy to do. Physical activity could be something as simple as walking. Physical activity offers protection from premature mortality, chronic diseases, and common mental health problems, such as depression and anxiety and Alzheimer's disease. For all of human history, physical activity was required for working, traveling, and obtaining food. Mechanization started during the Industrial Revolution, and physical activity has declined ever since. For example, automobiles replaced walking. Physical activity is likely to keep declining due to the increasing number of people who spend their leisure time on electronic entertainment. A recent analysis revealed that physical inactivity is responsible for over five million deaths annually worldwide, which is similar to the death toll of tobacco smoking. The World Health Organization estimates that physical inactivity is the fourth leading cause of death globally. One study found that physical inactivity accounts for 5.8 percent of deaths from coronary heart disease, 7.2 percent from type 2 diabetes, 10.1 percent from breast cancer, and 10.4 percent from colon cancer. In addition, a second study indicated that inactive adults would gain 1.3 to 3.7 years of life expectancy by becoming active at age 50.

88. Both proposals would definitely benefit the students. During my time in high school, I played football and ran track. I remember how annoying it was to play on a field with dirt patches and weeds. I'm sure all our teams would benefit from the artificial turf, which would probably make the field easier to maintain at high quality. At the same time, the auditorium urgently needs a renovation. The sound system and lights were cutting edge during the Korean War. The seats are so uncomfortable nobody can concentrate on the performance. The curtains don't always work.

Although it's a hard decision, I plan to vote for the auditorium renovations for two reasons. First, the auditorium is in dire straits, while the field is just less than optimal. We nearly had to cancel a dance recital last weekend due to the leaky roof. In contrast, our patchy fields didn't stop our girl's soccer team from winning the state championship. The field is playable, though we should probably keep the turf in mind the next time we have surplus funds. Second, the auditorium serves more students. The school assemblies and guest speakers are held in the auditorium and attended by the entire student body. More students also participate in the arts, like school plays, musicals, chorus, and band concerts, than sports. It'd be different if the field was also used for physical education, but it isn't.

89. My favorite city in the world is New York City. The city is the home of world-class monuments, culture, and food. My favorite monument is the Statue of Liberty. The Statue of Liberty was originally a gift from the French people, and it depicts the Roman goddess Libertas holding a torch and the Declaration of Independence. There are also chains at her feet, representing the immigrants who left their homeland to find freedom in America. Ferries leave from Battery Park in Lower Manhattan, stopping at the Statue of Liberty and Ellis Island. Further uptown is the Metropolitan Museum of Art. The Met attracts more than seven million visitors per year. Of its seventeen departments, I most enjoy the one dedicated to ancient Egypt. The main chamber has a life-size tomb and pyramid, which are my two favorite exhibits. The Met is also across the street from Central Park, an enormous public park with fields, a concert theater, playgrounds, a zoo, fields, and pedestrian paths. Whenever I'm in New York I always eat pizza and bagels. I don't even have a specific recommendation; everywhere is so much better than home. People say the city's water, which originates in the Catskills mountain system, is the reason why the pizza and bagels are so good.

90. We know vaccines are safe and effective, because they're subject to very high safety standards. The Food and Drug Administration (FDA) regulates licensing, and the Centers for Disease Control and

Prevention (CDC) makes recommendations for vaccine use. In addition, throughout the entire process, the FDA and CDC play an active role in monitoring the vaccines. Before a vaccine is ever recommended for use, it's tested in labs for several years. The FDA works closely with the company producing the vaccine to evaluate the vaccine's safety and effectiveness. Once the vaccine meets the safety threshold, the vaccine is tested on people who volunteer to get vaccinated for clinical trials, which start with 20 to 100 volunteers but can eventually grow to thousands of volunteers. These trials verify safety, determine optimal dosage, and study reactions in the immune system. Even after it receives a government license and recommendation, vaccines continue to be tested. The company is required to test each batch of vaccine for potency, purity, and sterility. The FDA, CDC, and other federal agencies continue to supervise this ongoing safety check.

Practice Test #3

Reading

Questions 1–5 are based on the following passage:

Christopher Columbus is often credited for discovering America. This is incorrect. First, it is impossible to "discover" somewhere where people already live; however, Christopher Columbus did explore places in the New World that were previously untouched by Europe, so the term "explorer" would be more accurate. Another correction must be made, as well: Christopher Columbus was not the first European explorer to reach the present-day Americas! Rather, it was Leif Erikson who first came to the New World and contacted the natives, nearly five hundred years before Christopher Columbus.

Leif Erikson, the son of Erik the Red (a famous Viking outlaw and explorer in his own right), was born in either 970 or 980, depending on which historian you read. His own family, though, did not raise Leif, which was a Viking tradition. Instead, one of Erik's prisoners taught Leif reading and writing, languages, sailing, and weaponry. At age 12, Leif was considered a man and returned to his family. He killed a man during a dispute shortly after his return, and the council banished the Erikson clan to Greenland.

In 999, Leif left Greenland and traveled to Norway where he would serve as a guard to King Olaf Tryggvason. It was there that he became a convert to Christianity. Leif later tried to return home with the intention of taking supplies and spreading Christianity to Greenland, however his ship was blown off course and he arrived in a strange new land: present day Newfoundland, Canada.

When he finally returned to his adopted homeland Greenland, Leif consulted with a merchant who had also seen the shores of this previously unknown land we now know as Canada. The son of the legendary Viking explorer then gathered a crew of 35 men and set sail. Leif became the first European to touch foot in the New World as he explored present-day Baffin Island and Labrador, Canada. His crew called the land "Vinland," since it was plentiful with grapes.

During their time in present-day Newfoundland, Leif's expedition made contact with the natives whom they referred to as Skraelings (which translates to "wretched ones" in Norse). There are several secondhand accounts of their meetings. Some contemporaries described trade between the peoples. Other accounts describe clashes where the Skraelings defeated the Viking explorers with long spears, while still others claim the Vikings dominated the natives. Regardless of the circumstances, it seems that the

Vikings made contact of some kind. This happened around 1000, nearly five hundred years before Columbus famously sailed the ocean blue.

Eventually, in 1003, Leif set sail for home and arrived at Greenland with a ship full of timber. In 1020, seventeen years later, the legendary Viking died. Many believe that Leif Erikson should receive more credit for his contributions in exploring the New World.

1. Which of the following best describes how the author generally presents the information?
   a. Chronological order
   b. Comparison-contrast
   c. Cause-effect
   d. Conclusion-premises

2. Which of the following is an opinion, rather than historical fact, expressed by the author?
   a. Leif Erikson was definitely the son of Erik the Red; however, historians debate the year of his birth.
   b. Leif Erikson's crew called the land "Vinland," since it was plentiful with grapes.
   c. Leif Erikson deserves more credit for his contributions in exploring the New World.
   d. Leif Erikson explored the Americas nearly five hundred years before Christopher Columbus.

3. Which of the following most accurately describes the author's main conclusion?
   a. Leif Erikson is a legendary Viking explorer.
   b. Leif Erikson deserves more credit for exploring America hundreds of years before Columbus.
   c. Spreading Christianity motivated Leif Erikson's expeditions more than any other factor.
   d. Leif Erikson contacted the natives nearly five hundred years before Columbus.

4. Which of the following best describes the author's intent in the passage?
   a. To entertain
   b. To inform
   c. To alert
   d. To suggest

5. Which of the following can be logically inferred from the passage?
   a. The Vikings disliked exploring the New World.
   b. Leif Erikson's banishment from Iceland led to his exploration of present-day Canada.
   c. Leif Erikson never shared his stories of exploration with the King of Norway.
   d. Historians have difficulty definitively pinpointing events in the Vikings' history.

Questions 6–19 are based on the following two passages:

Passage 1

Shakespeare and His Plays

People who argue that William Shakespeare is not responsible for the plays attributed to his name are known as anti-Stratfordians (from the name of Shakespeare's birthplace, Stratford-upon-Avon). The most common anti-Stratfordian claim is that William Shakespeare simply was not educated enough or from a high enough social class to have written plays overflowing with references to such a wide range of subjects like history, the classics, religion, and international culture. William Shakespeare was the son of a glove-maker, he only had a basic grade school

education, and he never set foot outside of England—so how could he have produced plays of such sophistication and imagination? How could he have written in such detail about historical figures and events, or about different cultures and locations around Europe? According to anti-Stratfordians, the depth of knowledge contained in Shakespeare's plays suggests a well-traveled writer from a wealthy background with a university education, not a countryside writer like Shakespeare. But in fact, there is not much substance to such speculation, and most anti-Stratfordian arguments can be refuted with a little background about Shakespeare's time and upbringing.

First of all, those who doubt Shakespeare's authorship often point to his common birth and brief education as stumbling blocks to his writerly genius. Although it is true that Shakespeare did not come from a noble class, his father was a very *successful* glove-maker and his mother was from a very wealthy land-owning family—so while Shakespeare may have had a country upbringing, he was certainly from a well-off family and would have been educated accordingly. Also, even though he did not attend university, grade school education in Shakespeare's time was actually quite rigorous and exposed students to classic drama through writers like Seneca and Ovid. It is not unreasonable to believe that Shakespeare received a very solid foundation in poetry and literature from his early schooling.

Next, anti-Stratfordians tend to question how Shakespeare could write so extensively about countries and cultures he had never visited before (for instance, several of his most famous works like *Romeo and Juliet* and *The Merchant of Venice* were set in Italy, on the opposite side of Europe!). But again, this criticism does not hold up under scrutiny. For one thing, Shakespeare was living in London, a bustling metropolis of international trade, the most populous city in England, and a political and cultural hub of Europe. In the daily crowds of people, Shakespeare would certainly have been able to meet travelers from other countries and hear firsthand accounts of life in their home country. And, in addition to the influx of information from world travelers, this was also the age of the printing press, a jump in technology that made it possible to print and circulate books much more easily than in the past. This also allowed for a freer flow of information across different countries, allowing people to read about life and ideas from throughout Europe. One needn't travel the continent in order to learn and write about its culture.

Passage 2

Now there is very good authority for saying, and I think the truth is so, that at least two of the plays published among the works of Shakespeare are not his at all; that at least three others contain very little, if any, of his writing; and that of the remainder, many contain long passages that are non-Shakespearean. But when we have submitted them all the crucible of criticism we have a magnificent residuum of the purest gold. Here is the true Shakespeare; here is the great magician who, by a wave of his wand, could transmute brass into gold, or make dry bones live and move and have immortal being. Who was this great magician—this mighty dramatist who was "not of an age, but for all time"? Who was the writer of *Venus* and *Lucrece* and the *Sonnets* and *Lear* and *Hamlet*? Was it William Shakespeare of Stratford, the Player? So it is generally believed, and that hypothesis I had accepted in unquestioning faith till my love of the works naturally led me to an examination of the life of the supposed author of them. Then I found that as I read my faith melted away "into thin air." It was not, certainly, that I had (nor have I now) any wish to disbelieve. I was, and I am, altogether willing to accept the Player as the immortal poet if only my reason would allow me to do so. Why not? . . . But the question of authorship is,

nevertheless, a most fascinating one. If it be true, as the Rev. Leonard Bacon wrote that "The great world does not care sixpence who wrote *Hamlet*," the great world must, at the same time, be a very small world, and many of us must be content to be outside it. Having given, then, the best attention I was able to give to the question, and more time, I fear, than I ought to have devoted to it, I was brought to the conclusion, as many others have been, that the man who is, truly enough, designated by Messrs. Garnett and Gosse as a "Stratford rustic" is not the true Shakespeare. . .

That Shakespeare the "Stratford rustic and London actor" should have acquired this learning, this culture, and this polish; that *he* should have travelled into foreign lands, studied the life and topography of foreign cities, and the manners and customs of all sorts and conditions of men; that *he* should have written some half-dozen dramas . . . besides qualifying himself as a professional actor; that *he* should have done all this and a good deal more between 1587 and 1592 is a supposition so wild that it can only be entertained by those who are prepared to accept it as a miracle. "And miracles do not happen!"

Excerpt from The Shakespeare Problem Restated by G.G. Greenwood

6. Which sentence contains the author's thesis in the first passage?
   a. People who argue that William Shakespeare is not responsible for the plays attributed to his name are known as anti-Stratfordians.
   b. But in fact, there is not much substance to such speculation, and most anti-Stratfordian arguments can be refuted with a little background about Shakespeare's time and upbringing.
   c. It is not unreasonable to believe that Shakespeare received a very solid foundation in poetry and literature from his early schooling.
   d. Next, anti-Stratfordians tend to question how Shakespeare could write so extensively about countries and cultures he had never visited before.

7. In the first paragraph in Passage 1, "How could he have written in such detail about historical figures and events, or about different cultures and locations around Europe?" is an example of which of the following?
   a. Hyperbole
   b. Onomatopoeia
   c. Rhetorical question
   d. Appeal to authority

8. In Passage 1, how does the author respond to the claim that Shakespeare was not well-educated because he did not attend university?
   a. By insisting upon Shakespeare's natural genius.
   b. By explaining grade school curriculum in Shakespeare's time.
   c. By comparing Shakespeare with other uneducated writers of his time.
   d. By pointing out that Shakespeare's wealthy parents probably paid for private tutors.

9. In Passage 1, the word *bustling* in the third paragraph most nearly means which of the following?
   a. Busy
   b. Foreign
   c. Expensive
   d. Undeveloped

10. In passage 2, the following sentence is an example of what?
"Here is the true Shakespeare; here is the great magician who, by a wave of his wand, could transmute brass into gold, or make dry bones live and move and have immortal being."

    a. Personification
    b. Metaphor
    c. Simile
    d. Allusion

11. In passage 2, the author's attitude toward Stratfordians can be described as which of the following?
    a. Accepting and forgiving
    b. Uncaring and neutral
    c. Uplifting and admiring
    d. Disbelieving and critical

12. What is the relationship between these two sentences from Passage 2?
Sentence 1: So it is generally believed, and that hypothesis I had accepted in unquestioning faith till my love of the works naturally led me to an examination of the life of the supposed author of them.

Sentence 2: Then I found that as I read my faith melted away "into thin air."

    a. Sentence 2 explains the main idea in Sentence 1.
    b. Sentence 2 continues the definition begun in Sentence 1.
    c. Sentence 2 analyzes the comment in Sentence 1.
    d. Sentence 2 is a contrast to the idea in Sentence 1.

13. The writing style of Passage 1 could be best described as what?
    a. Expository
    b. Persuasive
    c. Narrative
    d. Descriptive

14. In passage 2, the word *topography* in the second paragraph most nearly means which of the following?
    a. Climate features of an area.
    b. Agriculture specific to place.
    c. Shape and features of the Earth.
    d. Aspects of humans within society.

15. The authors of the passages differ in their opinion of Shakespeare in that the author of Passage 2
    a. Believes that Shakespeare the actor did not write the plays.
    b. Believes that Shakespeare the playwright did not in act in the plays.
    c. Believes that Shakespeare was both the actor and the playwright.
    d. Believes that Shakespeare was neither the actor nor the playwright.

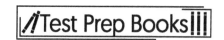

16. Which of the following would the two authors be most likely to disagree over?
    a. Readers of Shakespeare's plays should not care whether or not the "country Shakespeare" wrote the plays or not; the fact that they exist is reason enough for readers to be grateful.
    b. A person born into a lower socioeconomic class is not capable of writing plays with universal themes that creates new ways to use the English language.
    c. That a country education is not sufficient enough to have written the greatest plays in Western Civilization.
    d. That in order to write about the topography and civilization of a place, one must have travelled there and mingled with the people.

17. The author of Passage 1 believes that Shakespeare the actor *was* Shakespeare the writer because of which of the following?
    a. New evidence cites that Shakespeare did indeed travel a great bit between the years 1587 and 1592, suggesting that the playwright did have sufficient experience to write the great plays.
    b. There is sufficient evidence from Shakespeare's peers that proves that Shakespeare wrote the poems and plays that his name was signed to.
    c. An individual with Shakespeare's socioeconomic status and country education would be too limited in knowledge to write such brilliant plays.
    d. A country education and socioeconomic status do not deflect true genius if the individual is willing to absorb the textual and cultural knowledge surrounding them.

18. Which one of the following most accurately shows the relationship between the two passages?
    a. Passage 1 is written in concession with Passage 2.
    b. Passage 1 is written in opposition to Passage 2.
    c. Passage 1 is neutral to the stance of Passage 2.
    d. Passage 1 uses direct quotation from Passage 2 for contradiction.

19. The last phrase in this sentence in Passage 1 is considered what?
    William Shakespeare was the son of a glove-maker, he only had a basic grade school education, and he never set foot outside of England—so how could he have produced plays of such sophistication and imagination?

    a. Rhetorical question
    b. Literary allusion
    c. Hyperbole
    d. Symbolism

Questions 20–26 are based on the following passage:

"Mademoiselle Eugénie is pretty—I think I remember that to be her name."

"Very pretty, or rather, very beautiful," replied Albert, "but of that style of beauty which I don't appreciate; I am an ungrateful fellow."

"Really," said Monte Cristo, lowering his voice, "you don't appear to me to be very enthusiastic on the subject of this marriage."

"Mademoiselle Danglars is too rich for me," replied Morcerf, "and that frightens me."

"Bah," exclaimed Monte Cristo, "that's a fine reason to give. Are you not rich yourself?"

"My father's income is about 50,000 francs per annum; and he will give me, perhaps, ten or twelve thousand when I marry."

"That, perhaps, might not be considered a large sum, in Paris especially," said the count; "but everything doesn't depend on wealth, and it's a fine thing to have a good name, and to occupy a high station in society. Your name is celebrated, your position magnificent; and then the Comte de Morcerf is a soldier, and it's pleasing to see the integrity of a Bayard united to the poverty of a Duguesclin; disinterestedness is the brightest ray in which a noble sword can shine. As for me, I consider the union with Mademoiselle Danglars a most suitable one; she will enrich you, and you will ennoble her."

Albert shook his head, and looked thoughtful. "There is still something else," said he.

"I confess," observed Monte Cristo, "that I have some difficulty in comprehending your objection to a young lady who is both rich and beautiful."

"Oh," said Morcerf, "this repugnance, if repugnance it may be called, isn't all on my side."

"Whence can it arise, then? for you told me your father desired the marriage."

"It's my mother who dissents; she has a clear and penetrating judgment, and doesn't smile on the proposed union. I cannot account for it, but she seems to entertain some prejudice against the Danglars."

"Ah," said the count, in a somewhat forced tone, "that may be easily explained; the Comtesse de Morcerf, who is aristocracy and refinement itself, doesn't relish the idea of being allied by your marriage with one of ignoble birth; that is natural enough."

Excerpt from The Count of Monte Cristo by Alexandre Dumas, 1844

20. The meaning of the word "repugnance" is closest to:
    a. Strong resemblance
    b. Strong dislike
    c. Extreme shyness
    d. Extreme dissimilarity

21. What can be inferred about Albert's family?
    a. Their finances are uncertain.
    b. Albert is the only son in his family.
    c. Their name is more respected than the Danglars'.
    d. Albert's mother and father both agree on their decisions.

22. What is Albert's attitude towards his impending marriage?
    a. Pragmatic
    b. Romantic
    c. Indifferent
    d. Apprehensive

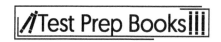

23. What is the best description of the Count's relationship with Albert?
    a. He's like a strict parent, criticizing Albert's choices.
    b. He's like a wise uncle, giving practical advice to Albert.
    c. He's like a close friend, supporting all of Albert's opinions.
    d. He's like a suspicious investigator, asking many probing questions.

24. Which sentence is true of Albert's mother?
    a. She belongs to a noble family.
    b. She often makes poor choices.
    c. She is primarily occupied with money.
    d. She is unconcerned about her son's future.

25. Based on this passage, what is probably NOT true about French society in the 1800s?
    a. Children often received money from their parents.
    b. Marriages were sometimes arranged between families.
    c. The richest people in society were also the most respected.
    d. People were often expected to marry within their same social class.

26. Why is the Count puzzled by Albert's attitude toward his marriage?
    a. He seems reluctant to marry Eugénie, despite her wealth and beauty.
    b. He is marrying against his father's wishes, despite usually following his advice.
    c. He appears excited to marry someone he doesn't love, despite being a hopeless romantic.
    d. He expresses reverence towards Eugénie, despite being from a higher social class than her.

Questions 27–32 are based on the following passage:

When I got on the coach the driver had not taken his seat, and I saw him talking with the landlady. They were evidently talking of me, for every now and then they looked at me, and some of the people who were sitting on the bench outside the door came and listened, and then looked at me, most of them pityingly. I could hear a lot of words often repeated, queer words, for there were many nationalities in the crowd; so I quietly got my polyglot dictionary from my bag and looked them out. I must say they weren't cheering to me, for amongst them were "Ordog"—Satan, "pokol"—hell, "stregoica"—witch, "vrolok" and "vlkoslak"—both of which mean the same thing, one being Slovak and the other Servian for something that is either were-wolf or vampire.

When we started, the crowd round the inn door, which had by this time swelled to a considerable size, all made the sign of the cross and pointed two fingers towards me. With some difficulty I got a fellow-passenger to tell me what they meant; he wouldn't answer at first, but on learning that I was English, he explained that it was a charm or guard against the evil eye. This was not very pleasant for me, just starting for an unknown place to meet an unknown man; but everyone seemed so kind-hearted, and so sorrowful, and so sympathetic that I couldn't but be touched. I shall never forget the last glimpse which I had of the inn-yard and its crowd of picturesque figures, all crossing themselves, as they stood round the wide archway, with its background of rich foliage of oleander and orange trees in green tubs clustered in the centre of the yard. Then our driver cracked his big whip over his four small horses, which ran abreast, and we set off on our journey.

I soon lost sight and recollection of ghostly fears in the beauty of the scene as we drove along, although had I known the language, or rather languages, which my fellow-passengers were

speaking, I might not have been able to throw them off so easily. Before us lay a green sloping land full of forests and woods, with here and there steep hills, crowned with clumps of trees or with farmhouses, the blank gable end to the road. There was everywhere a bewildering mass of fruit blossom—apple, plum, pear, cherry; and as we drove by I could see the green grass under the trees spangled with the fallen petals. In and out amongst these green hills of what they call here the "Mittel Land" ran the road, losing itself as it swept round the grassy curve, or was shut out by the straggling ends of pine woods, which here and there ran down the hillsides like tongues of flame. The road was rugged, but still we seemed to fly over it with a feverish haste. I couldn't understand then what the haste meant, but the driver was evidently bent on losing no time in reaching Borgo Prund.

Excerpt from <u>Dracula</u> by Bram Stoker, 1897

27. What type of narrator is found in this passage?
    a. First person
    b. Second person
    c. Third-person limited
    d. Third-person omniscient

28. Which of the following is true of the traveler?
    a. He wishes the driver would go faster.
    b. He's returning to the country of his birth.
    c. He has some familiarity with the local customs.
    d. He doesn't understand all of the languages being used.

29. How does the traveler's mood change between the second and third paragraphs?
    a. From relaxed to rushed
    b. From fearful to charmed
    c. From confused to enlightened
    d. From comfortable to exhausted

30. Who is the traveler going to meet?
    a. A kind landlady
    b. A distant relative
    c. A friendly villager
    d. A complete stranger

31. Based on the details in this passage, what can readers probably expect to happen in the story?
    a. The traveler will become a farmer.
    b. The traveler will arrive late at his destination.
    c. The traveler will soon encounter danger or evil.
    d. The traveler will have a pleasant journey and make many new friends.

32. Which sentence from the passage provides a clue for question 31?

a. "I must say they weren't cheering to me, for amongst them were "Ordog"—Satan, "pokol"—hell, "stregoica"—witch, "vrolok" and "vlkoslak"—both of which mean the same thing, one being Slovak and the other Servian for something that is either were-wolf or vampire."

b. "When I got on the coach the driver had not taken his seat, and I saw him talking with the landlady."

c. "Then our driver cracked his big whip over his four small horses, which ran abreast, and we set off on our journey."

d. "There was everywhere a bewildering mass of fruit blossom—apple, plum, pear, cherry; and as we drove by I could see the green grass under the trees spangled with the fallen petals."

Questions 33–36 are based on the following passage:

Smoking tobacco products is terribly destructive. A single cigarette contains over 4,000 chemicals, including 43 known carcinogens and 400 deadly toxins. Some of the most dangerous ingredients include tar, carbon monoxide, formaldehyde, ammonia, arsenic, and DDT. Smoking can cause numerous types of cancer including throat, mouth, nasal cavity, esophagus, stomach, pancreas, kidney, bladder, and cervical.

Cigarettes contain a drug called nicotine, one of the most addictive substances known to man. Addiction is defined as a compulsion to seek the substance despite negative consequences. According to the National Institute of Drug Abuse, nearly 35 million smokers expressed a desire to quit smoking in 2015; however, more than 85 percent of those addicts will not achieve their goal. Almost all smokers regret picking up that first cigarette. You would be wise to learn from their mistake if you have not yet started smoking.

According to the U.S. Department of Health and Human Services, 16 million people in the United States presently suffer from a smoking-related condition and nearly nine million suffer from a serious smoking-related illness. According to the Centers for Disease Control and Prevention (CDC), tobacco products cause nearly six million deaths per year. This number is projected to rise to over eight million deaths by 2030. Smokers, on average, die ten years earlier than their nonsmoking peers.

In the United States, local, state, and federal governments typically tax tobacco products, which leads to high prices. Nicotine addicts sometimes pay more for a pack of cigarettes than for a few gallons of gas. Additionally, smokers tend to stink. The smell of smoke is all-consuming and creates a pervasive nastiness. Smokers also risk staining their teeth and fingers with yellow residue from the tar.

Smoking is deadly, expensive, and socially unappealing. Clearly, smoking is not worth the risks.

33. Which of the following best describes the passage?

a. Narrative
b. Persuasive
c. Expository
d. Technical

181

34. Which of the following statements most accurately summarizes the passage?
    a. Tobacco is less healthy than many alternatives.
    b. Tobacco is deadly, expensive, and socially unappealing, and smokers would be much better off kicking the addiction.
    c. In the United States, local, state, and federal governments typically tax tobacco products, which leads to high prices.
    d. Tobacco products shorten smokers' lives by ten years and kill more than six million people per year.

35. The author would be most likely to agree with which of the following statements?
    a. Smokers should only quit cold turkey and avoid all nicotine cessation devices.
    b. Other substances are more addictive than tobacco.
    c. Smokers should quit for whatever reason that gets them to stop smoking.
    d. People who want to continue smoking should advocate for a reduction in tobacco product taxes.

36. Which of the following represents an opinion statement on the part of the author?
    a. According to the Centers for Disease Control and Prevention (CDC), tobacco products cause nearly six million deaths per year.
    b. Nicotine addicts sometimes pay more for a pack of cigarettes than a few gallons of gas.
    c. They also risk staining their teeth and fingers with yellow residue from the tar.
    d. Additionally, smokers tend to stink. The smell of smoke is all-consuming and creates a pervasive nastiness.

Questions 37–42 are based on the following passage:

I heartily accept the motto, "That government is best which governs least"; and I should like to see it acted up to more rapidly and systematically. Carried out, it finally amounts to this, which also I believe—"That government is best which governs not at all"; and when men are prepared for it, that will be the kind of government which they will have. Government is at best but an expedient; but most governments are usually, and all governments are sometimes, inexpedient. The objections which have been brought against a standing army, and they are many and weighty, and deserve to prevail, may also at last be brought against a standing government. The standing army is only an arm of the standing government. The government itself, which is only the mode which the people have chosen to execute their will, is equally liable to be abused and perverted before the people can act through it. Witness the present Mexican war, the work of comparatively a few individuals using the standing government as their tool; for, in the outset, the people would not have consented to this measure.

This American government—what is it but a tradition, though a recent one, endeavoring to transmit itself unimpaired to posterity, but each instant losing some of its integrity? It has not the vitality and force of a single living man; for a single man can bend it to his will. It is a sort of wooden gun to the people themselves. But it is not the less necessary for this; for the people must have some complicated machinery or other, and hear its din, to satisfy that idea of government which they have. Governments show thus how successfully men can be imposed on, even impose on themselves, for their own advantage. It is excellent, we must all allow. Yet this government never of itself furthered any enterprise, but by the alacrity with which it got out of its way. It does not keep the country free. It does not settle the West. It does not educate. The character inherent in the American people has done all that has been accomplished; and it would have done somewhat more, if the government had not sometimes got in its way. For

government is an expedient by which men would fain succeed in letting one another alone; and, as has been said, when it is most expedient, the governed are most let alone by it. Trade and commerce, if they were not made of india-rubber, would never manage to bounce over the obstacles which legislators are continually putting in their way; and, if one were to judge these men wholly by the effects of their actions and not partly by their intentions, they would deserve to be classed and punished with those mischievous persons who put obstructions on the railroads.

But, to speak practically and as a citizen, unlike those who call themselves no-government men, I ask for, not at once no government, but at once a better government. Let every man make known what kind of government would command his respect, and that will be one step toward obtaining it.

Excerpt from Civil Disobedience by Henry David Thoreau

37. Which phrase best encapsulates Thoreau's use of the term *expedient* in the first paragraph?
   a. A dead end
   b. A state of order
   c. A means to an end
   d. Rushed construction

38. Which best describes Thoreau's view on the Mexican War?
   a. Government is inherently corrupt because it must wage war.
   b. Government can easily be manipulated by a few individuals for their own agenda.
   c. Government is a tool for the people, but it can also act against their interest.
   d. The Mexican War was a necessary action, but not all the people believed this.

39. What is Thoreau's purpose for writing?
   a. His goal is to illustrate how government can function if ideals are maintained.
   b. He wants to prove that true democracy is the best government, but it can be corrupted easily.
   c. Thoreau reflects on the stages of government abuses.
   d. He is seeking to prove that government is easily corruptible and inherently restrictive of individual freedoms that can simultaneously affect the whole state.

40. Which example best supports Thoreau's argument?
   a. A vote carries in the Senate to create a new road tax.
   b. The president vetoes the new FARM bill.
   c. Prohibition is passed to outlaw alcohol.
   d. Trade is opened between the United States and Iceland.

41. Which best summarizes this section from the following passage?

"This American government—what is it but a tradition, though a recent one, endeavoring to transmit itself unimpaired to posterity, but each instant losing some of its integrity? It has not the vitality and force of a single living man; for a single man can bend it to his will. It is a sort of wooden gun to the people themselves."

a. The government may be instituted to ensure the protections of freedoms, but this is weakened by the fact that it is easily manipulated by individuals.
b. Unlike an individual, government is uncaring.
c. Unlike an individual, government has no will, making it more prone to be used as a weapon against the people.
d. American government is modeled after other traditions but actually has greater potential to be used to control people.

42. According to Thoreau, what's the main reason why government eventually fails to achieve progress?
a. There are too many rules.
b. Legislation eventually becomes a hindrance to the lives and work of everyday people.
c. Trade and wealth eventually become the driving factor of those in government.
d. Government doesn't separate religion and state.

Questions 43–47 are based on the following passage:

It has been pointed out by Boltzmann that the fundamental object of contention in the life-struggle, in the evolution of the organic world, is available energy. In accord with this observation is the principle that, in the struggle for existence, the advantage must go to those organisms whose energy-capturing devices are most efficient in directing available energy into channels favorable to the preservation of the species.

The first effect of natural selection thus operating upon competing species will be to give relative preponderance (in number or mass) to those most efficient in guiding available energy in the manner indicated. Primarily the path of the energy flux through the system will be affected.

But the species possessing superior energy-capturing and directing devices may accomplish something more than merely to divert to its own advantage energy for which others are competing with it. If sources are presented, capable of supplying available energy in excess of that actually being tapped by the entire system of living organisms, then an opportunity is furnished for suitably constituted organisms to enlarge the total energy flux through the system. Whenever such organisms arise, natural selection will operate to preserve and increase them. The result, in this case, is not merely a diversion of the energy flux through the system of organic nature along a new path, but an increase of the total flux through that system.

Again, so long as sources exist, capable of supplying matter, of a character suitable for the composition of living organisms, in excess of that actually embodied in the system of organic nature, so long is opportunity furnished for suitably constituted organisms to enlarge the total mass of the system of organic nature. Whenever such organisms arise, natural selection will operate to preserve and increase them, provided always that there is presented a residue of untapped available energy. The result will be to increase the total mass of the system, and, with

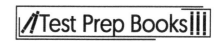

this total mass, also the total energy flux through the system, since, other things equal, this energy flux is proportional to the mass of the system.

Where a limit, either constant or slowly changing, is imposed upon the total mass available for the operation of life processes, the available energy per unit of time (available power) placed at the disposal of the organisms, for application to their life tasks and contests, may be capable of increase by increasing the rate of turnover of the organic matter through the life cycle. So, for example, under present conditions, the United States produces annually a crop of primary and secondary food amounting to about 1.37×10^{14} kilogram-calories per annum, enough to support a population of about 105 million persons (equivalent to about 88 million adults) at the present rate of food consumption (4,270 kilogram-calories per adult per day). Suppose, as a simple, though rather extreme illustration, that man found means of doubling the rate of growth of crops, and of growing two crops a year instead of one. Then, without changing the average crop actually standing on the fields, the land would be capable of supporting double the present population. If this population were attained, the energy flux through the system composed of the human population and the organisms upon which it is dependent for food would also be doubled. This result would be attained, not by doubling the mass of the system (for the matter locked up in crops, etc., at a given moment would be, on an average, unchanged) but by increasing the velocity of circulation of mass through the life cycle in the system. Once more it is evident that, whenever a group of organisms arises which is so constituted as to increase the rate of circulation of matter through the system in the manner exemplified, natural selection will operate to preserve and increase such a group, provided always that there is presented a residue of untapped available energy—and, where circumstances require it, also a residue of mass suitable for the composition of living matter.

Excerpt from "Contributions to the Energetics of Evolution" by Alfred J. Lotka, 1922

43. Judging by the content of the passage, Boltzmann (opening paragraph) is most likely which of the following?
 a. Physicist
 b. Dietician
 c. Anthropologist
 d. Agriculturalist

44. Which description best suits the use of "competing" in the first line of the second paragraph?
 a. Varying in diversity
 b. Fighting to the death
 c. Coexisting in the land
 d. Seeking to develop

45. What is the author's purpose behind writing this passage?
 a. To educate the reader on how energy conservation impacts genetic development
 b. To disprove the idea that energy is not essential to evolution
 c. To advocate the study of environmental enhancements to increase resource availability
 d. To prove that an organism's ability to capture and retain energy influences its survival and evolution

46. It would be reasonable to assume that a "species possessing superior energy-capturing and directing devices" would do which of the following?
    a. Die out from having too much energy
    b. Thrive and pass on these energy-directing devices to the next generation
    c. Be unable to pass on these specific traits
    d. Disrupt the flux of the natural world

47. Which is the best correlation among energy, mass, and evolution?
    a. Energy creates evolutionary trends that result in shifting mass amounts.
    b. In the end, evolution is influenced by, but not dependent on, the mass and energy consumed by organisms.
    c. More mass means more energy, which makes evolution happen faster.
    d. The amount of energy consumed by organisms influences the total mass of their system, in turn, evolving energy-retaining traits.

Listening

Directions: The Listening section measures your ability to understand conversations and lectures in English. In this test, you will listen to several pieces of content and answer questions after each one. The questions typically ask about the main idea and supporting details. Some questions ask about a speaker's purpose or attitude. Answer the questions based on what is stated or implied by the speakers.

Listen to all of these passages by going to testprepbooks.com/toefl or by scanning the QR code below:

Note that on the actual test, you can take notes while you listen and use your notes to help you answer the questions. Your notes will not be scored.

For your convenience, the transcripts of all of the audio passages are provided after the answer explanations. However, on the actual test, no such transcripts will be provided.

Passage #1: Lecture

- 50

- 480,000

- 5.6 million

- 20 million

- 600

- 69

48. How many chemicals in tobacco are known to cause cancer?

49. How many children alive in 2014 will die prematurely of a tobacco-related disease when they are adults?

50. Tobacco contains how many ingredients?

51. At the time of the article in 2014, how many years had it been since the original 1964 U.S. Surgeon General's report on smoking and health?

52. The Surgeon General reported in 2014 that cigarettes had killed over how many users?

53. When did the surgeon general first report on smoking and health?
   a. 1864
   b. 1914
   c. 1964
   d. 1978

Passage #2: Conversation

54. What is the major point of disagreement between the hockey fan and basketball fan?
   a. The basketball team that plays well at the end of a game always wins.
   b. Most of the talented basketball players are consolidated on a few teams.
   c. Basketball games last significantly longer than hockey games.
   d. Basketball tickets are cheaper than hockey tickets.

55. What point does the hockey fan doubt but not know enough about to dispute?
   a. Every basketball team has at least one talented player.
   b. Basketball teams can easily overcome massive deficits.
   c. Basketball games don't matter until the final few minutes of play.
   d. The outcome of hockey games are entirely dependent on luck.

56. Why does the hockey fan think only the last few minutes of a basketball game matter?
   a. Basketball teams can call timeouts and foul players to generate more offensive possessions.
   b. All the talent in professional basketball is consolidated on a few teams.
   c. Basketball teams can score ten consecutive points within a few minutes of game time.
   d. Basketball is dependent on luck, so the team that's lucky at the end wins.

57. Why does the basketball fan think luck is so decisive in hockey?
   a. Icy conditions
   b. Lack of skill
   c. Defective equipment
   d. Poor work ethic

58. According to the hockey fan, which two qualities allow hockey teams to overcome the icy conditions?
    a. Better coaching and strategy
    b. More money and talent
    c. High work ethic and skill
    d. Customized skates and sticks

Passage #3: Conversation

59. Which of the following did the professor wrongly assume?
    a. That the student is staying with friends and family.
    b. That the student recently moved into a new apartment.
    c. That the student is effectively homeless.
    d. That the student's parents bought a new house.

60. The professor and student plan to meet on _____ at 9:00 a.m.
    a. Monday
    b. Tuesday
    c. Wednesday
    d. Thursday

61. What does the teacher usually do during their downtime?
    a. Grades homework assignments
    b. Plays games on their phone
    c. Prepares lesson plans for the rest of the week
    d. Talks to students about their personal lives

62. The student has _____ in the evenings.
    a. Basketball practice
    b. Extra help
    c. Lacrosse practice
    d. Voice lessons

63. What does "bouncing between friends' and relatives' homes" most likely mean?
    a. The student is excited about having more sleepovers.
    b. The student is temporarily staying with their relatives' friends.
    c. The student is moving between homes after short stays.
    d. The student is exploring options before deciding where to stay permanently.

Passage #4: Conversation

For questions 64–65, match ALL of the student's remaining course requirements for the minor and major. Some questions might be matched with more than one answer.

    64. British literature minor

    65. Creative writing major

    a. Three 100-level courses

b. Four 100-level courses

c. Two 300-level courses

d. Three 300-level courses

e. One 400-level courses

f. Two 400-level courses

g. Capstone course

66. Why does the student want to finish their classes before 3:00 p.m. next semester?
    a. The student needs more time to study for their new major and minor.
    b. The student plans to work more hours to pay for the summer semester.
    c. The student has several extracurricular commitments in the evenings.
    d. The student is trying to complete their degree in four years.

For questions 67–68, complete the notes provided below.

Next semester: take three 100-level 67._____courses and a language course.

Summer semester: take three 300-level creative writing courses.

Next year: take one of the 68._____ courses to complete the general education requirement.

a. British literature

b. Capstone

c. Creative writing

d. English 101

e. History

f. Math

g. Science

Passage #5: Lecture

69. Who famously crossed the Rubicon in 49 B.C.?
    a. Julius Caesar
    b. Queen Cleopatra
    c. Pompey the Great
    d. Tiberius Caesar

70. Who was NOT a member of the Second Triumvirate?
   a. Lepidus
   b. Nero
   c. Mark Antony
   d. Octavian Caesar

71. According to the lecture, what heavily contributed to emperors replacing senators in Rome?
   a. Emperors used the military might of the legions to seize and retain power until a stronger faction overthrew them.
   b. Populist politicians railed against the corruption of senators and promoted authoritarianism.
   c. Emperors feared restoring the power of the Senate due to the failures of Octavian Caesar.
   d. Political alliances consolidated power to such a degree that only a truly dominant faction could govern Rome.

For Questions 72–73, complete the flowchart provided below.

72. _____ is stabbed to death.

Octavian Caesar defeats Mark Antony at the Battle of Actium.

Octavian Caesar rejects dictatorship and restores the 73. _____

   a. Augustus Caesar

   b. Etruscans

   c. God-king

   d. Julius Caesar

   e. Legions

   f. Marcus Aurelius

   g. Senate

74. _____ suffered a decisive defeat at the Battle of Actium to Octavian Caesar, his primary rival in the struggle for control over Rome.
    a. Claudius
    b. Lepidus
    c. Mark Antony
    d. Nero

Passage #6: Lecture

75. Which statement most accurately expresses the professor's opinion of philosophy?
    a. The professor favors philosophy for its rejection of unfamiliar possibilities.
    b. The professor is cautious about how philosophy interferes with common sense.
    c. The professor believes philosophy can help people lead more rewarding lives.
    d. The professor argues that philosophy is necessary to support instinctive interests.

76. What is the meaning of the professor's fortress analogy?
    a. The professor is explaining how philosophy can turn life solitary.
    b. The professor is illustrating the danger and futility of living in a solely private world.
    c. The professor is comparing philosophy to unfamiliar situations.
    d. The professor is arguing that living in a fortress is better than being in prison.

For Questions 77–78, complete the table below.

Benefits of Philosophy
Increases 77._____ about the outer world.
Challenges common sense ideas to reveal new possibilities.
78._____ people's sense of wonder.

   a. Danger

   b. Ignorance

   c. Knowledge

   d. Limits

   e. Prejudices

   f. Safeguards

   g. Tyranny

191

79. The professors asks the students to read several _____ to prepare for the next class.
    a. Essays
    b. Handouts
    c. Textbook chapters
    d. Treatises

80. The value of philosophy is mostly derived from how it handles _____.
    a. Analogies
    b. Culture
    c. Laws
    d. Uncertainty

Speaking

81. Imagine you are hosting an exchange student. Talk about your experience learning English and what you've found to be the most helpful.

    • Preparation Time: 15 seconds
    • Response Time: 45 seconds

82. Read the conversation between two students and then answer the question that follows.

    (Emily) I don't get it, Laura. Why would you want to take a public interest job? You're going to graduate at the top of our law school class.

    (Laura) I want to make a meaningful impact on the world. There's a lot of people who can't afford a lawyer. I was one of those people. Before I graduated college, my family could barely afford to keep a roof over our heads and put food on our table, let alone pay legal fees. I can help some of those families who are suffering.

    (Emily) I get it, but you're throwing away an opportunity to *really* make a difference. You could join the top law firm in the country and work alongside the people who set policies for the whole country.

    (Laura) That's true, but I wouldn't feel right accepting hundreds of thousands of dollars to represent multinational corporations.

    (Emily) Okay, but that money could set up your future. You could realistically save enough to open up your own public interest firm.

    (Laura) That is basically my plan, except for the bit about working for a big law firm. I want to start on the ground floor, doing advocacy work and really finding out what works and what doesn't in the public interest sector. I'll make less money, but the money I do save will go further when I start my firm.

    (Emily) It seems like you've made your decision. Best of luck. I'm sure you'll be a star wherever you go.

    (Laura) Thanks so much. That means a lot.

Question: Summarize the conversation. Talk about where the students go to school, Emily's future plans, Laura's two objections, and how the conversation ends.

- Reading Time: 30 seconds
- Response Time: 45 seconds

83. Read the passage from the lecture and then answer the question that follows.

- Reading Time: 50 seconds
- Response Time: 45 seconds

(History Professor) When the United States entered the World War I the Allied Navies appeared to be lacking in effective means for combating the German submarines which had started a campaign of unrestricted warfare two months previously. It was extremely important, therefore, that immediate American naval assistance be furnished to aid them in meeting the crisis.

The task facing the American Navy was one of tremendous difficulty. It had to assist as soon as possible in counteracting the submarine menace and in addition had to organize means of providing passage across the Atlantic for hundreds of thousands of American troops and enormous quantities of supplies.

Action against submarines was initiated at once by dispatching to Europe the limited number of destroyers then available. These were augmented by converted yachts, gunboats, small cruisers and revenue cutters, and immediate steps were taken to build additional destroyers.

The first fighting unit of the American Navy to arrive in European waters was a detachment of six destroyers which, on May 4, 1917, steamed into the harbor at Queenstown, Ireland, where a main base was established. This force was soon increased to 34 destroyers.

Soon after the United States entered the war, the Cruiser and Transport Force was organized to carry American troops overseas. The few suitable vessels available were taken over by the Government at once and the German liners interned in American ports were later added to this fleet. Every effort was made throughout the war to obtain additional ships for this service, which carried a total of 911,000 men to Europe, or a little less than half of the number sent. Most of the remainder were transported in ships under British control.

To guard against submarine attack, American transports making the trip to Europe were, as far as practicable, gathered into groups and escorted through the danger zone by destroyers and other armed vessels. This method of combating the submarine menace was most successful and the results obtained were remarkable. Not a single vessel of the Cruiser and Transport Force was lost on the eastward voyage, although three ships returning to the United States were sunk out of a total of five torpedoed.

As the number of troops overseas increased, the task of supplying them became more difficult. This problem was met by the formation of the Naval Overseas Transportation Service, which was a force distinct from the troop transport organization. It developed into a fleet of more than 400 vessels, manned by approximately 4,500 officers and 29,000 men. To form this great organization it was necessary to take vessels from every available source, and included in it were ships taken over from the Shipping Board, new tonnage resulting from the intensive building program of the Emergency Fleet Corporation, and a number of ships which were brought from the Great Lakes under

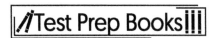

considerable difficulties. The convoy system was also used insofar as possible in the operation of this fleet, and only seven vessels were lost by enemy action. This was considered an exceptionally fine record.

As soon as the safety of the transports and supply ships had been reasonably assured, aggressive steps were taken against enemy submarines. This was done by the laying of mine barrages, the employment of a hunting force of small ships, supplemented by aircraft, and the use of submarines.

Source: American Armies and Battlefields in Europe: A History, Guide, and Reference Book, prepared by the American Battle Monuments Commission (2018), published by the Center of Military History (United States Army), found at https://permanent.access.gpo.gov/gpo92289/CMH_Pub_23-24.pdf

Question: Your classmate missed the lecture and asks you to catch her up. She asks you these questions: What challenges did the U.S. Navy face when the United States entered World War I? How did the U.S. Navy respond? Was the Navy successful?

- Preparation Time: 50 seconds
- Response Time: 45 seconds

84. You are a local politician, and the legislature is considering a new proposal. The proposal is to install red light cameras on Main Street in the busiest part of your electoral district. There has been a series of accidents in this area during the last year, and studies have shown that red light cameras significantly reduce accidents. But you also know the cameras would be wildly unpopular with your constituents, the people whose views you were elected to represent.

How do you vote? How will your constituency react to your decision, and what are the likely consequences?

- Preparation Time: 20 seconds
- Response Time: 45 seconds

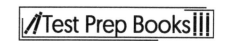

First Essay

1. First read the article below. Then click the link below the article and watch the TED Talk video. Then review the prompt and write an essay synthesizing the two sources.

"Confronting Opioids"

By the U.S. Centers for Disease Control and Prevention, (https://www.cdc.gov/features/confronting-opioids/index.html)

[1] Opioid overdoses continue to increase across all regions of the United States for both men and women and most age groups. Drug overdoses have dramatically increased over the last two decades, with deaths more than tripling between 1999 and 2016. In 2016, more than 63,000 people died from drug overdoses—more than 42,000 of these involved prescription or illicit opioids.

[2] The best ways to prevent opioid overdose deaths are to improve opioid prescribing, reduce exposure to both prescription and illicit opioids, prevent misuse, and to treat opioid use disorder. The Centers for Disease Control and Prevention (CDC) plays an essential role in opioid overdose prevention and takes a public health approach to address key aspects of the epidemic.

Timely, high-quality data are critical to help public health officials effectively respond to the opioid overdose epidemic. Data help us understand the extent of the problem, focus resources where they are needed most, and evaluate the success of prevention and response efforts. CDC recognizes the importance of data and is helping states track the epidemic and better focus their activities, as well as funding research to identify effective strategies to help prevent overdoses.

[3] States, local communities, and tribes play an important role in preventing opioid overdoses and related harms. They run prescription drug monitoring programs, regulate controlled substances, license healthcare providers, respond to drug overdose outbreaks, and run large public insurance programs such as Medicaid and workers compensation. CDC is funding state efforts to improve data collection and to implement evidence-based prevention strategies.

[4] Improving the way opioids are prescribed can ensure patients have access to safer, more effective pain treatment while reducing the number of people who misuse, abuse, or overdose from these drugs. Providers and the health systems in which they work are critical when it comes to promoting safer and more effective opioid prescribing. Providers and health systems can use the CDC Guideline for Prescribing Opioids for Chronic Pain to help address patient-centered clinical practices such as conducting thorough assessments, considering non-opioid treatments, monitoring risks, and safely discontinuing opioids as needed. Supporting healthcare providers and health systems with data, tools, and guidance for evidence-based decision-making related to opioid prescribing is an important component to patient safety.

[5] Helping Americans understand the severity of the epidemic and raising awareness about opioid use disorder and overdose is a key component of prevention. CDC launched the Rx Awareness communication campaign featuring testimonials from people recovering from opioid use disorder and those who have lost loved ones to prescription opioid overdose. The campaign's goal is educating people about the risks of prescription opioids and the importance of discussing safer and more effective pain management with healthcare providers. It also

promotes awareness of risks associated with recreational (non-medical) use of opioids and prevention.

[6] The opioid overdose epidemic has worsened with a rise in the use of illicit opioids. This fast-moving epidemic does not distinguish between age, sex, or location, and increases in deaths across states indicate the need for better coordination. Many different responders come together to prevent opioid overdoses and deaths, including health departments, law enforcement, and community-based organizations. Improving communication and collaboration between public health and public safety can help identify changes in illicit drug supply and coordinate a more timely and effective response. CDC recognizes that first responders including police, fire, and paramedics are on the frontlines of the epidemic and works to protect all public safety officials and provides guidance for those responding.

[7] Everyone plays an important role in preventing opioid overdose deaths through education, partnership, and collaboration.

2. Listen to the following lecture:
https://www.ted.com/talks/chera_kowalski_the_critical_role_librarians_play_in_the_opioid_crisis

3. Prompt: Apply the strategies to the situation described in the lecture and answer the following questions. What strategies could the library adopt? How would those strategies achieve the desired results? Who would be valuable and/or necessary partners in the library's fight against the opioid crisis? What obstacles will the library likely face?

Cite evidence found in the passage by placing the relevant paragraph number in parentheses at the end of the sentence.

Second Essay

Prepare an essay of about 300–600 words on the topic below.

> Margaret Atwood says "war is what happens when language fails." In an essay that is going to be read by educated adults, explain whether you agree or disagree with this observation. Support your argument with details and examples.

Answer Explanations #3

Reading

1. D: The passage does not proceed in chronological order since it begins by pointing out Christopher Columbus's explorations in America, so Choice *A* does not work. Although the author compares and contrasts Erikson with Christopher Columbus, this is not the main way in which the information is presented; therefore, Choice *B* does not work. Neither does Choice *C* because there is no mention of or reference to cause and effect in the passage. However, the passage does offer a conclusion (Leif Erikson deserves more credit) and premises (first European to set foot in the New World and first to contact the natives) to substantiate Erikson's historical importance. Thus, Choice *D* is correct.

2. C: Choice *C* is the correct answer because it is the author's opinion that Erikson deserves more credit. That, in fact, is the conclusion in the piece, but another person could argue that Columbus or another explorer deserves more credit for opening up the New World to exploration. Rather than being an indisputable fact, it is a subjective value claim. Choice *A* is incorrect because it describes facts: Leif Erikson was the son of Erik the Red and historians debate Leif's date of birth. These are not opinions. Choice *B* is incorrect; that Erikson called the land "Vinland" is a verifiable fact, as is Choice *D* because he did contact the natives almost 500 years before Columbus.

3. B: Choice *B* is correct because, as stated in the previous answer, it accurately identifies the author's statement that Erikson deserves more credit than he has received for being the first European to explore the New World. Choice *A* is incorrect because the author aims to go beyond describing Erikson as merely a legendary Viking. Choice *C* is incorrect because the author does not focus on Erikson's motivations, let alone name the spreading of Christianity as his primary objective. Choice *D* is incorrect because it is a premise that Erikson contacted the natives 500 years before Columbus, which is simply a part of supporting the author's conclusion.

4. B: Choice *B* is correct because the author wants the reader to be informed about Leif Erikson's contribution to exploring the new world. While several other answers are possible options, Choice *B* is the strongest. Choice *A* is incorrect because the author is not in any way trying to entertain the reader. Choice *C* is incorrect because the nature of the writing does not indicate the author would be satisfied with the reader merely being alerted to Erikson's exploration; instead, the author is making an argument about the credit he should receive. Choice *D* is incorrect because the author goes beyond merely a suggestion; "suggest" is too vague.

5. D: Choice *D* is correct because there are two examples of historians having trouble pinning down important dates in Viking history: Leif Erikson's date of birth the results of his encounter with the natives of Vinland. Choice *A* is incorrect because the author never addresses the Vikings' state of mind or emotions. Choice *B* is incorrect because the author does not elaborate on Erikson's exile and whether he would have become an explorer if not for his banishment. Choice *C* is incorrect because there is not enough information to support this premise. It is unclear whether Erikson informed the King of Norway of his finding. Although it is true that the King did not send a follow-up expedition, he could have simply chosen not to expend the resources after receiving Erikson's news. It is not possible to logically infer whether Erikson told him.

6. B: But in fact, there is not much substance to such speculation, and most anti-Stratfordian arguments can be refuted with a little background about Shakespeare's time and upbringing. The thesis is a

statement that contains the author's topic and main idea. The main purpose of this article is to use historical evidence to provide counterarguments to anti-Stratfordians. Choice *A* is simply a definition; Choice *C* is a supporting detail, not a main idea; and Choice *D* represents an idea of anti-Stratfordians, not the author's opinion.

7. C: Rhetorical question. This requires readers to be familiar with different types of rhetorical devices. A rhetorical question is a question that is asked not to obtain an answer but to encourage readers to consider an issue more deeply.

8. B: By explaining grade school curriculum in Shakespeare's time. This question asks readers to refer to the organizational structure of the article and demonstrate understanding of how the author provides details to support the argument. This particular detail can be found in the second paragraph: "even though he did not attend university, grade school education in Shakespeare's time was actually quite rigorous."

9. A: Busy. This is a vocabulary question that can be answered using context clues. Other sentences in the paragraph describe London as "the most populous city in England" filled with "crowds of people," giving an image of a busy city full of people. Choice *B* is incorrect because London was in Shakespeare's home country, not a foreign one. Choice *C* is not mentioned in the passage. Choice *D* is not a good answer choice because the passage describes how London was a popular and important city, probably not an underdeveloped one.

10. B: This sentence is an example of a metaphor. Metaphors make a comparison between two things, usually saying that one thing *is* another thing. Here, the author is saying that Shakespeare *is* "the great magician." Choice *A*, personification, is when an inanimate object is given human characteristics, so this is incorrect. Choice *C*, simile, is making a comparison between two things using *like* or *as*, so this is incorrect. Choice *D*, allusion, is an indirect reference to a place, person, or event that happened in the past, so this is also incorrect.

11. D: Remember from the first passage that anti-Stratfordians are those who believe that Shakespeare *did not* write the plays, so Stratfordians are people who believe that Shakespeare *did* write the plays. The author of Passage 2 is disbelieving and critical of the Stratfordian point of view. We see this especially in the second paragraph, where the author states it is a supposition "so wild that it can only be entertained by those who are prepared to accept it as a miracle." All of the other answer choices are incorrect.

12. D: Sentence 2 is a contrast to the idea in Sentence 1. In the first sentence, the author states that they, at one time, believed that Shakespeare was the author of his plays. The second sentence is a contrast to that statement by saying the author no longer believes that the author of the plays is Shakespeare. The other answer choices are incorrect.

13. B: This writing style is best described as persuasive. The author is trying to persuade the audience, with evidence, that Shakespeare actually wrote his own dramas. Choice *A*, expository writing, means to inform or explain. Expository writing usually does not set out to persuade the audience of something, only to inform them, so this choice is incorrect. Choice *C*, narrative writing, is used to tell a story, so this is incorrect. Choice *D*, descriptive writing, uses all five senses to paint a picture for the reader, so this choice is also incorrect.

14. C: Topography is the shape and features of the Earth. The author is implying here that whoever wrote Shakespeare's plays studied the physical features of foreign cities. Choices *A, B,* and *D* are

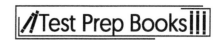

incorrect. Choice *A* is simply known as climate. Choice *B* would just be considered the "agriculture of a particular area." Choice *D*, aspects of humans within society, would be known as *anthropology*.

15. A: The author of Passage 2 believes that Shakespeare the actor did not write the plays. We see this at the end of the first paragraph where the author contends that the "'Stratford rustic' is not the true Shakespeare." The author does believe that Shakespeare was an actor, as the author calls this Shakespeare a "Player" throughout the text, so Choices *B* and *D* are incorrect. Choice *C* is incorrect, as the author does not believe that Shakespeare wrote the plays.

16. D: That in order to write about the topography and civilization of a place, one must have travelled there and mingled with the people. We are clear the two authors would disagree over this sentiment. The author of Passage 1 says that "[o]ne needn't travel the continent in order to learn and write about its culture." The author of Passage 2 says "that *he* should have travelled into foreign lands, studied the life and topography of foreign cities" is an assertion that the one who wrote the plays *must have* travelled into foreign lands and studied the life and topography of foreign cities. Choice *A* is something the author of Passage 2 quotes, but we can assume both the authors *do care* whether or not Shakespeare wrote the plays. Choices *B and C* are close. However, the author of Passage 2 does not mention the country education, so we do not know their opinion on Choice *C*. The author does hint that the socioeconomic status of the "rustic" actor would be a limitation to Shakespeare's abilities. However, the author of Passage 2 is most straightforward about Choice *D*.

17. D: This is the argument that the author voices in the second paragraph of Passage 2. A country education and socioeconomic status do not deflect true genius if the individual is willing to absorb the textual and cultural knowledge surrounding them. Choice *A* is incorrect; there is no "new evidence" mentioned in the first passage about Shakespeare having travelled. Choice *B* is incorrect; there is no evidence from Shakespeare's peers that he wrote the plays. Choice *C* is incorrect; this is the author's belief in Passage 2, not Passage 1.

18. B: Passage 1 is written in opposition to Passage 2. We can see the author of Passage 1 stating that it's likely that Shakespeare wrote his own plays. The author of Passage 2 says that it is unlikely that Shakespeare wrote his own plays. This makes Choices *A* and *C* incorrect. Choice *D* is incorrect because we have no direct quotation in Passage 1 that comes directly from Passage 2, only general concepts.

19. A: The last phrase is an example of a rhetorical question. Rhetorical questions are asked in order to make a dramatic effect or point rather than to receive an actual answer. Choice *B*, literary allusion, are indirect references to some historical event, person, or object. Choice *C*, hyperbole, is an exaggeration of something, so this is incorrect. Choice *D*, symbolism, is used to represent an idea or quality of something, like how a rose symbolizes love in western culture.

20. B: Strong dislike. This vocabulary question can be answered using context clues and common sense. Based on the rest of the conversation, the reader can gather that Albert isn't looking forward to his marriage. As the Count notes that "you don't appear to me to be very enthusiastic on the subject of this marriage," and also remarks on Albert's "objection to a young lady who is both rich and beautiful," readers can guess Albert's feelings. The answer choice that most closely matches "objection" and "not . . . very enthusiastic" is *B*, "strong dislike."

21. C: Their name is more respected than the Danglars'. This inference question can be answered by eliminating incorrect answers. Choice *A* is tempting, considering that Albert mentions money as a concern in his marriage. However, although he may not be as rich as his fiancée, his father still has a stable income of 50,000 francs a year. Choice *B* isn't mentioned at all in the passage, so it's impossible to

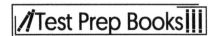

make an inference. Finally, Choice *D* is false because Albert's father arranged his marriage but his mother doesn't approve of it. Evidence for Choice *C* can be found in the Count's comparison of Albert and Eugénie: "she will enrich you, and you will ennoble her." In other words, the Danglars are wealthier but the Morcef family has a more noble background.

22. D: Apprehensive. As in question 7, there are many clues in the passage that indicate Albert's attitude towards his marriage—far from enthusiastic, he has many reservations. This question requires test takers to understand the vocabulary in the answer choices. "Pragmatic" is closest in meaning to "realistic," and "indifferent" means "uninterested." The only word related to feeling worried, uncertain, or unfavorable about the future is "apprehensive."

23. B: He is like a wise uncle, giving practical advice to Albert. Choice *A* is incorrect because the Count's tone is friendly and conversational. Choice *C* is also incorrect because the Count questions why Albert doesn't want to marry a young, beautiful, and rich girl. While the Count asks many questions, he isn't particularly "probing" or "suspicious"—instead, he's asking to find out more about Albert's situation and then give him advice about marriage.

24. A: She belongs to a noble family. Though Albert's mother doesn't appear in the scene, there's more than enough information to answer this question. More than once is his family's noble background mentioned (not to mention that Albert's mother is the Comtess de Morcef, a noble title). The other answer choices can be eliminated—she is obviously deeply concerned about her son's future; money isn't her highest priority because otherwise she would favor a marriage with the wealthy Danglars; and Albert describes her "clear and penetrating judgment," meaning she makes good decisions.

25. C: The richest people in society were also the most respected. The Danglars family is wealthier but the Morcef family has a more aristocratic name, which gives them a higher social standing. Evidence for the other answer choices can be found throughout the passage: Albert mentioned receiving money from his father's fortune after his marriage; Albert's father has arranged this marriage for him; and the Count speculates that Albert's mother disapproves of this marriage because Eugénie isn't from a noble background like the Morcef family, implying that she would prefer a match with a girl from aristocratic society.

26. A: He seems reluctant to marry Eugénie, despite her wealth and beauty. This is a reading comprehension question, and the answer can be found in the following lines: "'I confess,' observed Monte Cristo, "that I have some difficulty in comprehending your objection to a young lady who is both rich and beautiful.'" Choice *B* is the opposite (Albert's father is the one who insists on the marriage), Choice *C* incorrectly represents Albert's eagerness to marry, and Choice *D* describes a more positive attitude than Albert actually feels ("repugnance").

27. A: First person. This is a straightforward question that requires readers to know that a first-person narrator speaks from an "I" point of view.

28. D: He doesn't understand all of the languages being used. This can be inferred from the fact that the traveler must refer to his dictionary to understand those around him. Choice *A* isn't a good choice because the traveler seems to wonder why the driver needs to drive so fast. Choice *B* isn't mentioned in the passage, and doesn't seem like a good answer choice in the first place because he seems wholly unfamiliar with his surroundings, which is also why Choice *C* can be eliminated.

29. B: From fearful to charmed. This can be found in the first sentence of the third paragraph, which states, "I soon lost sight and recollection of ghostly fears in the beauty of the scene as we drove along."

Also, readers should get a sense of foreboding from the first two paragraphs, where superstitious villagers seem frightened on the traveler's behalf. However, the final paragraph changes to delighted descriptions of the landscape's natural beauty. Choices *A* and *D* can be eliminated because the traveler is anxious, not relaxed or comfortable at the beginning of the passage. Choice *C* can also be eliminated because the traveler doesn't gain any particular insights in the last paragraph, and in fact continues to lament that he cannot understand the speech of those around him.

30. D: A complete stranger. The answer to this reading comprehension question can be found in the second paragraph, when the traveler is "just starting for an unknown place to meet an unknown man"— in other words, a complete stranger.

31. C: The traveler will soon encounter danger or evil. Answering this prediction question requires readers to understand foreshadowing, or hints that the author gives about what will happen next. There are numerous hints scattered throughout this passage: the villager's sorrow and sympathy for the traveler and their superstitious actions; the spooky words that the traveler overhears; the driver's unexplained haste. All of these point to a danger that awaits the protagonist.

32. A: "I must say they weren't cheering to me, for amongst them were "Ordog"—Satan, "pokol"—hell, "stregoica"—witch, "vrolok" and "vlkoslak"—both of which mean the same thing, one being Slovak and the other Servian for something that is either were-wolf or vampire." As mentioned in question 39, this sentence is an example of how the author hints at evil to come for the traveler. The other answer choices aren't related to the passage's grim foreshadowing.

33. B: Narrative, Choice *A*, means a written account of connected events. Think of narrative writing as a story. Choice *C*, expository writing, generally seeks to explain or describe some phenomena, whereas Choice *D*, technical writing, includes directions, instructions, and/or explanations. This passage is persuasive writing, which hopes to change someone's beliefs based on an appeal to reason or emotion. The author is aiming to convince the reader that smoking is terrible. They use health, price, and beauty in their argument against smoking, so Choice *B*, persuasive, is the correct answer.

34. B: The author is opposed to tobacco. They cite disease and deaths associated with smoking. They point to the monetary expense and aesthetic costs. Choice *A* is incorrect because alternatives to smoking are not addressed in the passage. Choice *C* is incorrect because it does not summarize the passage but is just a premise. Choice *D* is incorrect because, while these statistics are a premise in the argument, they do not represent a summary of the piece. Choice *B* is the correct answer because it states the three critiques offered against tobacco and expresses the author's conclusion.

35. C: We are looking for something the author would agree with, so it will most likely be anti-smoking or an argument in favor of quitting smoking. Choice *C* is correct because the author is attempting to persuade smokers to quit smoking. Choice *A* is incorrect because the author does not speak against means of cessation. Choice *B* is incorrect because the author does not reference other substances. Choice *D* is incorrect; the author would not encourage reducing taxes to encourage a reduction of smoking costs, thereby helping smokers to continue the habit.

36. D: Here, we are looking for an opinion of the author rather than a fact or statistic. Choice *D* is correct as an opinion because smell is subjective. Some people might like the smell of smoke, they might not have working olfactory senses, and they might not find the smell of smoke akin to "pervasive nastiness," so this is the expression of an opinion. Thus, Choice *D* is the correct answer. Choice *A* is incorrect because quoting statistics from the Centers of Disease Control and Prevention is stating facts, not opinions. Choice *B* is incorrect because it expresses the fact that cigarettes sometimes cost more than a

few gallons of gas. It would be an opinion if the author said that cigarettes were not affordable. Choice *C* is incorrect because yellow stains are a known possible adverse effect of smoking.

37. C: This is a tricky question, but it can be solved through careful context analysis and vocabulary knowledge. One can infer that the use of "expedient," while not necessarily very positive, isn't inherently bad in this context either. Note how in the next line, he says, "but most governments are usually, and all governments are sometimes, inexpedient." This use of "inexpedient" indicates that a government becomes a hindrance rather than a solution; it slows progress rather than helps facilitate progress. Thus, Choice *A* and Choice *D* can be ruled out because they are hindrances or problems and would work better with inexpedient rather than expedient. Choice B makes no logical sense. Therefore, Choice *C* is the best description of *expedient*.

38. B: Choice *B* is the most accurate representation of Thoreau's views. Essentially, Thoreau brings to light the fact that the few people in power can twist government and policy for their own needs. Choices *A* and *C* are also correct to a degree, but the answer asks for the best description, which is Choice *B*. While Choice *D* is the only answer that mentions the Mexican War directly, Thoreau clearly thinks the war is unnecessary because the people generally didn't consent to the war.

39. D: Choice *C* and Choice *B* are incorrect. Thoreau is not defending government in any way. His views are set against government. As mentioned in the text, he appreciates little government but favors having no government structure at all. The text is reflective by nature, but what makes Choice *D* a more appropriate answer is the presence of evidence in the text. Thoreau cites current events and uses them to illustrate the point he's trying to make.

40. C: One of Thoreau's biggest criticisms of government is its capacity to impose on the people's freedoms and liberties, enacting rules that the people don't want and removing power from the individual. None of the scenarios directly impose specific regulations or restrictions on the people, except Prohibition. Prohibition removed the choice to consume alcohol in favor of abstinence, which was favored by the religious conservatives of the time. Thus, Thoreau would point out that this is a clear violation of free choice and an example of government meddling.

41. A: Choice *B* is totally irrelevant. Choice *C* is also incorrect; Thoreau never personifies government. Also, this doesn't coincide with his wooden gun analogy. Choice *D* is compelling because of its language but doesn't define the statement. Choice *A* is the most accurate summary of the main point of Thoreau's statement.

42. B: Thoreau specifically cites that legislators "are continually putting in their way." This reflects his suspicion and concern of government intervention. Recall that Thoreau continually mentions that government, while meant as a way to establish freedom, is easily used to suppress freedom, piling on regulations and rules that inhibit progress. Choice *B* is the answer that most directly states how Thoreau sees government getting in the way of freedom.

43. A: Even though it isn't clear who Boltzmann is, analyzing the content of the passage will reveal clues to what field he most likely studies. While anthropology, the study of humans, might be relevant further into the passage, the writer doesn't open his passage with a specific focus on human origins or studies, so Choice *C* can be eliminated. Choice *D* can also be eliminated because the passage isn't focused on how increasing the food supply would be done—this is presented more as an abstract example. Dietician is a very tempting choice, especially since the article deals with the need for organisms to consume resources for energy, but the correct answer is physicist. Boltzmann was, in fact, a physicist, but even without knowing this fact, there are clues that reveal his field. Note how this text emphasizes the perpetuating relationship between mass and energy. The field of physics is defined as the study of nature as well as the interplay of mass and energy. Choice *A* is correct.

44. C: This is another tricky question that doesn't give the precise answer but instead relies on the careful reading of the text and the knowledge of the reader. Essentially, the passage is discussing how energy consumption is a major factor in evolution and how this can apply to human sustainment and life in general. Living beings must consume food/resources to survive, and the food is converted to energy; energy consumption and conservation are key focuses of survival and evolution—the themes of the text. Organisms must then draw from resources where they live, which is occupied by other organisms. Therefore, in this case, competing doesn't necessarily refer to combat but to the fact that many organisms are trying to survive off the same or similar resources simultaneously. Essentially, they are coexisting together and struggling to live off the land. Choice *C* is the best choice.

45. D: Choice *A* is very tempting; it's clear that his goal is to educate the reader on a concept within evolution. Choice *B* is totally incorrect. Energy clearly does have an impact on evolution. Choice *C* is also compelling. The author does use an example of how environmental shifts can impact the population; he hasn't yet proposed a plan of study or urged the reader to support a specific environmental enhancement study. Choice *D* is actually very similar to Choice *A*. What makes Choice *D* the optimal answer is the specific use of capturing energy, which is more consistent with the text. The author also elaborates on how energy impacts evolution and the survival of key traits. He is educating the reader, but he's also trying to prove his point about energy and evolution.

46. B: Choice *A* can be immediately eliminated, as the passage specifically states, "whenever such organisms arise, natural selection will operate to preserve and increase them." This literally means that these positive traits will be passed on to following generations, increasing their chances of survival within the flux of the natural world. Choices *C* and *D* are incorrect for similar reasons.

47. D: Choice *B* is incorrect because the author goes into detail about how the three concepts are interconnected. On that note, Choice *A* is somewhat backward, as evolution is not a constant but a resulting trend. Energy does not create evolution, nor does evolution necessarily create shifting mass amounts. Rather, evolution occurs through a result of several key factors such as energy influencing the mass of an organism and the organism's successful use of that stored energy. Thus, Choice *D* is the accurate summary. Choice *C* is incorrect because no rate of evolution is mentioned specifically.

Listening

48. 69

49. 5.6 million

50. 600

51. 50

52. 480,000

53. C: The professor opens the lecture by saying the surgeon general first reported on smoking and health in 1964.

54. A: The major point of disagreement starts with the hockey fan's assertion that the basketball team playing well at the end of a game always wins. The basketball fan responds, "I strongly disagree." The basketball fan concedes that Choice *B* is a problem, and Choices *C* and *D* are never discussed.

55. A: The basketball fan claims every basketball team has at least one talented player. In response, the hockey fan says, "I doubt that's true, but I don't know enough to dispute you." The hockey fan believes Choices *B* and *C* to be true, and he disputes Choice *D*.

56. C: The hockey fan argues that a basketball team can easily score ten consecutive points within a few minutes of game time, which allows teams to overcome massive deficits; therefore, whoever plays well at the end of a game always wins. Choice *A* isn't part of the hockey fan's argument. Choice *B* is something the hockey fan also thinks, but it's an entirely separate issue. Choice *D* is what the basketball fan uses to argue against hockey.

57. A: The basketball fan contends that the icy conditions make hockey games dependent on luck. At the beginning of the conversation, the basketball fan says, "Hockey involves sliding a frozen puck around a sheet of ice that's constantly melting and getting cut up by skates." The other choices aren't part of the basketball fan's criticism.

58. C: The hockey fan believes that a high work ethic and skill mitigate the icy conditions. The remaining choices might also be true, but they aren't included in the hockey fan's rebuttal.

59. D: After the student mentions their family is in the process of moving, the professor wrongly assumes the student's parents bought a house. Thus, Choice *D* is the correct answer. It's true the student is staying with friends and family, so this can't be an incorrect assumption. Therefore, Choice *A* is incorrect. The professor asks if the student was moving to an apartment, which isn't an assumption. Therefore, Choice *B* is incorrect. The student is effectively homeless, but the professor doesn't make this assumption. So Choice *C* is incorrect.

60. B: Since the student can't make it to the professor's office hours, the professor offers to meet with the student on Tuesday morning at 9:00 a.m. Thus, Choice *B* is the correct answer. The professor has office hours on Monday and Wednesday, but the student cannot meet then. So Choice *A* and Choice *C* are both incorrect. Choice *D* is incorrect because a meeting on Thursday is never discussed during the conversation.

61. B: When the student says they don't want to trouble their professor by meeting with them, the professor explains it's not a problem because they typically waste time playing games on their phone during their downtime. Thus, Choice *B* is the correct answer. The professor doesn't mention grading homework assignments or preparing lesson plans. Therefore, Choice *A* and Choice *C* are both incorrect. The professor talks about the student's personal life during this conversation, but the professor doesn't say that's what they typically do during their downtime. Therefore, Choice *D* is incorrect.

62. A: The student says they can't attend the professor's office hours because they have basketball practice in the evenings. Thus, Choice *A* is the correct answer. The professor holds office hours in the evening, but the student isn't able to receive extra help at that time. So, Choice *B* is incorrect. Neither lacrosse practice nor voice lessons are mentioned in the conversation, so Choice *C* and Choice *D* are both incorrect.

63. C: The student says they've been "bouncing between friends' and relatives' homes" after their family was evicted. This most likely means the student is staying with a number of different people on a

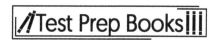

temporary basis. Thus, Choice *C* is the correct answer. The student mentions they're excited to have sleepovers with their cousins, but that doesn't explain the meaning of this phrase. Therefore, Choice *A* is incorrect. The student is temporarily staying with friends and relatives, but they don't mention relatives' friends. Therefore, Choice *B* is incorrect. Choice *D* is incorrect because the student doesn't characterize this issue as a search for a permanent home.

64. C: The conversation is about the possibility of the student changing majors. Since the student has already taken several British literature courses, the academic advisor suggests minoring in British literature because the student would only need to take two 300-level courses. Thus, Choice *C* is the correct answer. There are no other course requirements for the minor, so none of the other answer choices apply.

65. A, D, G: The student is only just beginning a creative writing major, so there are significant course requirements. The academic advisor mentions the student needs to complete three 100-level courses, three 300-level courses, and a capstone course. Thus, Choice *A*, Choice *D*, and Choice *G* are the correct answers. The student must take three 100-level courses, not four, so Choice *B* is incorrect. The two 300-level courses are a requirement for the British literature minor, not the creative writing major, so Choice *C* is incorrect. The academic advisor never mentions 400-level courses, so Choice *E* and Choice *F* are both incorrect.

66. B: The student asks the academic advisor whether they can finish their classes before 3:00 p.m. in order to pick up night shifts at work. Thus, Choice *B* is the correct answer. The student never mentions their study schedule or extracurricular commitments, so Choice *A* and Choice *C* are incorrect. The student does want to complete their degree in four years, which is why the student wants to take classes over the summer. However, the desire to finish classes earlier in the day is more directly related to their work schedule and finances, so Choice *B* is the better answer. Therefore, Choice *D* is incorrect.

67. C: The student needs to take three 100-level creative writing courses next semester so they can enroll in 300-level courses as soon as possible. Thus, Choice *C* is the correct answer. The student only needs to take two 300-level British literature courses to complete a minor, so Choice *A* is incorrect. None of the other answer choices are subjects in which the student needs to take a 100-level course.

68. F: The student needs to complete two general education courses: language and math. Language best fits in the student's schedule for next semester, so they're planning to take a math course next year. Thus, Choice *F* is the correct answer. British literature and creative writing aren't general education requirements; therefore, Choice *A* and Choice *C* are incorrect. Capstone courses are the final class to complete a major, not a general education requirement, so Choice *B* is incorrect. Choice *D* is incorrect because the student has already completed the English 101 general education requirement. History and science aren't mentioned during the conversation, so Choice *E* and Choice *G* are both incorrect.

69. A: At the beginning of the lecture, the professor describes how Julius Caesar moved his troops across the Rubicon to march on Rome in 49 B.C. Thus, Choice *A* is the correct answer. Cleopatra was an Egyptian ruler, and she never marched Roman legions across the Rubicon. Therefore, Choice *B* is incorrect. Julius Caesar crossed the Rubicon to overthrow Pompey the Great, so Choice *C* is incorrect. Tiberius Caesar served as emperor more than 50 years after Julius Caesar crossed the Rubicon; thus, Choice *D* is not the correct answer.

70. B: Shortly after describing the murder of Julius Caesar, the professor provides a short history of the Second Triumvirate, which included Lepidus, Mark Antony, and Octavian Caesar. So Choice *A*, Choice *C*,

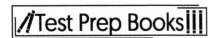
and Choice *D* are all incorrect. Nero ruled nearly a century after the end of the Second Triumvirate. Thus, Choice *B* is the correct answer.

71. A: At the end of the lecture, the professor describes how all of the emperors from Tiberius Caesar to Marcus Aurelius were "emperors of the legion" because their regimes were created and occasionally destroyed by Roman soldiers. Thus, Choice *A* is the correct answer. Roman populists did rail against corruption and promote authoritarianism; however, the professor doesn't mention either populism or corruption. So Choice *B* is incorrect. Emperors refused to restore the power of the Senate because their right to rule depended on military might. In addition, Octavian Caesar was one of the most successful emperors in Roman history. Therefore, Choice *C* is incorrect. Choice *D* is incorrect because the professor emphasizes military power over political alliances.

72. D: In the middle of the lecture, the professor describes Julius Caesar's murder in front of a statue of Pompey the Great during protests against his dictatorial governing style. Thus, Choice *D* is the correct answer. Augustus Caesar is the name adopted by Octavian Caesar, and he ultimately succeeded Julius Caesar. Therefore, Choice *A* is incorrect. Likewise, Marcus Aurelius served as emperor after the murder of Julius Caesar; therefore, Choice *F* is incorrect. The other answer choices don't list individual people, so they don't fit the sentence and must therefore be incorrect.

73. G: In the middle of the lecture, the professor contrasts the temperament of Octavian Caesar with that of his uncle, Julius Caesar. Unlike his uncle, Octavian Caesar didn't desire dictatorial control, so he restored some power to the senate, which was a more democratic form of governance. Thus, Choice *G* is the correct answer. The Etruscans lived in Rome five centuries before Octavian Caesar rose to power, so Choice *B* is incorrect. The lecture repeatedly refers to Octavian Caesar's rejection of the concept of a Roman God-king; therefore, Choice *C* is incorrect. Legions were large units of Roman soldiers. Octavian Caesar leveraged the power of the legions to defeat his rivals, but his restoration of the Senate limited the political influence of the legions. So, Choice *E* is incorrect.

74. C: Approximately halfway through the lecture, the professor describes how the Second Triumvirate collapsed during the aftermath of Julius Caesar's murder, and the civil war ended after Octavian Caesar defeated Mark Antony at the Battle of Actium. Thus, Choice *C* is the correct answer. Claudius and Nero are mentioned at the end of the lecture, but they both served as emperor long after the Battle of Actium and Octavian's reign as emperor. Therefore, Choice *A* and Choice *D* are both incorrect. While Lepidus was part of the Second Triumvirate, the professor specifically names Mark Antony as Octavian Caesar's chief rival and the loser of the Battle of Actium. So, Choice *B* is incorrect.

75. C: The professor repeatedly argues that philosophy frees people by showing them new possibilities. Therefore, the professor definitely has a positive view of philosophy and finds it rewarding. Thus, Choice *C* is the correct answer. The professor favors philosophy because it embraces the uncertain and unfamiliar, so Choice *A* is incorrect. At the beginning of the lecture, the professor asserts that philosophy frees people from prejudices related to common sense, and this claim isn't cautious. Therefore, Choice *B* is incorrect. Choice *D* is incorrect because the professor believes philosophy weakens instinctive interests.

76. B: The professor makes the fortress analogy at the end of the lecture. In this analogy, the professor claims that life without philosophy reduces people living in a private world of instinctive interests, which can never join up with anything larger. The fortress is "beleaguered," meaning it is under attack; it is endangered, and the "garrison" or troops inside cannot escape because of the enemy outside. The troops will die in the fortress, and the people who lack philosophy will end their days without ever

seeing a wider world than their private instincts. Thus, Choice *B* is the correct answer. Choice *A* is incorrect because it states the opposite of what the professor believes. The professor is arguing that philosophy helps people escape the metaphorical fortress. While the professor argues that philosophy helps people navigate unfamiliar situations, the fortress represents the private world in this analogy. Therefore, Choice *C* is incorrect. The professor doesn't compare living in a beleaguered fortress and a prison; instead, he uses both to illustrate the dangers of living in a private world. Therefore, Choice *D* is incorrect.

77. C: In the middle of the lecture, the professor discusses how philosophy increases knowledge about possibilities in the outer world, which helps people escape their private world of instinctive interests. Thus, Choice *C* is the correct answer. The professor repeatedly characterizes living in the private world as more dangerous than the outer world, so Choice *A* is incorrect. Choice *B* is incorrect because it reverses the professor's argument about how philosophy makes people more knowledgeable about the outer world. Tyranny doesn't make grammatical sense, and the professor would argue that philosophy reduces the tyranny of living in a private world. Therefore, Choice *G* is incorrect.

78. F: The correct answer must be a verb to properly complete the sentence. During the middle of the lecture, the professor describes how philosophy helps people continuously feel a sense of wonder by showing them familiar things in unfamiliar ways. In other words, philosophy safeguards people's sense of wonder by preventing everything from becoming familiar. Thus, Choice *F* is the correct answer. The professor contends that philosophy introduces people to new possibilities and frees their thoughts, which is close to the opposite of limiting people's sense of wonder. So, Choice *D* is incorrect. The professor asserts that the private world of instinctive thoughts prejudices people's sense of wonder, and philosophy is argued to be the cure. Therefore, Choice *E* is the correct answer.

79. A: At the very end of the lecture, the professor asks students to read essays by Jeremy Bentham and John Stuart Mill in order to prepare for their upcoming unit on Utilitarianism. Thus, Choice *A* is the correct answer. Handouts, textbook chapters, and treatises are never mentioned; therefore, Choice *B*, and Choice *C*, and Choice *D* are all incorrect.

80. D: Near the beginning of the lecture, the professor directly states that the value of philosophy is derived from its uncertainty. Furthermore, the professor repeatedly praises the value of philosophy in its treatment of uncertainty. Thus, Choice *D* is the correct answer. The professor uses analogies about fortresses and prisons to make a point about private worlds being dangerous, but the professor never claims that philosophy is most valuable for its handling of analogies. Therefore, Choice *A* is incorrect. Choice *B* is incorrect because culture isn't discussed during the lecture. Customs are discussed but only in the context of philosophy helping people overcome customs and navigate uncertainty. Likewise, the professor doesn't discuss philosophy's implications for laws or legal systems, so Choice *C* is incorrect.

Listening Transcripts

<u>Passage #1</u>
(Narrator) Listen to the professor's lecture and then answer the questions.

(Professor) It has now been more than 50 years since the original 1964 U.S. Surgeon General's report on smoking and health. In 2014, tobacco use, primarily the combustible tobacco products dominated by cigarettes, is estimated by the Surgeon General to prematurely kill even more users than ever before: 480,000 adults annually; furthermore, it is estimated that 5.6 million children alive in 2014 will die prematurely of a tobacco-related disease unless more is done. The Surgeon General also reports that

cigarettes have killed over 20 million users, more American deaths than in any of the wars since the founding of the Nation. Moreover, the effects of combustible tobacco have been underestimated because analysts combined disease-specific causes of death rather than considering all-cause mortality…

…The enemy is the combustion or burning of tobacco…Cigarettes have approximately 600 ingredients; when burned, they create carbon monoxide, particulate matter, and more than 7,000 chemicals, commonly referred to as tars. At least 69 of these chemicals are known to cause cancer, and many are poisonous…

…A renewed call to action through the lens of social justice is needed now more than ever. This is not only for the sake of the current generation of adult tobacco users and for the current generation of vulnerable children, adolescents, and young adults who are potential users, but also especially for priority populations in whom cigarette use is highest (i.e., economically disadvantaged people and ethnic and racial minorities), those with comorbid mental and substance abuse disorders, and finally, for the generations to come.

There is great excitement at the prospect of the global eradication of smallpox, polio, and measles, and dramatic inroads and investments have been made into reducing the impact of malaria and HIV/ AIDS, as well as increasing concerns about global warming and carbon footprints. Why not place the wholly preventable deaths and disease burdens of tobacco use behavior on the same priority list of scourges to be eradicated? We can plausibly imagine a world where our families and generations to come will all grow up free of the known preventable harms of using tobacco products, especially the lethal and addictive combustibles like cigarettes, cigars, and hookah.

"Cigarettes: The Rise and Decline But Not Demise of the Greatest Behavioral Health Disasters of the 20th Century" by David B Abrams et al. Population Health: Behavioral and Social Science Insights, edited by Robert M. Kaplan et al. (2015), published by the Agency for Healthcare Research and Quality (National Institutes of Health)

Passage #2

(Narrator) Listen to the conversation between the basketball fan and hockey fan and then answer the questions.

(Basketball Fan) Hockey involves sliding a frozen puck around a sheet of ice that's constantly melting and getting cut up by skates. This means that the results are heavily influenced by luck.

(Hockey Fan) That's true, but the luck isn't determinative. The team with the higher work ethic and skill will always be in a much better position to win. Plus the icy conditions make the games more exciting. In contrast, most basketball games don't matter until the final few minutes of play.

(Basketball Fan) What are you talking about? Of course the entire basketball game matters. All the points count just the same.

(Hockey Fan) A basketball team can easily score ten consecutive points within a few minutes of game time, allowing teams to overcome massive deficits. So, whoever plays well at the end of the game always wins.

(Basketball Fan) I strongly disagree, and I watch basketball every night during the season.

(Hockey Fan) Why do you watch basketball every night? From the very start of the season, it's painfully obvious which team is going to win the championship every year. All the league's talent is consolidated in a handful of teams.

(Basketball Fan) There are admittedly some overpowering teams, but every team has at least one fun player to watch.

(Hockey Fan) I doubt that's true, but I don't know enough to dispute you.

(Basketball Fan) How about you come over to watch tomorrow night's game?

(Hockey Fan) I will if you come to a hockey game with me next week.

(Basketball Fan) That sounds like a plan.

Passage #3

(Narrator) Listen to a conversation between a professor and student, and then answer the questions that follow.

(Professor) Thank you for waiting after class. I've been meaning to speak to you for a while.

(Student) No problem, I have some time before basketball practice. What's up?

(Professor) Your performance on our last few assignments has not been up to your usual standard. Is there anything I can help you with?

(Student) No, my sleep schedule is just really off.

(Professor) That happens to me sometimes, too. It's really helped me to get into a bedtime routine, and to limit my screen time as I wind down for the night.

(Student) Thanks, but that's not the problem.

(Professor) Okay. What is the problem?

(Student) Our family has been in the process of moving.

(Professor) Oh, I see. That's great your parents were able to buy a house. Interest rates are historically low right now.

(Student) They didn't buy a house.

(Professor) Oh, I see. Sorry I assumed; that was wrong of me. Did you move into an apartment?

(Student) Kind of.

(Professor) What does that mean?

(Student) My mom lost her job last month, and we were evicted from our apartment. We've been bouncing between friends' and relatives' homes ever since.

(Professor) I'm sorry to hear that. Are you doing okay otherwise?

(Student) Yeah, it's a nice change of pace to have sleepovers with my cousins, but I don't like not knowing where I'll be staying every night. It stresses me out.

(Professor) That's very understandable. Is there anything I can do to help?

(Student) Could I have extra time on my tests? I always have difficulty finishing in time.

(Professor) I can't do that without a doctor's note, but I have office hours every Monday and Wednesday at six o'clock. Why don't you stop by?

(Student) I have basketball practice in the evenings, and coach benches us if we're late. I need to stay on the field to have a chance at playing professionally.

(Professor) What if I talked to your coach?

(Student) No! That'd make everything worse. I don't want him to know I'm struggling in class or anything about my home life. Basketball is my escape from everything, and I need to keep it that way.

(Professor) Education should come first, but I see your point. Do you have any free time in the morning?

(Student) Yeah, I don't have class or work before 10:00 a.m.

(Professor) That's perfect. I have Tuesday mornings free. Why don't you stop by my office around 9:00 a.m.?

(Student) No, you don't have to do that. I don't want to trouble you.

(Professor) It's no trouble at all. You're one of my best students, and I don't want to see you fall behind. Plus my New Year's resolution was to stop playing games on my phone, and that's typically all I do during my downtime.

(Student) Well, in that case, I could use the help. Thank you so much. I really appreciate it.

(Professor) No problem, I'll see you next Tuesday at 9:00 a.m.

(Student) Great, thanks again.

Passage #4
(Narrator) Listen to a conversation between a student and an academic advisor, and then answer the questions that follow.

(Student) Hey, thank you for meeting with me. I have a couple questions about my major and schedule for next semester.

(Academic Advisor) Sure thing.

(Student) I'm currently majoring in British literature, but I'm thinking about switching to creative writing. Is that possible?

(Academic Advisor) Yes, that's definitely possible. They're in the same department, so all you'd have to do is file the paperwork to make it official. You won't need to reapply to anything.

(Student) Great, but will my credits count toward my new major?

(Academic Advisor) Let me pull up your transcript and take a look.

(Student) Thanks.

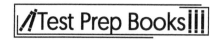

(Academic Advisor) Hmm, it looks like most will apply. British literature and creative writing both have the same general education requirements, so all of those will count the same as before. The only issue is some of the high-level British literature credits aren't applicable to creative writing.

(Student) So I should enroll in 300-level creative writing courses next semester?

(Academic Advisor) No, you need to start with 100-level courses. Once you complete three of those courses, you can start taking 300-level. Once you've taken three 300-level courses, then you'll qualify for a 600-level capstone course.

(Student) Oh man, I didn't realize I'd be so far behind. Can I take the 100-level and 300-level courses simultaneously? For example, next semester can I take all three 100-level courses and then one 300-level courses?

(Academic Advisor) No, like I said, the 100-level course requirement must be met before enrolling in a 300-level course.

(Student) Oh, man, I really can't afford to stay for a fifth year to complete my degree.

(Academic Advisor) We do offer an abbreviated semester over the summer. If you take the three 100-level courses in the Spring, then you could start taking 300-level courses this summer. That way, you could finish the 300-level courses next Fall and enroll in the capstone course the Spring semester of your senior year.

(Student) That could work. Can my British literature courses count as general education requirements?

(Academic Advisor) You've already completed English 101, so that won't work. British literature can't be substituted for the language, science, or math general education requirements that you're still missing. However, you could minor in British literature since you're only two 300-level courses short.

(Student) I'll definitely keep that in mind. Would it be possible to finish my classes by 3:00 p.m. next semester if I take the three 100-level creative writing classes and one class to meet my general education requirements? I'll need to pick up some night shifts if I'm going to take classes this summer.

(Academic Advisor) Yeah, but only if you take a language course. All the open math courses are in the evening.

(Student) Great, I'll sign up as soon as I get home. Thanks so much.

(Academic Advisor) You're welcome. Please let me know if you have any more questions.

(Student) Will do.

Passage #5
(Narrator) Listen to the lecture and then answer the questions.

(Professor) Today we'll be continuing our discussion of Rome's transition from a republic to an empire. We last left off with Julius Caesar's conquest of Gaul and his decision about whether to disband his legions as commanded by Pompey or to seize dictatorial power by marching on Rome.

It was illegal for a general to bring his troops out of the boundary of his command. The boundary between Caesar's command and Italy was a river called the Rubicon. In 49 B.C., Caesar crossed the

Rubicon, saying, "The die is cast," and he marched upon Pompey and Rome. Since then, "crossing the Rubicon" has become a metaphor for making an irrevocable decision.

After his overthrow of Pompey, Caesar was made dictator first for ten years and then (in 45 B.C.) for life. In effect he was made monarch of the empire for life. There was talk of his becoming a king, a word abhorrent to Rome since the expulsion of the Etruscans five centuries before. Caesar refused to be king, but he adopted the throne and scepter as symbols of his rule. After his defeat of Pompey, Caesar went on into Egypt and romanced Cleopatra, the last of the Ptolemies, the goddess queen of Egypt. She seems to have turned his head very completely. He brought back to Rome the Egyptian idea of a god-king. His statue was set up in a temple with the inscription "To the Unconquerable God." The expiring republicanism of Rome flared up in a last protest, and Caesar was stabbed to death in the Senate at the foot of the statue of his murdered rival, Pompey the Great.

Thirteen years more of this conflict of ambitious personalities followed. There was the Second Triumvirate, which consisted of Lepidus, Mark Antony and Octavian Caesar, the latter the nephew of Julius Caesar. Octavian like his uncle took the poorer, hardier western provinces where the best legions were recruited. In 31 B.C., he defeated Mark Antony, his only serious rival, at the naval battle of Actium, and made himself sole master of the Roman world. But Octavian was a man of different quality altogether from Julius Caesar. He had no foolish craving to be a god or a king. He had no queen-lover that he wished to dazzle. He restored freedom to the senate and the people of Rome. He declined to be dictator. The grateful senate, in return, gave him the reality of power instead of its mere forms. He was to be called not king, but "Princeps" and "Augustus." He became Augustus Caesar, the first of the Roman emperors (27 B.C. to 14 A.D.).

He was followed by Tiberius Caesar (14 to 37 A.D.), and he by others: Caligula, Claudius, Nero and so on up to Trajan (98 A.D.), Hadrian (117 A.D.), Antonius Pius (138 A.D.) and Marcus Aurelius (161- 180 A.D.). All these emperors were emperors of the legions. The soldiers made them, and the soldiers destroyed some of them. Gradually the senate fades out of Roman history, and the emperor and his administrative officials replace it.

Next class we'll begin discussing the fall of the Roman Empire. Please read pages 110 to 155 in the textbook to prepare.

This lecture has been adapted from A Short History of the World by H.G. Wells, 1922, found at https://www.gutenberg.org/files/35461/35461-h/35461-h.htm#chapXXXIII.

Passage #6
(Narrator) Listen to the lecture and then answer the questions.

(Professor) Hello class, today we'll be concluding our introductory lessons on general tenets of philosophy. This lecture will focus on the value of philosophy, particularly in the context of its relationship to our lived experiences.

The value of philosophy is, in fact, to be sought largely in its very uncertainty. The man who has no tincture of philosophy goes through life imprisoned in the prejudices derived from common sense, from the habitual beliefs of his age or his nation, and from convictions which have grown up in his mind without the co-operation or consent of his deliberate reason. To such a man the world tends to become definite, finite, obvious; common objects rouse no questions, and unfamiliar possibilities are contemptuously rejected. As soon as we begin to philosophize, on the contrary, we find, as we saw in our opening chapters, that even the most everyday things lead to problems to which only very

incomplete answers can be given. Philosophy, though unable to tell us with certainty what is the true answer to the doubts which it raises, is able to suggest many possibilities which enlarge our thoughts and free them from the tyranny of custom. Thus, while diminishing our feeling of certainty as to what things are, it greatly increases our knowledge as to what they may be; it removes the somewhat arrogant dogmatism of those who have never travelled into the region of liberating doubt, and it keeps alive our sense of wonder by showing familiar things in an unfamiliar aspect.

Apart from its utility in showing unsuspected possibilities, philosophy has a value—perhaps its chief value—through the greatness of the objects which it contemplates, and the freedom from narrow and personal aims resulting from this contemplation. The life of the instinctive man is shut up within the circle of his private interests: family and friends may be included, but the outer world is not regarded except as it may help or hinder what comes within the circle of instinctive wishes. In such a life there is something feverish and confined, in comparison with which the philosophic life is calm and free. The private world of instinctive interests is a small one, set in the midst of a great and powerful world which must, sooner or later, lay our private world in ruins. Unless we can so enlarge our interests as to include the whole outer world, we remain like a garrison in a beleaguered fortress, knowing that the enemy prevents escape and that ultimate surrender is inevitable. In such a life there is no peace, but a constant strife between the insistence of desire and the powerlessness of will. In one way or another, if our life is to be great and free, we must escape this prison and this strife.

Next class we'll have a quiz covering what we've discussed so far and then we'll start our unit on Utilitarianism. To prepare, please read the essays by Jeremy Bentham and John Stuart Mill I've posted on the class website.

This lecture has been adapted from *The Problems of Philosophy by Bertrand Russell*, 1912, found at https://www.gutenberg.org/files/5827/5827-h/5827-h.htm#link2HCH0015

Speaking

81. It's so exciting for us to be hosting you. I'm originally from Argentina and spent a semester abroad in the United States during college. I didn't know very much English when I moved to New York City to study Spanish literature at New York University. We spoke Spanish in the classroom, but everywhere else I tried to speak only English. It helped a lot that my roommates were bilingual students who spoke English as a first language. I could always ask them questions, and I had a ton. Some of the biggest difficulties weren't even related to language. They were more cultural, like where to stand in the subway or on escalators. The pace of life was much faster than I'd ever experienced before. Plenty of strangers were nice enough to point me in the right direction, but the vast majority didn't have time to answer my questions as they rushed around. Still, this type of immersion is what worked the best for me. I did have a safety net at NYU, especially with my roommates, but otherwise I had to fend for myself. Learning English wasn't just my goal, it was a requirement to function every day. And I did just that. I learned more English in those three months than I did in four years of high school English classes.

82. The students are currently in law school. Laura is at the top of her law school class, and she's planning to take a public interest job. She wants to make a meaningful impact on the world, helping people who can't afford legal representation, and she thinks a public interest job is the best opportunity to do so. Emily is a concerned friend who wants Laura to consider taking a different career path. Emily has two specific objections. First, she says Laura could join a top law firm in the country and work alongside the people who set policies for the whole country. By influencing policy, Laura could have a meaningful impact on even more people. Second, Emily thinks Laura could realistically save enough

money from her corporate job to launch her own public interest firm. Laura admits she wants to start a public interest firm, but she wants to start on the ground floor, doing advocacy work to gain insight into which practices work best. The conversation ends with Laura wishing Emily all the best on her future success.

83. The America Navy faced the challenge of combating the German submarines, which had started a campaign of unrestricted warfare two months previously. The situation needed to be addressed immediately since the Navy was responsible for providing passage across the Atlantic for hundreds of thousands of American troops and enormous quantities of supplies. The first response was to establish a main base at Queenstown, Ireland with 34 destroyers. The Cruiser and Transport Force was organized to carry American troops overseas, and to do so, the government acquired every available suitable vessel. When crossing the Atlantic, the transporting ships gathered into groups and were escorted through the danger zone by destroyers and other armed vessels. As soon as the safety of the transport and supply ships had been reasonably assured, aggressive steps were taken against enemy submarines. This was done by the laying of mine barrages; the employment of a hunting force of small ships, supplemented by aircraft; and the use of submarines. The American Navy was very successful in executing its plans to mitigate the submarine threat. The Navy carried a total of 911,000 men to Europe, and the Naval Overseas Transportation Service only lost seven vessels.

84. I will vote yes on the pending proposal to install red light cameras on Main Street. Our community has recently suffered a series of tragic accidents. Studies have shown that red light cameras significantly reduce accidents, and our law enforcement officers think that red light cameras likely would've prevented those recent accidents. People are less likely to run a red light when they know it'll cost them money. It's the same reason people generally obey parking rules, except in the case of red lights, it's even more imperative to do something because people are getting hurt. I don't want anyone to lose a loved one because we refuse to safeguard against known dangers. I know many of my constituents will not be happy with this decision. Despite these disagreements, I hope they can at least understand where I'm coming from. I expect that my opponent will use this against me in the next election, but I stand by my decision. I will always support policies that protect the people I'm elected to represent.

Dear TOEFL Test Taker,

We would like to start by thanking you for purchasing this study guide for your TOEFL exam. We hope that we exceeded your expectations.

Our goal in creating this study guide was to cover all of the topics that you will see on the test. We also strove to make our practice questions as similar as possible to what you will encounter on test day. With that being said, if you found something that you feel was not up to your standards, please send us an email and let us know.

We would also like to let you know about other books in our catalog that may interest you.

TOEFL Study Guide

This can be found on Amazon: amazon.com/dp/1637753462

GRE Study Guide

amazon.com/dp/162845900X

GMAT Study Guide

amazon.com/dp/1637753829

MCAT Study Guide

amazon.com/dp/1637752997

We have study guides in a wide variety of fields. If the one you are looking for isn't listed above, then try searching for it on Amazon or send us an email.

Thanks Again and Happy Testing!
Product Development Team
info@studyguideteam.com

FREE Test Taking Tips Video/DVD Offer

To better serve you, we created videos covering test taking tips that we want to give you for FREE. **These videos cover world-class tips that will help you succeed on your test.**

We just ask that you send us feedback about this product. Please let us know what you thought about it—whether good, bad, or indifferent.

To get your **FREE videos**, you can use the QR code below or email freevideos@studyguideteam.com with "Free Videos" in the subject line and the following information in the body of the email:

      a. The title of your product

      b. Your product rating on a scale of 1-5, with 5 being the highest

      c. Your feedback about the product

If you have any questions or concerns, please don't hesitate to contact us at info@studyguideteam.com.

Thank you!

Milton Keynes UK
Ingram Content Group UK Ltd.
UKHW031817280823
427650UK00004B/41